Confessions of a Lapsed Librarian

by
R.C. Benge

The Scarecrow Press, Inc.
Metuchen, N.J., and London
1984

Library of Congress Cataloging in Publication Data

Benge, Ronald C.
    Confessions of a lapsed librarian.

        Includes index.
        1. Benge, Ronald C. 2. Librarians--Great Britain--
Biography. 3. Librarians--Africa--Biography. L Title.
Z720. B46A36   1984   020'. 92'4 [B]   83-20405
ISBN 0-8108-1676-8

For

Maryvonne

Acknowledgments

I wish to acknowledge the encouragement of colleagues in Ahmadu Bello University, notably Brian Downes, Tony Olden and Michael Ward. Lary Amey of Dalhousie University made valuable comments on library objectives in Africa, while Wilfred Saunders and Douglas Foskett reassured me about my mystiques of information--a contribution prompted by Russel Bowden. Martyn Goff and Clive Bingley managed to persuade me that one chapter was too boring to be admissable and Sani Muazu helped to clarify for me so much that was obscure.

For the typing I have to thank Lilian Rossignol and Elaine Ward who completed the final version. I must also record my debt to the eloquence of Bala Usman who inspired me to leave Nigeria. Finally special thanks to Eric Moon who instigated the work and without whose advice I would not have had the temerity to proceed.

R. C. B.

CONTENTS

Introduction   vii

I.   Libraries: A Choice of Career   1

II.   My War   21

III.   My Colleges
1.   London: North Western Polytechnic   87
2.   Tropical Transfers: Trinidad & Ghana   94
3.   College of Librarianship Wales   104
4.   Postscript   111

IV.   My Africa
1.   Campus Expatriates   113
2.   Marie   119
3.   Racial Interactions   127
4.   The Other Eighty Per Cent   140
5.   Ideological Dilemmas: The Call of the Wild   147
6.   The Struggle for Education   154

V.   My Publications   171

VI.   Professional Concerns
1.   The Mystiques of Information   185
2.   Library Objectives in Africa   206

INDEX   221

INTRODUCTION

In Part V I have explained why these "memoirs" came to be published; there is no need to duplicate that explanation here. One factor which I might have stressed more is that I had returned from active involvement in the official world earlier than would have been the case if I had pursued a more "normal" life style. My career had not ended; it simply stopped as if a switch had been turned off. Mine was a special kind of redundancy, a common enough predicament just now. It became necessary, therefore, not only to cultivate the garden but to carry on with something else as well.

There is a professional context, represented by two chapters (in Part VI) which were left over from my other life: these are included here because we did not know what else to do with them. Those who are not involved in such matters can ignore them. Otherwise this is not a professional work nor is it an autobiography in the straight sense. This is where an explanation is due, since the method is experimental and tentative. It would be impossible to justify the publication of a direct record of my life and times since my contribution to the sum of things scarcely merits it. The approach is thematic, not chronological, and is meant to be cumulative: perhaps it could be called a kind of systems analysis. It follows that what is collected here is part of a Work in Progress and there is no good reason why it should ever stop.

I suppose this strategy is more or less equivalent to the traditional personal essay, which is no longer fashionable or possible, except in journalism: I have used myself to hang a theme upon. Montaigne, perhaps, had the same intention although he declared: "I am myself the subject of my book." Yet, as he knew perfectly well, one cannot isolate the self in that fashion and if one tries, then the self disappears. On the other hand, these pieces are not descriptions about a particular War or Colleges or Africa or Libraries, or anything else. Those who require data on such matters

vii

must go elsewhere. What has concerned me is mainly the relationship between what seems to be myself at any given time and whatever is "Out There" in the world or beyond. The Buddhists, if I understand them correctly, claim that there is nothing out there, only the Void, but even so that interaction remains Reality for me. Personal relationships are especially significant for the same reasons but, unless one is a novelist, these are much more difficult to deal with without being dishonest or offensive. (Total honesty is, of course, impossible: the sins are mainly those of omission.) As Somerset Maugham wrote (in the Summing Up,) the novelist is the only free man: he can invent his reality. This difficulty accounts for the absence of several installments which have been left for later publication.

One cannot know where a personal exploration like this may lead or who else will be interested in the outcome. In the chapter on my publications I have discussed that problem of readership. My answer now has to be that although there may be something here for specialists, I have written as if I were writing for Everyman, who is, after all, often a specialist as well.

Finally, I should explain that there are a number of irritating references which refer to "elsewhere." In many cases this tends to mean nowhere, since those are the parts which are not completed. The gaps, subject to Time and Circumstance, will eventually be filled.

R. C. Benge

CONFESSIONS OF A LAPSED LIBRARIAN

PART I

A Choice of Career

One of the more dubious advantages of being born near the bottom of the social heap is that the future is not mapped out or predictable but a blank. Nobody provides the signposts or registers one for a private school. Everywhere in the world, but especially in Britain where the class system is almost biological in its persistence, the children of the poor have to become long-distance runners. Their parents have some knowledge of their own world but can rarely imagine that another one could have any relevance for them. So when at the age of 17 the time came for me to leave school there was no career counseling and parental guidance was absent. My father was at sea and could not have advised me even if he had not been; indeed he had resented my education, such as it was, because he had left school at 12 himself and furthermore had observed that his employers were mostly idiots --perhaps because they were educated. My mother, on the other hand, believed firmly in schooling but knew nothing about careers; severely practical at a domestic level, she was aware of little beyond the great houses where she had worked. She imagined (not without cause) that the gentry ran the country and nobody else really counted, so that it didn't make much difference what post I applied for. Because of this she would never vote Labour and in retrospect her position was not all that misguided since the same archaic social relations remain fifty years later and the equivalent of the same people are in the British Cabinet today. For her the employers were giant trees and we were part of the undergrowth. It was not class consciousness but an acceptance of dependency; domestic servants were naturally parasitic, mentally as well as materially.

As for me, all that I wanted was some occupation connected with Literature so that I could make my own contribu-

1

tion to it. Accordingly I applied for a post with the Kent and
Sussex Courier but heard no more, which was just as well
since a passion for poetry is hardly the best qualification for
reporting petty crime and weddings and funerals and other
rites of passage. Tunbridge Wells was then not a place where
much ever happened, although there was an underworld of
sorts: indeed communities of that kind tend to produce ac-
tivist minorities and at that time or somewhat earlier Tom
Driberg, according to his own account, was pursuing his
"cottage" life, especially in the one opposite the Central Station.

Next I applied for a post in the public library and was
appointed at a salary so low that there were probably no other
applicants. The good folk at my secondary school expressed
misgivings but I could not appreciate them since practical
considerations were beyond my understanding. When Lloyd
Morgan, the avuncular Headmaster, delivered his final bene-
diction in his sonorous lilting voice--almost a Welsh hwyl--
he said: "Remember my lad, however far you travel, wherever you may be, even when you become President of the
Library Association, you will always remain a Judd Boy."
Whether the Judd boys were any different from other boys is
open to doubt, but certainly if I had gone to the other more
famous school at Tonbridge this would be a record of quite
another kind.

My choice of librarianship was appropriate enough.
I was emphatically not academically brilliant and during the
thirties there were few opportunities for secondary school
leavers and I was, in any event, not interested in most of
them: I knew what I didn't want and that was sufficient. One
imagines that this was and is how many others choose a career. It was, of course, largely a negative response but how
many major decisions are anything else? As Auden noted,
"We are lived by Powers we pretend to understand," and perhaps the pretense is necessary. Apart from Literature my
other abiding interest was in the Biological Sciences, or what
was then called Natural History (to distinguish it presumably
from the unnatural history of mankind). Somewhere among
the animals I had wanted to be but when the time came to
join them it was clear that I had studied the wrong subjects.
It is probable that I might, in any case, have been incapable
of dealing with the appropriate disciplines, at least in the
form which the curriculum then provided. My development
had seemed to be lopsided and non-scientific in the extreme.

Life in the Royal Borough

Since the animals were ruled out, the important thing
was to be among books, and so for the next five years I was.
That was my education, an undisciplined, wasteful, and exciting process.   They were the proverbial formative years
and for them I have been forever grateful.   It was a heady
adventure, not related to the "real" world at many points but
nevertheless a valuable preparation for it.   Sexual, religious
and political obsessions, most of which have remained with
me ever since, were mediated by reading about them or by
wallowing in the poetry of passive grief as distinct from re-
volt.   The experience is typical enough, an elegiac concentration on the idea of Death.   On an ideological level this exposure to pluralism could only produce chaos since the pundits
spoke with many contradictory voices and I responded to them
all.   In a university setting such excesses are supposed to be
moderated not only by academic "discipline" but also by contact with staff and other students.   But in that public library
the available human intercourse could only increase the disorder in my jungle mind.   Those of the readers who had intellectual interests were mostly preoccupied with what a later
age would call "way-out" topics.   For example, from a highly
articulate but possibly demented Parsee called Tarachand I
acquired a detailed smattering of Eastern doctrines and some
real understanding of the philosophy of Schopenhauer.   This
gentleman brought a bag of sweets everyday for at least three
years and produced a horoscope which turned out to be un-
cannily accurate as a prediction for the next decade; after
that it was lost, which is perhaps just as well.   Why he
came to Tunbridge Wells nobody ever discovered, and like
many of our readers he had no visible means of support.

The other influences naturally came from colleagues,
who were few in number because it was a small library.
Dr. Johnson once observed that "meek young men" were to
be found working in libraries, but in his time libraries were
institutions of another kind.   In that library we were all products of that haunted decade and each in his or her own way
was "committed."   Several of us were members of the Left
Book Club, and there was an officer from the Salvation Army,
a high Anglican pacifist, a methodist lay preacher and so on.
There were no stock responses apart from those of the librarian himself and he was tolerant of the wild ideals of his staff
because he did not take them seriously.   Those long lost colleagues certainly provided a heady but healthy stimulus for

me and their oddities could best be celebrated in the manner
of Charles Lamb, a method which alas is no longer possible.

Meanwhile the most persistent voices were echoes in
my head and the derivative verse I was writing was an echo
also.   A surviving photograph from that time suggests someone who might have been Narcissus but was not because the
gaze is unfocused and fixed not on a reflection but on something far away or on nothing at all.   If I had drunk the milk of
paradise, as I doubtless believed, then other more substantial
fare would seem to be required.   Eventually this roughage
would be rationed out by the army.

Officially I was a library apprentice.   All professions
have their symbols, mystiques, rituals and exclusive jargon.
The older professions wear gowns, robes, uniforms, cas-
socks, miters, bearskins, busbies and wigs; they swear oaths
and undergo initiation ceremonies.   Librarians are too self-
conscious to dress up in all this drag but they do have their
own private language and there are mysteries which, as an
apprentice, I had to learn.   The first ones to be encountered
were time-hallowed, even atavistic, routines.   One imagined,
therefore, just as the layman imagines now, that library work
went on mainly at a technical level.   Distracted by my reading, I did my best to master these secret procedures and accepted that they were part of the structure of the world.   Our
first duty every morning was to put on the shelves books
which had been returned the day before and dumped on a long
trough running down the middle of the room.   The purpose
of this exercise was to get them away before other readers
could take them out again, a practice which we deplored as
an act of moral turpitude.   In fact we spent much of our
time preventing the readers getting the books they thought
they wanted because other people had read them.   After this
we had to check that all of the books were in their allotted
places, and I suffered daily because a sadistic superior would
follow me round turning down horizontally those many books
which were out of order.   His other responsibility was to stop
me from reading as I proceeded.   Such duties are now carried
out by non-professional persons but then it was instinctively
felt that the repetition of routines was an end in itself, or if
they had a purpose it was to strengthen our moral fibre.   It
was a Dickensian atmosphere and we made entries in enormous ledgers which contained the same records in many different forms.   These were activities which demanded human
sacrifice: as Kipling observed, "The Gods of the Copybook
Headings I notice outlast them all. "

These procedures were being abandoned elsewhere even then, but one could hardly expect the Royal Spa to rush on ahead in the vanguard of human endeavor. It was, after all, a place where the afflicated came to be cured of physical and spiritual maladies, and was it not possible that we too were in need of redemption by hard labor? It is difficult to caricature the town as it then was, or the library which mirrored its eccentricities. A legion of old ladies naturally visited the library almost daily. Retired rentiers at bay, they were awaiting the End and sustained themselves by incessant mutual bickerings--such as those which are to be found in Old People's Homes. Several of them became attached to me and, accustomed as they had been in better times to a personal service in subscription libraries like Harrod's or Boot's, they would insist that no one else should select their books for them. This irritated my colleagues, who suspected darkly that one of these old creatures would leave me a legacy, but alas the beneficiaries were the usual cats and dogs and distressed gentlefolk. In this manner I acquired a comprehensive knowledge of popular female writers, particularly those who were writing half a century earlier. When I went to the ex-colonies some twenty years later, I was astonished to find that some of these writers, notably Marie Corelli and Bertha Clay, were still much in demand. Among these novelists a common element was a tone of heavy religiosity which must have been considered suitable as a civilizing influence in the Colonies. The missionaries and/or publishers who introduced these distortions of Christianity have much to answer for.

But to return to this town where so many of the Imperialists had come home to die, it should not be supposed that I was discontented there. I thought the place was most delightful and my education was proceeding as I had hoped. Along with many others, E. M. Forster made some uncharacteristic savage remarks about it. But I did not feel that way and my Reality was my own. True, I was surrounded by Reactionary Persons but that is how my world had always been and I had never belonged to it.

The library, then in a back street called Dudley Road, was an old two-story house which had not been converted. It was in a state of decay and when the trains to London rumbled underneath, books would fall off the shelves. One memorable morning a large chunk of the reading room ceiling fell on the slumbering souls below, and in accordance with their Heritage they shook off the plaster and continued with their reveries. Doubtless, at that very moment some would be hearing again the far-off Frontier bugle call ("Trumpeter, what are you sounding now"). And one with an Ancient Mariner gleam in his eye dramatically would recite to me stanzas from Francis Thompson's Hound of Heaven, just as once he had done, no doubt, on the road to Mandalay. Finally, an incident of a different order is worthy of note. One of our many clergymen brought into the lending library a dead cat, put it on the counter and said he would return for it later.

The small businessmen of the town, well represented on the Council, had selected a librarian who met their requirements and who had every qualification except a professional one. On Saturdays, resplendent in his plus fours, he played golf with them and from him they borrowed the books which were not on the shelves because of their alleged obscenity. Surreptitiously I also made use of this collection. (This "blue" library included typical continental novels of the thirties such as Céline's Voyage au Bout de la Nuit.) Confident of his employers' backing, the librarian permitted his minor eccentricities to flourish: these included a ferocious enforcement of quaint regulations. Dogs, naturally, were not allowed and when they were tethered to the railings outside and began to bark he would rush out and take them up the road and tie them up elsewhere. Books naturally had to be given official ownership marks and one of his self-imposed tasks was fiercely to stamp all the nudes in the art books with the rubber stamp of the Royal Borough. There was scarcely a navel to be found which was not encircled in this way. Yet although somewhat choleric, especially after his visits to the golf club, he was a kindly man who looked after his staff well and had a soft spot for the children and the ladies, so much so that all through Saturday evenings his acting wife would stand--a grim sentinel beside him at the library counter--to watch over his dealings with his female patrons. (No trips to the blue room on those evenings.)

The rest of us were also allotted peculiar functions. Our main duty was to staff the counter, a formidable structure with a heavy grill, behind which in declining order of seniority we stood in a row. When the readers, who came in queues during rush hours, returned their books, the senior person (who was allowed the privilege of speaking to them) would call out in a loud voice the book's number and the date when it was due for return. Whereupon those further down the line would locate the required ticket and fling it to the other end, an operation which involved throwing straight.

Any failure to do so was a sign of professional incapacity.
When not throwing we were allowed to read, although we had
to remain standing. This extraordinary procedure, which
could go on for several hours, possibly strengthened my ability to live on more than one level at once. Suddenly, with
some lines of verse exploding in the mind for the first time,
perhaps one would also hear the relentless digits; "I should
have been a pair of ragged claws scuttling across the floors
of silent seas" would erupt from the page and meanwhile the
numbers had gone unheard, only to be angrily repeated.
Sometimes at such moments wrong tickets were thrown, and
to avoid mistakes the senior person would intone the reader's
name and then say "thank you." (Years later, when handing
out money to soldiers on pay day they would be puzzled when as
an automatic reflex I sometimes said "thank you" once again.)

One relief during the three-hour evening stint was af-
forded by the arrival of the evening papers, which we were
allowed to read before they were put on on the old-fashioned
slopes. I especially recall how, night after night, we followed the struggles of the Republicans in Spain with agonized
attention ("What am I doing here?").

The "service" for the children in the basement was no
less bizarre. When they wanted a book they had to ring a
hand bell which would summon some reluctant soul from the
ledgers in another room. They made a great deal of noise
and would often be found piled up like puppies on the floor.
Sometimes superior mothers were present and in a Joyce
Grenfell voice would demand the novels of Angela Brazil
(pronounced like bra), who must have been the original
"who's for hockey?" lady. The only times the children paid
fines for returning books late was when we needed more
spoons or a new teapot--a humane and flexible system.

At this point perhaps I should emphasize that the above
selective account is not intended for vocational guidance and
that it happened a long time ago. If I had written an account
at the time the oddities I have described would have been
wholly peripheral--indeed I might have regarded them as
normal and unworthy of comment. Somehow, as an apprentice I found time to study for Library Association examinations; we were even granted at least two hours a week for
that purpose. I regarded the L. A., with its headquarters
at Chaucer House (as it then was) in Malet Place, London,
with awe and veneration. My attitudes were still bucolic and
provincial, and none the worse for that. The middle years of

life should be spent in a metropolis but the end, and especially the beginning, should be pastoral and primitive. Those who have been denied these advantages often seem to have been--somewhere along the line--lobotomized as it were.

By the time I was half qualified I had been at the library for five years. What would have happened if the war had not come is now beyond all speculation, but in retrospect it seems that I had been there long enough. From that womb-like existence an unfinished creature had emerged and there was still a long way to go before it became fully human. I had, after all, never left the Home Counties. *

Military Interlude

When I was called up for the Army in 1940 (an experience described in Part II of this book) my qualifications for anything but foot slogging were not apparent either to me or to the authorities. The ledgers I was familiar with were the wrong kind and I could not do the clerical work which might have landed me a soft job, or what we called a cushy number. Some librarians eventually found themselves in the Intelligence Corps or even in an army library, but for me no such opportunties arose and I would not have taken them if they had, since such a move could not have been reconciled with my politics. So for six decisive years libraries were forgotten and I learned little that could be of any professional use thereafter.

During our infantry training we absorbed a few rudimentary techniques like Henry Reed's famous "Naming of Parts" ("And this is the piling swivel which in your case you have not got"). We also learned by rote mystical invocations and formulae from military manuals, designed to produce not conscious responses but instinctive reflexes, so that when we eventually encountered the Enemy we would not have to think. I probably missed little of practical value in not going for an officer's course but the banality and boredom experienced through two years of "training" as an infantry private soldier must have blunted my mental responses.

Four years more on active service made the past and especially the future wholly unreal. Because of those he has

---

*The Home Counties are those counties surrounding London.

left behind him, the soldier dreams of "home" but that is all. We could not imagine carrying on from where we left off so long ago. In my own case, the minutiae of so much library work--indeed of almost any peace-time labor--became unthinkable. How could a vista of wild horizons be reduced to a disciplined concentration on the immediate and palpable and small? Consciously, I probably did not consider the matter in such a fashion. Very likely there were no clear formulations and I existed in a cloud of unknowing, intensified by the fact that I had not expected to survive. It was like emerging dazed and dazzled from a tunnel which had seemed to be without end. It was also, I suppose, a kind of exhaustion which would last a long while.

Rehabilitation and the Civil Service

In 1946, however, I was officially alive and likely to remain so. It is true I had not gathered up any more professional qualifications, but some of my experience could be presented as relevant to the needs of the post-war world. I had, after all, presided over a military training school in Austria and what really happened there need never be disclosed.

This seemed to indicate that I might have teaching ability, so I applied for teachers' training, but was rejected, possibly because I was already half qualified as a librarian. The failure may have been a merciful dispensation since I would have been unsuitable for teaching children, as I later discovered with my own. Minority minded persons are not often good teachers, because they resent the need of children to conform. By then it was becoming evident that I would have to return to libraries--but not, I was determined, to Tunbridge Wells. It represented, I thought, a Past I had outgrown.

Accordingly I was appointed to a library post at the Central Office (formerly the Ministry) of Information, then housed in Crawford Street, just off Baker Street in London, where I wanted to be. "What a splendid opportunity, " one of the old ladies, a retired missionary, exclaimed ecstatically. "There you will be at the heart of the Empire. " I had misgivings about the Civil Service but these were allayed when I discovered that my colleagues in the Department were misfits all. Left over from the war, most of them later went on to higher realms in journalism and literature. They in-

cluded the Yeatman of 1066 and All That and the original
Christopher Robin Milne and Paul Jennings and Laurie Lee,
and at least one of Bertrand Russell's children, who spent
the time knitting. The head of our section was a formidable
but kindly old lady who closely resembled the then Queen
Mother; her regal mein served as well in dealing with our
anarchic clientele. Our function was to "project Britain" at
home and abroad; vulgar propaganda was left to other official
agencies. We gave out the right kind of information, inter
alia, about the right kind of novelists, such as the George
Orwell of Animal Farm or the J. B. Priestley of the Good
Companions. By and large it was a civilized setting and hard
work was frowned upon. What friction there was mostly developed from the unnatural co-existence of two people in the
same rooms. In our case my assistant, a young lady who
attracted our colleagues to the library for improper reasons,
was sent to a psychiatrist because she developed the habit of
throwing books at me across the room. She alleged that she
was sexually frustrated because her husband was a Plymouth
Brother. She was required to apologize to me for her provo-
cations but it may well have been that I also had provoked
her. It was a far cry from the tiresome power struggles
which characterize human relations in most organizations.

But restless I remained and obscurely felt that the
Civil Service, even in this humanized form, was not for me.
I was not a proper civil servant nor a real librarian, or
rather, I was conscious of being both or neither. Nearly
always one of the limitations of library work is that the scope
for independent action is restricted, nowhere more so than
in the civil service. There were also certain disadvantages
inherent in that kind of information activity. Our human encounters were mostly by telephone: they were personal to
some degree, especially when one already knew the owners
of the voices at the other end, but many of them we never
met and they remained disembodied sounds. One naturally
would have preferred corporeal relationships and it sometimes
came as a shock eventually to discover that one had been
chatting up unsuitable persons who would be equally discon-
certed when a visual confrontation finally came. The telephone speech of people may indicate their personalities very
well but apart from their appearance it is their age which is
disguised.

But these were minor frustrations; the main missing
element was that I had no sense of direction and the future,
obscure as it was still, obviously lay elsewhere. The war

was still only two years away and I remained something of
a somnambulist, so much so that it was a friend who in-
duced me to apply for a post in St. Marylebone Public Library (since then it has become part of Westminster).

St. Marylebone

When I became Reference Librarian (a senior but
specialized post) at St. Marylebone I was inspired by the
thought that I would be dealing not just with the bland voices
of the Civil Service but with the infinitely varied information
needs of metropolitan man. This was an advance and also a
return to my original allegiance to public libraries as distinct
from others. In public library work a degree of political
commitment is possible for people with strong radical convictions. To the outsider the political impact of a public library may seem to be minimal, but those who provide literature or information for "the masses" know (if they are politically aware) that small political decisions are made all
the time, and it is these which affect the quality of the library service. Historically public libraries were part of
the democratic and social movements of the nineteenth century which produced the Labour Party and some degree of
liberation for the common people. They could therefore be,
and still can, a progressive influence, whereas the other
historical library tradition, which goes back to the beginnings
of recorded history, is naturally conservative, if only because it involves the conservation of materials. These opposing left and right principles are inevitably in conflict as
they are in all social endeavor, and that is how it should be.
That particular reference library can be used to illustrate
the point.

When the Department was built around 1938 it was
a small but exact replica of the circular British Museum
reading room, including a central desk where a hapless at-
tendant had to sit. There were even uplifting mottoes running round the dome, although we never discovered their
literary source. All this had been done in accordance with
conservative principles and without any reference to the social needs of the people of Central London. In the main the
users of that library were not of course doing research; they
were either using it as a reading room, often for personal
academic study, or seeking practical information. It was
therefore obvious that the quasi- or pseudo-religious atmosphere of silence had prevented the kind of service which

should have been provided. All we had to do was to set up
an information center outside of this hallowed room and organize it to meet the need which was very much there.

This was done and the response was dramatic: there
was a great deal of noise and bustle, including the clatter of
typewriters, and people (unofficially) were allowed to smoke.
In the silent regions students were encouraged and the opening hours were extended until 9:00 p. m. (Most of them, including many foreign students, were in lodgings where the
cost of heating was prohibitive. On this issue the conservative argument was that we should not provide for them since
they didn't pay taxes.) As a final example of the care with
which "progressive" changes had to be made, it became desirable to design a desk and an adjoining office in such a
way that, if late at night, an assistant were to be attacked
by a maniac, an escape route was available. Incidentally an
office of that kind is also advisable, as we had realized in
Tunbridge Wells, when from time to time some members of
staff would become helpless with laughter.

Under certain favorable circumstances the provision
of information in public libraries can be a most rewarding
activity, especially for those whose dominant urge is to help--
rather than interfere with--other people (whether this trait
is admirable or not is irrelevant here). It is not an academic activity--far from it--nor is it just bibliographical (the lo-
cating of items), nor is it literary or scholarly or even intellectual except in the sense that curiosity is necessary. It
appears that I have now defined the nature of the work by
noting what it is not. On the face of it, all that one does
is to answer questions by looking up the answer in a book
or periodical or some other source such as another information worker. Dubious ethics are often involved here, since
some insoluble questions are passed around from place to
place and eventually return. That is how it appears to the
observer, and on one level that is how it is. Indeed, during
the 1950 Festival of Britain (that brave Jamboree dreamed up
to show that the Welfare State was also fun), it was officially
arranged that some of us in London should set up a temporary
library--at the National Book League it was--and guarantee to
provide within minutes an answer to any query that anyone
could conjure up. (Needless to say, many of the questions
asked came from other librarians trying to catch us out.)
Naturally, the rules of the game had to exclude certain categories of information since our sources were silent or contradictory about many human dilemmas. Work at this level

is mostly factual or practical and has an urgency and immediacy arising from what people are doing every day; it is essentially an <u>urban</u> activity and especially important in great cities where so much is happening that nobody can encompass the whole of it.   In rural places everywhere there is also a need for "information" but the facts required are often not to be found in books, or if they are, nobody seeks them there.

We noted above that many human predicaments were beyond our ministration.   We were not priests, nor psychiatrists or doctors.   Yet those other dimensions were always there and would not go away.   So many people who came to the library for information were really searching for something on another level altogether.   They were either lonely and needed someone to talk to, or mildly dotty or quite mad. (It was those who were wholly demented who seemed at first to be the most sane and whose requests were most convincing.)   One was evidently not only passing on ill-considered trifles but also contributing to the wild visions of the mentally dispossessed.   Legal obsessions were frequent, often involving legacies or an injustice perpetrated on them long since by an uncomprehending world.   Religious manias were almost as common.   One lady requested that all books which had been published prior to the date when she had been converted to whatever it was should be removed from the shelves. A man wearing a fez demanded that all reference to the Trinity should be obliterated.   And so on.   Mostly we humored them as far as possible, but the important thing was to learn how to distinguish between the sane and the insane without wasting too much of the taxpayers' money.

There was also regular trouble caused by those who were present in the reading room every day and all day. They would complain that the library was being taken over by black people or that other readers had sinister designs upon them or were casting spells: this last accusation was provoked by a man who made hierarchic repetitive gestures, doubtless some kind of St. Vitus' dance.   One evening at 8:45 p. m. there was an unearthly primeval scream, and when the assistant said in quiet tones, "Who did that?" a young man (equally quiet) replied, "I did. "   Our rules and regulations made no precise provision for such matters: they mentioned <u>talk</u> but there was nothing about screams.

We were, of course, accidentally involved in realms where information was irrelevant.   We were dealing, usually by default, because there was no one else to bother, with the

tattered legions of the lost who congregate in every capital
city: they included many senior citizens. "You'll be far better off in a home, " we used to sing in the army, but nobody
ever really believes that. Doggedly these people wanted to
be in a world which had rejected them. At that time the
complicated structure of the Welfare State was already in
place but there are those who have no wish to qualify for its
benefits.

Most of them were harmless but one who was not
slashed a number of books with some sharp instrument, and
eventually a plain-clothes policeman had to be called in to
watch. After more than 40 books had been irretrievably
damaged the man was caught in the act and a court case followed. Apart from the police I was the only witness for the
prosecution and the trial was by jury. It was farcical from
start to finish. On the first day the police forgot to bring
the evidence (three of the slashed books) and the judge said
to the prosecuting lawyer, "You are very naughty, Mr. So
and So, you have wasted our valuable time. " When we reassembled a week later, the barrister set out to prove that
the man couldn't possibly have been reading the books which
he had allegedly slashed. Now this was very odd, because
there is no legislation at all which lays down that he need
be reading. Charitably one could only suppose that the court
was in need of light relief as a change from its usual dreary
proceedings. The first item presented in evidence was a
collected edition of the works of Thomas Love Peacock and
the prosecution was able to prove that the accused was wholly
unfamiliar with Peacock's characters. The second item was
a work on the Dehydration of Food and it was eventually established also that the man's ignorance of dehydration was
total. "What, " the man was asked, "do you remember about
this book?" The reply was that he had noticed that there
were a great many letter Z's on the first page. Whereupon
the court adjourned while officials solemnly counted the number of Z's, and when we were reassembled it was agreed
that they were indeed plentiful. (No doubt American spelling
was responsible.) And so for the third item the catechism
continued and the man was slightly more successful since he
had noticed something about Picasso's paintings. By this
time I was beginning to feel like Alice, a condition which was
intensified when I noticed that several members of the jury
were asleep. But when I went into the witness box they all
woke up and glared horribly at this bullying bureaucrat who
was persecuting a harmless citizen. After he was eventually
pronounced not guilty I was present when the police returned

to him his entire worldly possessions, which consisted of two razor blades and a pair of scissors. As Alice remarked, every story should have a moral, and the only moral I can offer here is that the destruction of books should not be taken too seriously.

Ten years later, Joe Orton, the dramatist, was convicted of removing art books from public libraries and decorating the walls and ceilings of his room with the plates, a collage which rivalled the Sistine Chapel in its complexity. Not only this, but Orton and his friend Halliwell (later to be his murderer) "modified" illustrations on book jackets and also typed hilarious false blurbs on the convenient blank spaces on Gollancz covers, particularly those on the books of Dorothy L. Sayers. They were convicted of stealing 72 library books and removing 1, 653 plates from others, and were sentenced to six months imprisonment. In this instance Orton supplied his own moral, which was that their crime had been not so much the damage to books but that they had made fun of the bourgeoisie. (It was, after all, a light sentence.) As Orton observed, "One of the greatest things at the trial, the greatest outrage, the one for which I was sent to prison, was that I had stuck a monkey's face in the middle of a rose. " His biographer noted, somewhat portentously, that "in its ruthlessness the caper displayed the solitary's groping to connect. " Well, yes, but Orton and Halliwell were also fortunate enough to be able to dramatize or transcend their predicament. For our man and thousands like him, no such remedy is available and all connection has been broken.

Must we then conclude that the essence of library work is to be found in these encounters with the homeless mind? Certainly not: I am simply reporting some of my own experience in that particular place, an experience which was limited since after two years there I left libraries to take up the teaching of Library Studies. Yet this emphasis on the therapeutic value of public libraries is not entirely frivolous. One could show that, if we leave out reading which is done for practical and necessary purposes, most recreational reading is mildly therapeutic in so far as it mitigates boredom. On another level the same individuals may be heavy readers during adolescence or middle age or at other times when they encounter the Disturbing or the Unknown. Meanwhile, for many Life is always a crisis and reading helps to make it more tolerable or even rewarding. Otherwise such crises are dealt with by various professionals (legal, medical, religious, psychiatric) who almost without exception thrive upon the "problems" or miseries of their fellow men. It is also a way of dealing with their own. All of these need literature and information to follow the latest developments in the world. The rewards, being based on personal encounters, should include a decisive psychological satisfaction, whereas businessmen in their human relations cannot afford to go beyond the old-boy level where the uses of literature are not very important. Somewhere in between are the politicians, who have to deal with collective disorders and non-existent norms: for them literature, like everything else, may be useful in the pursuit of power.

However, professions have collective responsibilities too, and it is time to return to those of our generation. Reflecting the political preoccupations of the thirties, we tried to apply our social commitment to our professional area. (At that time even pig keepers and undertakers were applying Marxist categories to themselves.) The public library, as an institution which had grown up partly to make reading matter available to all instead of a privileged few, reflected the dilemmas and pluralistic confusions of capitalist liberal democracy. Many of the librarians and the local government politicians responsible for library development wanted to "educate" their masters, the voters, and bring them cultural development: at the same time the voters were, in theory, offered the freedom--even the right--to read whatever they chose. The fact that the masses were not in a position to choose was awkward, but this doubtless would be overcome as education became more widespread. Other librarians, especially the conservative elements already discussed, were more likely to become obsessed with bibliographical rather than political processes, and for them the Great Bibliographer in the sky was already classifying us according to his own special scheme. But the rest of us regarded library provision as a weapon in the advance towards socialism, and Lenin himself had said so. How within the liberal tradition this could come about was not examined too closely. Years later, after the war, the Unesco Manifesto for Public Libraries mirrored this dilemma when it declared that the public library should not tell people what to think but should help them to decide what to think about. This statement was, of course, a necessary evasion and it was dropped from a later edition. (One is reminded of the subsequent polemics surrounding the Euro-Communists.)

At that time, though, we thought we had satisfactorily

gone beyond the liberal bourgeois tradition, and that was the
title of one of our texts, Stephen Spender's Forward from
Liberalism.   Personally I was mainly influenced by Christopher Caudwell's Studies in a Dying Culture, a key work in
my development.

It seemed possible then that as their way of life was
threatened, a significant proportion of the middle classes
were about to cooperate in bringing about their own Doom.
(This was an illusion which was to recur thirty years later
in France in 1968.) The approach was apocalyptic: the Way
had been revealed by the inexorable march of History and
the orange volumes of the Left Book Club.

After the war when these grandiose hopes had faded,
the radical tradition among librarians got a bit lost, and
former members of the Communist Party were safely absorbed into established structures where they did very well.
But radicalism is inherent in the human condition and its
energies passed into the psychedelic dreams of the anarchic
sixties.   Some young librarians suffered from guilt feelings
that they might have hangups about the battered traditions of
High Culture and might even want to influence other people's
reading habits.   More recently a harder left has reappeared
and a militant tendency has influenced some library staff to
enter the political arena on behalf of the disadvantaged minorities; there is even a journal called The Socialist Librarian.
These trends are healthy and necessary and I have sum-
marized them in this remote way because this account is supposed to be about myself and I was not there but overseas.
A significant difference between these more recent manifestations and our pre-war ideologies is that they are limited to
specific areas and nobody now puts forward grand or total
designs.

To return to my small role, in 1950 I was necessarily
involved with the ideological implications of information work.
That sounds impressive, if not pompous, but it was not,
since I didn't know what these implications were.   What I
did know was that however interesting that work might be, I
was disturbed by its limitations and it was damaging my
brain.   My mind had always been afflicted with grasshopper
tendencies and at different times would be distracted almost
into hysteria by impacts from all directions.   I suppose
academics would have classified it as undisciplined.   However
you define it, the condition was intensified by the jumping
about process which happens in that kind of information work.

The point, of course, is that nothing adds up or develops:
I probably would have described it then as "uncreative. "
That was partly why I applied for a teaching post, although
at that time I had not realized that this would be a final
break with library work as such.   The alternative could have
been to proceed up the ladder in the usual way and no doubt
many other "job satisfactions" would have emerged. Any administrative post which makes it possible to build up an institution is exciting and management functions are seldom dull.
I had already found that the process of book selection itself
could be of tremendous interest.   But I was impatient of a
slow advance and also had misgivings about the local government setup in which I had to operate: the people within it
frightened me because they were so alien.

Finally there was a practical reason which my professional colleagues will at once appreciate.   In any walk of
life ambitious people instinctively understand that they should
always stay in the mainstream where the current is strongest.
Those who ignore this precept are left to play about in the
shallows or they explore some minor tributary or (to change
the metaphor) get shunted into sidings where they are soon
forgotten.   Many, of course, prefer it like that since they
are not prepared to pay the heavy price which a successful
career so often demands.   (Also, they may live longer that
way.)   In any case, I was, I suppose, ambitious at least
some of the time, and I had become aware that if I stayed in
that specialized post I might remain an information officer
forever.

And so my library role came to a premature end,
and thereafter I was involved with libraries only in a teaching capacity: it was a different job that required quite other
abilities.   However, I feel compelled to add a postscript.
Ten years later I completed a book about the "flow" of information as a social phenomenon.   I then considered that if
various obstacles (which I listed) could be removed this flow
would happen.   I would not deal with the matter in that way
now and it may well be that there was a failure in perception
associated with an approach which was altogether too mechanistic.   At that time the social function of information was
something I could not fully analyze.   I might do better now,
but this is a personal narrative, not a professional diagnosis.
The documentalists have defined information as "the meaning
attached to data. "   It is probable that I became distressed
because I hankered after meanings which the data could not
bear.   Subsequently, when I was lecturing about reference

sources it appeared to me that the pure data which they provide--precisely because no meaning is attached--can be most alarming. At any rate the disconnected facts frightened me and represented a preoccupation with the Absurd which I later preferred to abandon.

Meanwhile the equivalents of the lost souls who haunted those reading rooms are still around, their ranks now multiplied by recent recruits thrown out by political processes they do not understand. Somewhere up above hundreds of communication satellites are whirling unseen around the globe and data banks have already stored billions of facts which technologists, businessmen, warmongers and policemen may use but which are not available to the rest of us and would have no meaning even if they were. The librarians and information workers of the future will not be able to continue where we left off: they will have to start again.

PART II: MY WAR

1. BETWEEN THE WARS

British and American writers have not produced anything of epic significance on the European front in the Second
World War. Referring to the 1914-1918 conflict, J. B.
Priestley remarked in his autobiography that he felt unable
to write about his experience because it was an impossible
combination of horror and farce. The second time around
this comment was equally applicable: the farcical element
is perhaps constant in all wars but in our part of the war
the horror was not so prolonged or constant. If there can
be degrees of the horrific, then the depths were sounded on
the Russian front and not in our theater; our experience was
marginal to the gigantic struggles in the East, although
naturally we did not feel like that ourselves.

With certain well known exceptions, poets and novelists on active service were largely silent both at the time
and since. They had good reason to be: not many of them
were in the infantry and those of us who were rarely saw
the enemy. In our own case we spent the best part of three
years "pushing on" from one hole in the ground or one hill
top to the next. But in the 1914-18 horror the millions who
were slaughtered included a high proportion of infantry soldiers who never moved out of the mud. The experience of
those who were not infantry (as exemplified by the splendid
accounts by Spike Milligan, who was an artilleryman in our
theater) was of a different order. Our writers, or potential
writers, found themselves in Cairo or some mobile bath unit
of a Mediterranean grove; they too were conscious of a marginal role. For them, and even more for us, there were
long stretches of boredom. Can boredom be recollected in
tranquillity? Almost certainly not. That too should be added
to Priestley's list, and there also remains one other factor
which must be peculiarly characteristic of mountain warfare:

that is the <u>exhilaration</u> which we often felt briefly on reaching the top of yet another hill. If that were not recorded this account would be falsified. Yet it was a transient state and almost childish, so that afterwards more sober reflections would ensue. Altogether these conflicting reactions produced a kind of numbness. I recall writing on some lost set of verses that "I am dumb again about the war." What also contributed to this not untypical response was the fact that many of us had anticipated the predicament for so many years, before it had come about. The writers of the First World War spoke for their generation; those of the second could only report a <u>private</u> experience and their appropriate public role was <u>silence.</u>

So much has been said and written about the events leading up to our war and the political climate of the thirties that it need not be described here (my own ideological conflicts are described in Part I). The five years after leaving school until I was called up in January 1940 were spent in a fever of political indecision. Like most members of the Left Book Club I was swayed by an emotional anti-war gut reaction which was accompanied by equally intense anti-Nazi convictions. These confused responses were of course intensified by the fate of the Spanish Republicans, which profoundly affected us all. Torn by these conflicting attitudes I imagined that I would eventually reach the right conclusions by incessant reading and debate. As Auden noted, "It was a low dishonest decade," and to the extent that we were blind to the true nature of the Soviet Union we were not exempt from self-deception. Nevertheless, the idealism and commitment derived from states of mind which have had no parallel in the generations since. In retrospect our involvement was necessarily futile--even pathetic--yet it determined and conditioned my life from that time to this. Everybody was wrong because it was too late to be right--what was happening in Europe (especially the right-wing support of fascism in the interests of anti-communism) stemmed from the long lunacy of capitalist nationalism and class war. Europe had been planning its suicide for half a century, if not more: it was an age of betrayal.

It so happened that when the war came my pacifist inclinations (as distinct from the shifting communist party line) were uppermost. I was the Secretary of the Peace Pledge Union in Tonbridge, Kent and automatically registered as a Conscientious Objector. Such persons had to attend Tribunals which were set up to authenticate our consciences.

(I even attended a mock tribunal as a kind of rehearsal.
This was presided over by Professor Joad, who declared
that I would pass the test.) But, one week before the real
tribunal was due, I informed His Majesty's Government that
my objection was withdrawn and I wished to join the navy:
it was a decision I never regretted. Now that the war had
arrived at last my personal attitudes could make no difference and had become irrelevant. The long debate was over.

2. INITIATION

When I was called up in January 1940, I was summoned to the Royal West Kent regiment at Maidstone. My
recollections of the winter of 1940-41 are phantasmagoric.
Off duty we blundered about in our new boots and with our
useless rifles in the black-out. Our basic training also
seems to have been done either in the dark or in the snow--
an appropriate background since this was the time when the
Finns were struggling with the invasion from the Soviet Union,
the only real war which was then going on. The shock of
my experience was no doubt salutary, but shattering. In
spite of the poverty, I had led a sheltered and secret life,
unlike my fellow recruits, who were either working class--
it was a term which could still be used--or a very small
minority who had a public school O. T. C. * background. In
either case, they were used to a communal existence and
some degree of regimentation. My individualism had rendered me almost unfit for military consumption; automatically
when they said turn right, I turned left, and so on.

It was all symbolized by the boots: formerly I had
worn sandals and now there were these enormous weights,
which had to be not only worn, but polished and, if one did
it properly, spat upon. The main consolation was a variation in the nightmares: the horrors of drill were different
from those arising from standing about shivering in groups
in Maidstone Park and repeating mumbo jumbo about weapons
we did not have, or sighting an enemy at 6 o'clock right of
a bushy topped tree, an enemy we could not envisage. My
psychological condition can be imagined, but fortunately the
flesh was less troubled than the spirit and I enjoyed rude
health for the first time for years. Route marches through

---

*Officers' Training Corps, a British equivalent of R. O. T. C.

the wet lanes of Kent were salutary and physical fatigue is an excellent remedy for mental stress. There were some psychosomatic disorders, notably a loss of voice and, later, impetigo on the hands, which didn't go away until we landed in North Africa, but these symptoms were superficial. At a deeper level, the army was "doing me good," although I didn't appreciate it then.

The only healthy life (not the same thing as a "good" life) is a social one, and for the first time it was a genuine communality that I found: it was like being immersed into a warm bath, a condition only briefly felt before in the boy scouts at summer camps on the Isle of Wight. Theoretically on the side of the workers, I had no experience of the industrial working class. I had been intellectual or highbrow to a priggist degree and had no knowledge of current popular culture--Clementine and Shenandoah at boy scout camp fires was a different thing. My companions were astounded that I had never heard of "She'll be coming round the mountain." Route march singing was part of this warm experience, one in fact which literally "kept us going." Nobody in the forces at that time can forget the ridiculous songs we sang with such gusto, the "patriotic" ones being the most absurd and characteristic of the illusions of the phony war: "Roll out the barrel," "Run rabbit run," and (most ironic of all) "We'll be hanging out the washing on the Siegfried line." The non-martial ones were better, if even more sentimental, like "South of the border down Mexico way."

Then there was the world of Vera Lynn, which carried on the traditions of Ivor Novello in the first world war: "Keep the home fires burning," "It's a long way to Tipperary," etc. Sad songs from the nineteenth-century regular army also survived. (We were of course trained by regular soldiers, many of them semi-literate.) Typical of these was "My love is for a soldier boy who sailed away across the sea." The singer was supposed to be the girl he left behind him, but the homosexual component is apparent: it was always unacknowledged, but understood. Among all these the drawn-out cadences of "Nellie Deane"--the English national anthem--had a special place. It was typical of the British (or rather the English) attitudes that these songs, although maudlin, were never militaristic: jingoism was a temporary aberration. Ballads like "Fuck them all--the long and the short and the tall" or "Kiss me good night Sergeant Major" or "When this bloody war is over" were far from martial; they could not have been more different from the songs the Nazis sang with such prevision--no drooling there.

It was only the politicians who had to be blood-thirsty and they were forgiven because it was their job. As an ex-pacifist, I was impressed that nobody hated the war more than the soldiers. Bayonet practice made me literally sick --plunging the blade into a sack ("in--out--on guard")--but they treated it as a joke or game, which it was, because modern war, as a rule, was not like that. Mixed up with all those ditties, there was the public school rugby song tradition, an emanation from another class. At that time we did not sing them. The crude sexual preoccupations which they reflect came uppermost more when we went overseas beyond womankind.

There was in the army an extraordinary tolerance toward individual aberrations. There were, of course, sadistic NCOs but in most cases their roaring was a professional act. One of our recruits had an identical twin sister and every month when her period was due he would take to his bed with sympathetic pains. Nobody thought this odd and he was exempted from duty. Homosexuals were accepted without comment except for crude but kindly badinage--it was only obviously "effeminate" or passive types of homosexuals who were noticed at all. One reason for this tolerance was of course that we were "all in it together." Until then I had probably not encountered the wilder kinds of human oddity except in novels--I had read my Dostoievsky thoroughly--or among the old ladies of Tunbridge Wells. Such manifestations were, by normal standards, freakish, but here were the foibles of the average man. Toward the end of our basic training we were billeted in the town, in my own case in a poor quarter. There, the hosts for two of us were Will and Lil, whose lives were humdrum but enlivened by a mild Saturday night spree. On Saturdays also they would always have, as they informed us, a good cry together, which they looked forward to. My roommate was himself odd enough: he had a compulsive habit of punning and each new excruciating invention was followed by maniacal laughter. He made them up during the night as well and would wake me up to tell the latest one.

Altogether two long years were to be spent in various training exercises. Dunkirk came and went without our participation. (True, we sailed out from Southampton, but it was so late that on approaching the French coast we had to turn around and come back along with those in the little ships who had actually been there.) We became familiar with remoter parts of Britain; for example, we were exposed to the

mad peasantry around Haverfordwest in Pembrokeshire.
Without much justification, I and a friend, Bruce Copp,
identified the population there with the demented creatures
of Cold Comfort Farm, Stella Gibbons' minor classic. This
fantasy threatened to grow out of control. We identified the
quivering brethren at public prayer and Effie the fey heroine
wandering in the water meadows, watched over by Big Bas-
ness the bull. In fact most of the ladies there were not at
all fey and although cautious, were most lascivious. In the
novel, whenever the Sukebind bloomed, animals and humans
were in heat, and in Haverfordwest we decided it bloomed
all the year round. Twenty years later I revisited that town
and could not recognize it at all.

We also spent several months in the genteel purlieus
of the Malvern Hills, which, inter alia, provided great opportunities for our sadistic sergeant to march us up and down
with constant about-turns. It was this same sergeant, a regular soldier, who once tried to insert his penis--much battered
by twenty years overseas--into my ear. I was sitting in a
chair at the time and, incensed, I hit him with the chair.
The outcome was predictable: he finished me off with a judo
scissors leg grip across the stomach, but his subsequent behavior was a little less bizarre.

We also--just after Dunkirk--sat about among the
curlew-haunted moors of Cumberland, while the brass hats
tried to put the army together again. We were near a village
called Wark where there was only one young eligible lady
surrounded by the sex-starved soldiery. When she consented
to go for a walk with me--only a walk it was--my status was
secured and I was invited to the saloon bar of the village
pub, a place normally out of bounds to other ranks, but our
officers were too drunk to notice the anomaly.

By way of contrast, we survived another bitterly cold
winter in Nissen huts in Pollockshaws in Glasgow: I recall
their distinctive meat pies and traveling on the late night
trams. Every morning twenty or so soldiers washed in a
kind of soup out of a bucket which was heated all night over
the central stove. The soldiers were appropriately licentious
and rough; some of them had been juvenile delinquents. I
used to think--was it then or since?--how absurd it was for
T. E. Lawrence, in his last incarnation as Aircraftsman
Shaw, to shrink from the coarseness of their air force
equivalents. The reasons are made plain in his writing,
yet the behavior of such men is always more straightforward

than was his; they are possessed by a peculiar innocence. Or did one, even then, regard them as children the way that some of the colonialists saw the natives? It was at the Pollockshaws camp that an incident occurred to illustrate the point. When the guards one morning checked the number of "prisoners," who were charged with various offenses, they found there was one extra: he had broken in through the roof to be with his friends.

Also in Scotland we went to the Hydro in Creiff in Perthshire. From there we launched ferocious attacks into the clouded hills (I suppose they were the Lowlands). By this time we were using live ammunition and stumbling through the rain over that soggy bog moss with our ammunition was an exhausting process, so much so that I can now recall nothing else of Perthshire. Then we went to sea on combined operations and mounted more confused attacks against various harmless islands in the Hebrides--Harris and Rum and Eigg and others we couldn't even name. By this time everybody, especially the navy, had been exercising for far too long. In consequence, the sailors ceased to care whether we had landed at the correct piece of shore or even the right island. There were ludicrous "errors" and sometimes what was supposed to be shallow water where we plunged was not shallow at all and bren carriers disappeared between the waves along with their crew.

It was on one of these dawn assaults that I heard a corncrake. While I was peering about trying to locate it, my companions--so they later claimed--were entertained by a half-witted maiden. I thought of Wordsworth's highland lass whose voice, he thought, was like the cuckoo bird "breaking the silence of the seas among the farthest Hebrides."

During our war village idiots were much in demand. By this time we were all heartily sick of playing soldiers and no longer responded to its absurdities. When we heard that our invasion was to be real at last, it was with relief, tempered by a sensible dread. We could not, of course, be told where we were going.

3.   ON BEING RECONSTRUCTED

A balanced verdict on those years must not fail to

record that it was an existence almost wholly without meaning. Being a private infantry soldier for that length of time under those circumstances was an experience no one would wish to repeat. The total lack of responsibility could not compensate for the boredom and the frustration of being eternally buggered about for reasons which were unknown and unknowable. What made it bearable was the time off duty. After a day's route march almost any kind of beer tasted better than any before or since, and even the most unlikely ladies became desirable, but sex or romance was probably less important than domestic comfort. It was every soldier's ambition to "get his feet under the table," as the saying went. Often the husband of the house was away doing the same thing elsewhere. In short, we were still cushioned by some of the lineaments of home.

Naturally, life's more subtle refinements were not very relevant or possible: the mind was no longer in tune with the infinite. We made efforts--some of us: a few choice spirits went to chamber music concerts in the more elevated parts of Glasgow. There were musical soirées in Malvern and kind ladies would take us home to tea and Tchaikovsky. In Haverfordwest, in the drill hall, we sometimes managed to play records and I recall my distress at going to sleep immediately following the dramatic opening chord of the Emperor Concerto: it was after a heavy army dinner. I continued to read a little when I could, mostly poetry, often in one of those comforting anthologies compiled for soldiers under fire. ("These I have loved" by General Somebody.) They usually included such splendid nonsense as Binyon's "For the Fallen," "They shall not grow old as we that are left grow old," etc. There was always the New Statesman, constant prop for so many alienated souls, and regular doses of more rigorous literature such as the paper of Labour Monthly, where the great Marxist guru Palme Datt thundered his anathemas and pursued his abstractions, first about the wicked Imperialist war, and later, after the German attack on the U.S.S.R., about the need for a second front; but I remember nothing vividly except for reading Byron's Don Juan on the banks of some clear Scottish burn. Or was it the Cottar's Saturday Night by the national bard? You will note that these matters were no longer central but peripheral concerns, devised to make life tolerable: that is how it should have been.

I must also explain that for some time I worked in the intelligence section of our Battalion--the 6th Battalion of the Royal West Kent regiment. This was a relatively cushy number, as we called it, and our role was supposed to be that of collecting information. There was only the officer, one sergeant and six privates, of whom I was one. Two of them, including the officer, were subsequently killed in action. Being better educated than the others, we were all misfits, but not--emphatically not--regarded as officer material. We were anarchic and inefficient and the bores of our rifles were black: nobody much cared, as it was all make-believe anyway. Collecting military intelligence is awful enough, but producing imaginary intelligence was impossible. Does it matter if a non-existent enemy is in the wrong place on the map?

I became unhappy with this role and managed to get transferred to a field company as an ordinary footslogger rifleman. The move was inspired by my interpretation of Marxism, which required that I should be at the center of the action. As a result of basic activity, my being would be transformed and I would be well placed to make my contribution to the destruction of Nazidom and ultimately to the revolution, which would then lead to the liberation of mankind. It was an almost mystical conception.

This "motivation" remained throughout the war and that is why I have to mention it here. I "knew" what I was fighting for, whereas most of my companions only knew what they were fighting against. (To be correct, if you had asked them, they would probably have mentioned national survival, which is fair enough.)

In Practice, of course, it didn't work out entirely as intended: I tried to conform but there were lapses, some of them were caused by an acute awareness that much of our training was stupid and irrelevant. Because of this, my behavior was not always cooperative. Other incidents were accidental, the worst being on the loch at Inveraray in Invernessshire. As I was peering over the edge of our ship, my steel helmet dropped into the water and sank into the depths. This crime was second only to losing one's rifle and I had to be disciplined. I must have been one of the last to undergo seven day's pack drill, which consisted of running to and fro with a heavy pack on one's back, pursued by a savage sergeant major: at such times I almost forgot my resolve to confirm outwardly whatever went on within. Incidentally, it was at Inveraray that discipline broke down when soldiers refused to take up guard duties at the castle.

The ghost on the ramparts frightened them, female though it was: for such encounters they had not been trained. They were also demoralized because that feudal potentate, the Duke of Argyll, would not allow French letters (condoms) into his domain.

Then, to return to the matter in hand, there was the terrible incident of the forgotten sausage. When we were being inspected by some visiting Brigadier or General, there was a horrified hush when this withered sausage was revealed in my unpolished mess tin: the company was disgraced. Because of such misdemeanors, together with my inability to hit a target, let alone a bull's eye, on the rifle range, our company commander recommended that I should not proceed overseas. Probably he considered that the wrong people might get shot. Fortunately, in the confusion that always prevailed, the report was lost or never sent and I embarked with everyone else. The long preparation was over. They had not wholly succeeded in producing the happy warrior, but I was not the only imperfect soldier and there had been many worse cases who had been transferred to less exacting spheres. Reconstructed or not, I had survived.

4. NORTH AFRICA

Preliminaries

As I was not a general this is not a history of our times nor even a footnote to them, but a personal record. There will, therefore, be no place names or dates or descriptions of battles. More than normal life, warfare is phantasmagoric, with dream sequences that have no linear time or geographic space. Official histories present a vast impersonal panorama where armies move around like hordes of ants upon a map. But at the time the individual soldier cannot know whether his side is winning or losing. His battle is only one confused episode in a campaign and his part in it is confined to one ridge, perhaps, or one hole in the ground. A peculiar feature of war is that it turns that small place into a universe.

So it was that in our "invasion" of North Africa, although we had been told roughly where we were supposed to be, we could not know what was happening. To begin with, in fact nobody knew because it was not clear whether the

French, particularly those with General Giraud, would "cooperate" or not. However, we appreciated well enough the
fact that our landing had been unopposed; there was no one
there to greet us in the dawn. Quite an anti-climax after
the Hebrides, it was. At first, in the half light, some of
us thought that the beaches were littered with corpses, but
they were only sleeping soldiers. We then marched aimless-
ly around and, when night came again, re-embarked on a
destroyer which, zig-zagging down the Mediterranean, took
us to Algiers. This time, they said we were going to where
the action was. When in doubt, infantry soldiers should move
to higher ground, so we toiled up to a hill overlooking Algiers. From this grandstand view we witnessed the pyro-
technics of enemy air attacks on our ships and those that
went to the bottom included the one with our equipment together with the top part of our uniforms. It was hot, they
said, so we landed in shirt sleeves, to be boiled by day and
to shiver in the cold nights. From an abandoned bungalow
of a French "colon," therefore, we collected clothes and I
was fitted out with some kind of woolly female garment. In
retrospect it may seem appropriate that my war began as a
kind of drag show. But at the time no such sophisticated notions ever surfaced: we had warm clothing and that was
enough.

Whoever was in charge of the First Army then decided
that we should proceed along the coast to Tunis--a "rush"
that eventually took six months.

However, all unconscious of our doom etcetera, we
began our bizarre preparations to move within hours. Bizarre they were, because although officially we were motor-
ized, at that time we had no vehicles. As we could not proceed to Tunis on foot, we set about commandeering trucks.
This meant that somebody would have to speak to the natives
and it emerged that nobody in our company, including the
commander, could speak French except myself. (Many of our
comrades could scarcely speak English.) In my schoolboy
French I started negotiations with owners and drivers of
trucks, but they kept repeating "pas d'essence, pas d'essence,"
and when the captain impatiently asked what they were saying,
in good faith I translated that he had no sense. The only
way to fuel the vehicles apparently was to burn charcoal in
them, although the science of this escapes me still. This
process was time-consuming and nerve-racking because the
consequent fires betrayed us to enemy planes which had already started their shuttle bombing and strafing flights from
Tunis.

While this was going on one of the French drivers said he wanted to go home to say goodbye to his wife and to collect some belongings. He said it was some distance but that we could return before preparations for moving off were finished. Without permission, I set out with him through territory apparently controlled by French units. It was indeed a long way and on the return journey we were stopped by the soldiers and taken to their commander. There followed a confused explanation in my halting French. He seemed too weary to care and let us go, maybe not knowing whether or not we were officially friends. In any event he must have thought I was a harmless idiot and therefore as English as I claimed. We arrived back just in time to join the grand advance on Tunis.

In my memory the following days and weeks are all mixed up. At first there was no enemy except for the planes. Because of them our truck overturned in the ditch and we never saw it again. The planes did a kind of shuttle service from Tunis and with our feeble entrenching tools we burrowed frantically away at our little slit trenches, the first of the multitude that were to be dug from there all the way to Austria three years later. The ground was hard and the trenches were shallow, and we prayed for night to come. The passive business of being machine-gunned from low flying planes--Stukas I suppose they were--is demoralizing in the extreme and the only way to stop shaking is to fire whatever weapons one has into the empty air. In our war gestures, however futile, were very important.

The First Encounter

In addition to the planes, signs of resistances began to appear on the ground. A few tanks fired at us and went away; it was, presumably, a delaying operation while they prepared their stand. This defensive operation was to be decisive and they took up positions near a place called Mateur for a battle which we called Green Hill. Almost relieved that this was a proper war at last, at dawn we advanced up the hills with more enthusiasm than in our Scottish rehearsals. With traditional panache one of our young officers led the way blowing his hunting horn. Like many others on that day, he was never seen again; some, we hoped, had been taken prisoner. When full daylight came, we discovered that our objectives, if they existed at all, were far away and we were sitting on the open hillside in full view of the enemy machine-

gunners opposite. A stream of bullets poured into our midst
and shattered my rifle, which I still held on to in a stupid
kind of way, watching it splinter to bits. Afterwards they
said how calm I was, but it was really more like hypnosis.
A friend to whom I was very devoted was severely wounded
and I took him back to where the stretcher bearers were. I
had forgotten, or had never been told, that this was a breach
of discipline punishable by court martial--our business was
with the enemy, not our friends. Him also I never saw again,
but I still remember his name.

It soon became apparent that pinned down up there we
were serving no useful purpose. Messages were supposed
to be sent over the air in some kind of improvised code,
and to our astonishment we received this extraordinary query
(or was it a command?): "Gentlemen, shall we join the
ladies?" The English class system had reared its silly head
again. What ladies? However, it didn't really matter what
the message meant as we were running down hill fast. That
was the end of our rapid rush to Tunis and the first of many
such encounters, most of which were far less catastrophic.
Some who had made mistakes were dead: those who survived
would not make them again.

The Green Hills of Africa

During that campaign our later skirmishes were more
conventional and the other bits of a proper army began to
catch up. Artillery appeared and even air support and tanks,
although our part of Tunisia was never really tank country as
they didn't like crawling about on steep slopes. For some
of the time not much would happen and we felt, if not quite
forgotten, then somewhat neglected. Rather than blunder
about in our muddy hills, war correspondents preferred to
go to the more glamorous desert where Montgomery and his
8th Army could put on a more exciting show. Now that we
had some protection from air attack, the Stukas had gone
away and the great advantage of being on a hill is, so long
as you keep out of the valleys and on the right side near the
top, that the artillery shells go over your head. With mortars it was quite otherwise: what we dreaded most was that
sudden vertical swish and that was all. If the hit was direct,
there were no more dreams of home: that was how I lost
my false teeth. I used to place them on the side of the
latest trench, and when a mortar bomb just missed our hole
it buried my teeth in soil and we could not stay to retrieve

them. (Unlike artillery shells, mortar bombs come down twice in the same place.) Toothless, but triumphant, I continued my war.

We had settled down to a life which, for the time being, was a little more static and humdrum. In consequence, our attention shifted to more earthly concerns like food. In the first world war they had bully beef and plum-flavored turnip jam with wooden pips. But in our war, perhaps because the army was partly American, we were much better served, probably more so than the folks back home. As no fires could be lit, there were special standard wooden boxes whose contents exhibited minor variations, especially among the meat and pudding tins. Our idea of heaven was the box which contained steak and kidney pudding instead of Irish Stew. The containers were perhaps foolishly distinguished by marks, so the nightly stint downhill to get the boxes was a time of drama and competitive commotion. (Woe betide anyone who could not see in the dark.) The boxes were just light enough for one man to carry--on level ground--but toiling up the mountain men would stagger and slip so that the night resounded with crashing boxes and horrible maledictions --"Mother, where are you now?" The boxes also included our cigarette rations in packets called "Camel." Our other idea of heaven was to crouch womb-like in our holes and light up one of these noxious weeds beneath our gas capes, whose original purpose was fortunately never to be realized: they also kept out the cold and the rain.

Formerly regarded as a nuisance and dispensable, I was now sent on important minor errands and peculiar patrols. It was a welcome relief and the enemy was not often directly involved since he was living in the same fashion on the other side of the hill and there was plenty of room. Wandering about at night we mostly ignored our adversary, who went another way. As the troops of either side patrolled through hill-top villages surrounded by prickly pears the dogs would bark so that we knew and they knew where everybody was; in this manner we avoided noisy encounters. There were even walks in the daytime and I remember a rare moment of illumination in a valley where flowers had burst like jewels out of the mud, apparently overnight when the rains came. At such a place and time the war seemed unthinkable and remote except that at the end of the valley there was a crashed plane and the dead pilot was overgrown with hair.

I was also still sometimes required as interpreter.

Once I was sent to guide three high-ranking French officers through a mine field. Never good at topography, I lost the way, but they were never informed how close they had been to Kingdom Come.

I was sent to liaise with Moroccan soldiers called Goums (an Arabic term for supplementary French native military formations). They were paid a bonus based on the number of ears they could deliver. Had I joined an anti-Nazi crusade to become a collector of severed ears?

At this time we became fully aware of the local peasantry, inevitably called wogs by the soldiers. I often thought how much more civilized they were than my comrades in arms. We were given orders to shoot at them as they were all spies, and it was true that they did not care which side we were on: all marauding soldiers were the same to them. A solitary figure would silently emerge out of nowhere to sell us eggs (when they were lucky, they were paid). Hoping for polite conversation, they were taught lurid obscenities and in return we picked up some of their words. I thought I was learning Arabic, but later it emerged that it was a local dialect that was almost useless elsewhere. Rough practical jokes were played on them, like shaving off their beards: it was all harmless fun.

Promotions

"You'll get no promotion this side of the ocean, " the soldiers sang in two world wars. For some of us this was accurate enough; indeed we said we didn't want it this side of the ocean or any other. However, it was a common experience that as soon as we came under fire our attitudes had to be changed. It was, I suppose, a turning point in my earthly career. Always naive, I had assumed that tough soldiers, many of them regulars who had been made sergeants and sergeant majors, were what they claimed to be; often they could boast of exploits in other theaters of war. Whereas, as an ex-pacifist formerly devoted to poetry and dreams, I took it for granted that battles were not my thing. I had assumed that my contribution, if any, would remain marginal and obscure. In anticipation:

> I had seen the eternal Footman hold my coat
> > and snicker
> And in short, I was afraid.

After our first encounter it emerged that these notions were
illusions: others with a similar background had similar reactions.   When so many of their NCOs had run away, they
were astounded.   To be more precise, when the "show" began, they would become "pinned down" and get lost, reappear-
ing only after it was all over.   The bullshit which a peace-
time army had engendered was no longer of any avail.   What
we discovered was that, roughly speaking, in every attack it
was only one-third of our unit which reached the top of the
hill.   Those who did were always the same men.   There
were some casualties, of course, but others either disappeared for some days or, like the troops of the Grand Old
Duke of York, they were only half way up the hill, etcetera.
That is how it was and in consequence some of us had to take
on responsibilities we had not bargained for.

During those first months my rank changed from private to lance-corporal, to corporal, to sergeant.   My perception of myself had to be modified and it would be less
than honest to pretend that I was not gratified.   There were
naturally a number of other emotions swilling about, but most
important was a crude satisfaction that certain qualities, hitherto unsuspected, had emerged.   If this was their game which
we had to play, then we could play it better.   In my case the
clue to the transformation was that, as soon as I became responsible for other people, my natural terrors subsided.   If
there are such things as military virtues, then this is the
main one.

Eventually I came to believe that the "leadership" role
at this level was the most difficult of all.   A corporal responsible for controlling a small group of men (an infantry
section) bears the final burden of all the necessarily mad
orders that somehow filter down from far above.   He is face-
to-face not just with the enemy, who is impersonal anyway,
but with his own ten recalcitrant individuals, none of whom
wants to die.   It is much easier, I used to think, to be a
brigadier, and easier still to be a general.   It was a simple
belief, but not without some validity.

Usually subalterns or junior officers were thought of
in this role but in my way they were often not available.
There was a shortage, partly because they were accident-
prone, especially those who had just arrived from their officer training units back home.   Foolishly they got in the way
of bullets and bombs or they succumbed to mysterious maladies like jaundice, which never affected other ranks.

Later Encounters

Most of the time what we had to do in our new capacity was not at all dramatic. The infantry's role was not
mainly to shoot at the enemy but to fill up successive holes
in the ground. Somehow we had to keep up the morale of the
men so that, weighed down with weapons and ammunition,
they could plod doggedly on to the next positions. Most of
the fire power came from the artillery and mortars and tanks.
There were, in fact, some perfectly good soldiers who, all
the way from Algiers to Tunis, never fired their rifles once.
Much of our slow progress consisted of advances to positions
which the enemy had prudently abandoned. Even so the terrain naturally favored the defenders and we were never sure
whether the infantry would remain to fire at us or not.
Compared to our war the conflict in the desert must have
been very simple and a bit like the military textbooks. But
among our mountainous hills our intelligence system often
failed. Our maps seemed to be wrong or were wrong and
frequently we arrived at the top of our hill only to witness
further ranges stretching interminably ahead. Sometimes we
were sent to take up positions behind hills which were not
there, and when morning came we were in full view of the
enemy. Once we were ordered to a map reference which
turned out to be far away in the Mediterranean Sea. Also
it happened that when we were officially informed that the
enemy had retreated, he was in fact awaiting us. If it had
been a game it would have been most exhilarating since the
uncertainty factor was so great.

Usually of course it was not a game, but on one famous occasion it almost was. Our platoon was to "advance"
on to the next hill, which was known to be unoccupied. We
began our daylight ascent in a relaxed and rambling fashion,
carrying non-military items like parcels just received from
home, as if it were a picnic. But when we were almost at
the summit the enemy was obviously very much present. Because we were so close the usual heavy fire-power could not
be brought down from friend or foe. For once then, there
was no overwhelming din and a foolish euphoria took possession of us; we jumped around and threw grenades over the
hilltop and fired our puny weapons into the blue. Whenever,
over the ridge, I saw faces like targets at a fair, I threw
my little bombs and when they bobbed down into their trenches
I thought they were dead: we were like children playing soldiers. With much difficulty I fastened my bayonet and ran
up and down. From the other side several rushed over the

hill, not to attack but to surrender. Polish conscripts they
were, who had at last found the opportunity they had been
waiting for. "Don't fire," I was screaming to our troops,
because I was in the way.

Meanwhile the enemy was still there and doubtless
puzzled by our antics. Then the ammunition so recklessly
expended ran out and we had to retreat. I could not unfasten
my bayonet (a short pig-sticker thing) and when, in our head-
long rush down hill, it stuck in the buttocks of the man in
front he cried out that he would surrender. On the way we
were prudently joined by our platoon officer who had been
shouting encouragement from halfway up the hill. He had not
shared our excitement; he possessed what is called a cool intelligence and later became a staff officer.

When this battle was over we examined ourselves as
usual and found that casualties were light and none fatal. On
my back I had been carrying a parcel of Marxist literature,
mostly news sheets called World News and Views. Embedded
in it was a nasty looking bullet and I suppose it was appropriate that it had played the role of the proverbial Bible.
For this performance as the platoon sergeant I was awarded
the Military Medal.

Night Attack

That was the quasi-farcical bit: the horror part followed that same night. One of the reasons for making these
notes personal is that infantry battles, as distinct from campaigns, are wholly indescribable. The "war diaries" compiled in the field, some of which I later wrote myself, are
no more reliable than the historical accounts based upon
them. When the noise subsides, various units, if they are
still intact, find themselves in a different place from where
they began; that is all. What happened precisely during that
time no one can ever know. The confusion is, naturally,
greatest in night operations.

On that night, instead of our little platoon which, because of its earlier role, was kept in the rear, those same
enemy positions were attacked by a much larger force. By
not making a great show of resistance the opposition had deceived us about their numbers. It was part of their training
to be more cunning than we were. Starting out at midnight
we were to surge once more up the several hills. "Surge"

suggests an invading flood and is perhaps not the right word.
What we were ordered to do was to <u>proceed</u>, which is even
less appropriate. By definition night attacks are nightmarish
because of the dark. Everyone gets lost more rapidly than
usual; friend is confused with foe and the scene is lit up by
the streaking lights of tracer bullets and flares in the sky
and often by burning grass. That is the visual part of the
show: the noisy element is naturally more shattering to the
ear drums and the nerves. The sound of modern warfare
has been likened to a symphony, a post-Wagnerian one of
total cacophony, and the various instruments cannot be distinguished, especially as there are two orchestras, theirs
and our own. They may be anybody's bombs or shells, but
at least we would sometimes be comforted by the recognizable
steady supporting notes of our supporting heavy machine-guns
--theirs made an evil crackling sound. Beneath the din of
these modern percussion instruments one could hear primeval
human voices: the shouting of frantic directions, the groans
of the wounded, and the anguished cries of "stretcher bearers." In the early movement of this devil's symphony we
could hear also the exalted keening of the bagpipes of the
Argyll and Sutherland Highlanders. At such a time those
wild notes among echoing hills added an unearthly motif
which is beyond description.

I suppose it might have been called martial music,
which was also meant to frighten the enemy. If so, he was
evidently unmoved and unsurprised. Sitting in his trenches
up there, he heard us blundering about in all directions and
we were pinned down by deadly fire. He also adopted the
then unfamiliar tactic of shouting in perfect English, "'C'
Company over here," and we were confused or deceived.
The havoc produced on such occasions caused us to imagine
in the dark that half our comrades were gone, but the casualties in fact were seldom heavy. It was not like the first
World War or the holocaust on the Russian front. For those
who were hit, however, this was scarcely a consolation.

When dawn came it was established that we had "won"
after all, since the enemy had retired (as was his intention).
Sometimes there would be a counter-attack but this time all
was quiet. There were the usual feelings of almost animal
peace; we heard a small bird singing and we could begin to
count ourselves. ("Who are you and where is your unit?")
Another battle was over; another ridge was taken and for the
moment we forgot all the other hills extending away from
there to Eternity, as it were.

The Last Round-up

     There were other variations on the theme I have just recorded. In terms of strategy, it was a prolonged delaying operation by our antagonists, who knew that defeat was inevitable. (Every one of us was caught up in something which we did not understand.) Elsewhere, in the great campaigns that really mattered, there was consolation: the Russian tide had turned. (When we heard the news of these vast encounters our sergeant major would refer to "Them Lovely Russians.") But on our front, in terms of our experience, the resistance was real enough.

     The last decisive battle at "Long Stop" Hill has been described in the official literature, for example in the history of our own 78th Division, whose insignia was a battle-axe. For the first time our confrontation was not an intimate or isolated event. It was reassuring and at the same time sobering to become part of an attack where we were at last integrated into some grand design. Eventually our side prevailed as it should have done and the enemy surrendered at last. He had done well--jolly good show. Nobody had ever imagined that the Germans were bad soldiers, only that they were prepared to fight with maximum efficiency on behalf of an evil cause or no cause at all, since the core of Nazism was wholly nihilistic.

     This time every possible instrument in the orchestra was present, including the planes and the tanks, since the hill was long as well as high. This was not our battle therefore: we did not have to do anything except stumble on amidst the noise. Somnambulistic zombies, we staggered upwards in the sun. From a dead man, who could have been the unknown soldier from either side, I took a water bottle which contained half boiling rum, and thus fortified and out of habit we struggled on. The main adversary was now the intense heat and exhaustion. When night came those of our platoon who were left found themselves gathered together in one large hole somewhere way up high. Then we were ordered to make one last effort and put in a final attack. Our company commander came to transmit these orders but we knew and he knew that we could go no farther. He was doubtless relieved when I said that our endurance was at an end. Meanwhile the remnants of another of our three platoons had just been wiped out by a direct mortar hit. All that was possible was a kind of oblivion, and when consciousness returned in the morning they told us it was all over. We did not believe them but at least we understood that they were asking no more of us.

It had been a long march. In warfare six months is a lifetime and many of us had not expected another. Instead we had survived and other lives were still to come.

Aftermath

After everything was over, there was a lull while we prepared for the next invasion, wherever that might be. I can recall nothing of this interlude except for the "victory" parade through Tunis. There were cheering crowds, but what they were cheering about it is impossible to say, except that they were relieved that a war which was not theirs had ended. All mass emotion of any kind for whatever reason makes me cry. As a tough battle-"hardened" infantry sergeant I felt particularly foolish on this march as I blubbered in the boiling sun. As Auden said:

> Our tears well from a love
> we have never outgrown.

That is how I usually interpret this unfortunate trait, but precisely what these lines mean has never been clear to me. However, like all good verses they have a consoling quality.

Although the Tunisian campaign was only the beginning of my war, I have had to resist the temptation to leave the rest out altogether. Later it was a more confused experience, while the first part was somehow pure and uncomplicated: we were not, for example, mixed up with the destruction of cities and civilians, but moving over lonely hills where nothing else was. Also we were young and unimportant enough to be immune from the corruptions of a world which had been abandoned before we had properly become a part of it. What we had instead was an unreality which may have suited my kind of neurotic temperament. I had never been fully absorbed into any daily round or common task and was not so much indifferent to, as unaware of, material considerations: I had nothing to lose. The personal feelings of love I had experienced were real enough but they had been set aside and were now sublimated into a total commitment.

But commitment to what? To an anti-Nazi crusade? To dreams of glory? To my comrades in arms? Or was it simply to necessity, the recognition of which had brought a temporary peace? We lived on a level beyond analysis, and explication now would be tedious and probably wrong. It may be that I have already overdone the "innocence" theme; we were, after all, killing other people like ourselves. In view of my pacifist past, was that a matter for congratulation? Obviously not. It appears that what I have done is to distance myself emotionally from the experience, as if it happened to someone else. It is a strategy for survival which has always been part of my temperament, a combination of detachment on one level, together with total involvement on another. Apart from these personal reactions, it seems to me now that the campaign itself had a kind of dramatic unity, ending appropriately with the largest bang of all. The rest of my war became much more complex and ultimately faded away with a dying fall: it was bad theater.

In this account I have also been aware that those who missed that war (which was the last of its kind) naturally get exasperated or bored with the nostalgia which is so often expressed by ex-combatants. If that was our war, why make such a fuss? If we apparently "enjoyed" the fighting, where is the horror and why should anyone else be impressed? Yet these natural reactions miss the point. Most of us would stress the significance of a feeling of human solidarity which transcended all other emotions and can never be found again. It is, after all, something to which every religious and secular creed aspires, mostly in vain. (The vanity is brought sharply home to anyone who has attended an old comrades' reunion.) This almost oceanic feeling is not sentimental but an experience of meaning. Whether one is aware of it or not, that is the universal human quest, life as such has no meaning, and we have to create it for ourselves. That it can so often only be found in such circumstances is a most tragic irony.

This element for some of us was paramount at that time and place in that particular war. This has to be said because it is not true that twentieth-century war has normally been like that at all. There were the special factors I have mentioned. In other conflicts during that war and in other fighting since, it would be wholly misleading to write in such terms. Our war was entirely impersonal and most soldiers never saw the enemy at all. When you get a combination of modern techology and personal hatred inspired by racism, as in Vietnam and more recently in Rhodesia/Zimbabwe, it is a different phenomenon altogether. Those wars, perhaps be-

cause of the racist attitudes, were brutal, bestial and de-
grading to all who were involved in them.   We were fortunate
to be spared such dereliction and, with a few rare exceptions,
knew nothing of such matters.   Nobody would be so stupid as
to maintain that gentlemanly wars are ever possible, but
there certainly are degrees of barbarity.

Even in that conflict other elements could have been
dwelt upon and what I have written is a gross over-simplification.   The poet Keith Douglas, who was killed in North
Africa, wrote:

> Remember me when I am dead
> And simplify me when I am dead.

That is what I have done.   Naturally there were the times
when one was overwhelmed by wholly other reactions.   I recall, for example, burying in a shallow and temporary grave
(the bodies were collected later by the War Graves Commission) a very young man who had been with us for not more
than a week.   He had the improbable name of Oblovsky and
as I lifted him up, I found that the mortar bomb had broken
all his bones.   There came to me all at once a rush of
normally suppressed feelings about the appalling waste and
evil of all our enterprise and our entire existence.   This
could have no meaning; there was only the mocking blankness
of death.   This was the theme of Wilfred Owen's Futility:

> Was it for this the clay grew tall?
> --O what made fatuous sunbeams toil
> To break earth's sleep at all?

I have also written nothing about fear: there is little
that needs to be noted.   Hannah Arendt has made us familiar
with the concept of the banality of evil: the same can be
said about fear.   It can only be driven out by some kind of
activity.   Most of the time when involved in action one felt
nothing at all.   For example, during one encounter, as we
were running up-hill the platoon commander next to me went
on running some yards after his head had been blown off.
I remember thinking vaguely how strangely the blood bubbled
from his neck.

It is only afterwards that a reaction sets in.   The
other thing about fear was that it never bore the slightest relation to the degree of danger we were in.   Furthermore, it
cannot be overcome indefinitely.   As Vernon Scannell wrote
in Any Complaints:

> Lawrence said something about courage: Courage
>   is like
> A bank account; you keep on writing cheques
> Until the day comes when there's nothing there,
> No more to draw.   You're broke.   What next?

During the following campaigns in Sicily and Italy that is
what happened to most of us: that is the part of the story
which remains to be related.

5.   THE MOUNTAINS OF SICILY

Our war in Sicily was the same thing again except
that the resistance, although lighter, was formidable in a
different way.   Because of the mountainous terrain which
suited the defense even more than that of Tunisia, quite
small groups of fanatical troops were able to hold up our
advance for hours or even days.   The Sicilian mountains are
a continuation of the Apennines, where we later found ourselves.   Churchill had announced that this formidable barrier was the "soft underbelly of Europe" and when the post-
war election ultimately came that phrase alone must have
lost him the vote of ninety per cent of the soldiers who went
through the Italian campaign.

By this time, our 78th Division was part of General
Montgomery's 8th Army which was formerly in the Western
desert.   Our landing was unopposed; indeed I cannot remember it except that there was some confusion about the island
of Pantellaria, where we thought we were going and didn't:
it must have been too flat.   We had to "advance" over terrain
which was the start of an experience of the spectacular, the
opening salvos of our Grand Tour of the Italian Alps.

Almost immediately, our battalion was held up in the
dark when trying to "proceed" through a mountain pass.   As
our platoon, which was the advance unit, was approaching
this pass the enemy machine guns opened up when we were
at a distance of only a hundred yards or so and exposed in
a narrow defile.   The bren gunner with me was hit and in
any event he had apparently fainted from shock.   While I
was trying to bandage him up with the field dressing we all
carried, their tracer bullets set fire to the grass and for
horrifying minutes the light grew brighter and brighter.   This
time, I thought, it really is the end: there was no way for-

ward or back and a long delayed but inexorable doom had overtaken us. At that crucial moment the man's machine gun jammed and we could hear him banging it to start it up again. His efforts failed and once more we had been preserved.

It is because of such incidents, in my case often repeated, that soldiers become fatalistic. Some statistical law seemed to have been suspended and some preserving principle was at work instead. This had nothing to do with any merits or skills or abilities, not even a faculty for keeping out of the way. If one was a survivor once, that was a comprehensible accident: if that unexpected survival was repeated over and over, what then? There may have been some simple souls who believed that God looked after them, but to most of us this was a blasphemous concept. There is, of course, an almost universal tendency at such times to pray, whether one is a believer or not (officially all declared atheists were recorded as Church of England, which was perhaps appropriate). Nearly always I was too doctrinaire or stiff-necked to call on God in this manner, but there is a kind of unconscious prayer, a dialogue which continues always. A dialogue with what or whom? Most of the time I have believed that this question may well be irrelevant.

These natural human tendencies were sometimes very awkward. One of our comrades at that time was an almost stage-Irish private from Dublin. He was called Paddy O'-Flynn, which may have been his real name; he was a butcher in "civvy street" and much given to poetic dialogue apparently taken from The Playboy of the Western World. All this was fine but he had this habit--especially alarming when we went on patrols in the dark--which was to mumble his prayers in a very loud voice. We were of course trying to be stealthy and still and there was no way of shutting him up without making even more noise. In addition he had a shambling gait which made him blunder into obstacles, so that curses would mingle with his supplications. When he was wounded there was an emotional farewell: "Keep your head down," he said as he went, and that was the end of his war. We envied the wounded but not for long: in his case we subsequently learned that he had lost an eye.

During our part of the campaign in Sicily the casualties were not heavy as the opposition was a delaying rearguard action by quite a small force. However there were some very noisy incidents; for example, I remember an attack at a place called Bronte where we went forward toward the objectives accompanied by tanks. We never liked this because they attracted mortar and artillery fire; also, when they were firing the noise was so deafening that we were reduced to a scarcely conscious state. When I reached the top of this hill I had no weapon--the captured German automatic rifle I was carrying had failed to work and I had thrown it away. Then there was a peculiar personal encounter when a man stepped out from behind a rock and, looking as dazed as I was, threw a grenade which went over my head. He was shot down by someone else and it was as if I had lost a Doppelgänger. In this attack, too, some of our men over-ran the objective and were never seen again. This was the result not so much of enthusiasm as of their bemused condition.

A more bizarre episode was a sort of battle which took place on Mount Etna, the highest mountain in Sicily. We received these puzzling orders that we should "proceed" up the slopes of this volcano as far as we could go. We were not told why but it may have been something to do with observation--it was in the daytime. All that we could see was, not the enemy, but the other side of the mountain. However, they could see us and when their explosives came down we were showered with black cinders--an artificial eruption. There we encountered the flying dustbins called Minnewerfers, which were most demoralizing since they arrived in multiple numbers and made a fearful wailing sound. An officer who had survived the North African campaign was killed but nothing else happened.

It would be tedious to go on about the other skirmishes, which in any event are all mixed up in my memory. Sometimes these young men who were holding us up would surrender without firing and other times not. There was always this vivid contrast between the sight of these bewildered boys--they were little more--and the havoc they could cause. Whenever the personal side of the experience obtruded the absurdity became more noticeable. Five minutes after blazing away at us they would ask for a cigarette.

In the first World War there was sometimes fraternization because the infantry on either side had more in common with each other than they had with the idiotic Generals who sent them there, or with the even worse politicians back home: they were fighting a European civil war on someone else's behalf. But our reactions were necessarily more complex. It was difficult to regard these fanatical boys as "the enemy, " yet Hitler, their mentor, emphatically was and so were the hordes that had devastated Eastern Europe. We sang "Lili Marlene" just as they did, but we knew they would be singing it as they were carrying out their "reprisals" against the "untermenschen," the civilians in Yugoslavia and elsewhere. We never had any doubts about such matters. Whatever the ultimate rights and wrongs it was not an issue then. There were wholly indefensible policies from our side, like the bombing of Dresden, but they were mostly later and we knew too little about them. Meanwhile these products of an evil system did their small bit--spiritual mercenaries--and their reward was a shattered dream. However, it could not last long and soon it was all over again and we were able to rest once more and prepare for the next time around.

It was during this Sicilian lull, among these arcadian groves, that some of us were promoted "in the field." Overnight we became officers and gentlemen and discarded our stripes on the arm for pips on the shoulder. There was a shortage of officers and since we had been doing their job anyway, we accepted this dubious honour (second lieutenants were often thought of as the lowest form of life). In our war such elevations were rare and commissioned officers went through the Officer Cadet Training Units (O. C. T. U.). I had long been aware that I would never have successfully passed out of such an establishment. We accepted on condition that we could stay with our own unit. This promise was given but subsequently broken, no doubt as a result of orders from higher up. (The theory was that those who had known us so well would find it difficult to start calling us "Sir" and saluting, etcetera.) Eventually we had no choice but there was some resistance. (My close friend Danny Lenihan, an ardent I. R. A. supporter, was in hospital with malaria at the time and when the news was announced he became violent, as was his wont, and destroyed his new insignia--but these were gestures. Delirious he was, they said.) We resigned ourselves to a posting to another battalion in the same Brigade and I moved from the 6th Battalion Royal West Kent Regiment to the 5th Buffs. At the time it was a depressing event.

Before the move there was a curious interlude when we were sent for a week to the Divisional Headquarters to eat in the Officers' Mess. It was not clear who had thought up this strange move and the assumption appeared to be that we had to learn how to use knives and forks and to eat soup.

There were, of course, arcane rituals and tribal rites in officers' messes, but their observance under such circumstances was scarcely possible or important. The General, who was a civilized man, was clearly embarrassed by these arrangements and did his best to make us feel at home.

After that we returned to our new units and I found the transition easier than anticipated since it was a relief to the Company I joined that I was not one of those untested officers straight out from the training unit. It was significant that even in that democratic war the British class system was still reflected. We had discovered that the aristocratic principle still had its value. Officers out of the top drawer were generally more popular and more effective. In accordance with their life style they were permitted certain eccentricities, particularly in their dress, which would have been frowned upon from others. During the boredom and the longueurs when we were sitting about, they were in demand to keep the troops amused. For instance, the Hon. John Prentice had an inexhaustible fund of probably apocryphal stories about his father, the Lord. The "higher ups" turned a blind eye on another who had collected a flock of sheep which were driven about together with the men of his platoon: the excuse was that they were to supplement a monotonous diet. Officers from the middle, especially the lower middle, classes were often tense and insecure and therefore found it difficult to gain the confidence of the men. Like bad schoolmasters they tried to be authoritarian and it didn't work. As I shall relate, in Italy we were sent on a great many night patrols and this was always a severe test for those in charge of them. On one occasion the men refused to go--a not uncommon experience--and the officer, an ex-bank clerk, threatened them with his revolver. So the man with the bren gun said, "You have that little pop gun and I have this automatic weapon, so what?" Stories that some of these officers were shot in the back by their own men were never substantiated. At that time also, I recall another who played chess with me one night and lost: the next morning he committed suicide. I was disturbed that this might have been some symbolic game, like the throwing of a die to assist his divided mind: I am not a good chess player anyway.

One last anecdote to illustrate this theme may be appropriate. One of my colleagues, an ex-professional golfer, developed a strategy of almost hysterical clowning. As they were trying to "advance" he would wave his revolver and scream, "Get on up the hill--on to your Doom--the Fuehrer

will get you, " etcetera. Eventually they became exasperated
by his constant threats of Doom delivered with fearful intensity and he had to be removed. He had finally gone mad
and maybe in some Institution still threatens Doom today.

The interesting thing about these strategies to overcome boredom--which were naturally of great military value
since they helped to maintain morale--is that they were not
overtly inspirational: there were no pep talks or official
calls to duty or appeals to patriotism. This was the aesthetic principle, a supreme justification for art. Mostly we
could not sing because of the need to keep quiet, so the art
of conversation and anecdotage had to be revived. At the
other end of the social scale, members of the working, especially the criminal, classes kept the Foul Fiend at bay.
Their sexual exploits, real or imaginary, were a never-fail-
ing source of pleasure. Above all, the cockney sense of
humor came into its own. Perhaps their stories would not
seem funny now: we had not yet been spoiled by television.
However, I will risk one example. Private Pickles--yes,
that was his name--provided his own sociological survey of
Bermondsey (a working-class area of London). Many of his
tales referred to his old woman, to whom he was obviously
devoted. She was an inveterate gossip, he said, and would
lean out of the upstairs window to chatter to people in the
street. On one occasion, if not more, he banged down the
sash window on her shoulders and "back scuttled" her, and
she had to continue to wave and shout to her neighbors as if
nothing was happening. On another he seized her long hair,
rolled it up in the rollers of the mangle, and did the same.
It was all very innocent.

Even in my own case, when we were sitting cramped
in some ridiculous hole, they would say, "Tell us some more
stories about your dad. " These were mostly drunken exploits. He did more to help win the second war than he did
the first, when he rode about on a horse in Mesopotamia.
(Later he claimed they rode on bicycles, but I never believed
this.)

These generalizations about class behavior are of
course not scientific--I cannot provide a statistic. This was
our experience: and how typical these things were I cannot
say. As for me, I did not have to think of myself in this
way since I had always been déclassé. I had, and have, a
prejudice against the middle classes: that is all, and because of my six months in the Tunisian hills, I did not feel

insecure. (However, from time to time there were appalling moments of desperation when I imagined I could not continue.) This would seem an appropriate note on which to close this Sicilian interlude. Beyond all this there was for me an acute awareness of a most beautiful countryside and a people to whom I was instinctively attracted; if I discussed them now it would throw things out of perspective. Later they will have to be included because they became part of my war.

6. A GAY MEDITATION

Some bits of my war were left out of the official records and this is one of them. What happened was that our Battalion was almost taken over by a fifth column which had not, fortunately, any links with the enemy. A percentage of homosexuals much higher than the national average had somehow found its way into our Battalion. This was not apparent at first, except that when we were out of the line there were disturbing banshee cries at night. It was assumed that they were made by coyotes or wild dogs. Only later, as the Italian campaign progressed, did it become evident that an ideological liberation had overtaken us.

We should not have been surprised. Almost without exception they were good soldiers and naturally devoted to their comrades. During the fighting there was a simple law: one was either, within that military context, a good fellow or not. All other considerations were irrelevant or secondary and any prejudices brought about by social life in a particular place had disappeared. They were, therefore, accepted without reservation. Another factor was that several of them were officers in key positions, one of whom, a company commander, was much admired. He had the kind of courage which took him out of the closet dimension twenty years before such responses became fashionable. These influences naturally affected us all, but the most important fact was that we were in the front line for almost three years and there was therefore no feminine competition. The real ladies in uniform, whatever they were called, were reserved for the fortunate soldiery back at the base. The result was inevitable, but it is important that no one should imagine that we had become an army of raving sodomites. The faute de mieux element was not unhealthy as it is in prisons, but largely a matter of a conscious attitude, which was gay in the ordinary sense. Doubtless the proper homosexuals did not go unsatisfied but that was almost incidental.

Many of these manifestations were largely fantasy and a means of providing color to an existence which would otherwise have been emotionally drab. For example, on the rare occasions when we rested out of the line, attempts would be made to set up a rudimentary officers' mess with all its ludicrous trappings. (Even this was a kind of parody.) The relevant thing was that some of the batmen who were transformed into temporary waiters wore makeup and were given appropriate names. Just before ceremonial drinks were served--we used to drink copious draughts of vermouth out of a bucket--the officers would shout in unison, "We want Nellie" (or Diana or Lucy as the case might be). Then the ladies would flounce in with the potent brew in enamel mugs. It was the only kind of theater we could manage, and quite therapeutic. Another curious fact which didn't seem odd at the time was that throughout the Division--not just in our unit--the normal greeting shouted as we passed some other trudging file of men was "suck mine. " Needless to say, such injunctions were not taken seriously.

It is possible that some of all this may strain credibility--the next item in this record seems scarcely credible to me even now. It concerns an incident at the highest level when we were waiting in some idyllic olive grove. By that time I was the unit intelligence officer and the Colonel had just received disturbing news. His batman (whom we knew as Lucy), according to a medical report, had contracted gonorrhea, apparently in the anus. The Colonel was totally nonplussed by this document and demanded an explanation. Soon after I started to explain I realized that, even after twenty years in the regular army, he was unaware of the facts of life. He was a sensitive man, if somewhat limited in his perceptions, and I felt obliged to proceed cautiously in my elementary description. It took a long time and he was difficult to convince. Striding up and down among the ancient olive trees he shouted, 'I won't believe it, Benjy, I won't believe it, I won't. " He meant that he couldn't accept that such phenomena existed. (His attachment to me, incidentally, could have been regarded as excessive.) As the shadows lengthened in that shady grove his resistance subsided and he became almost calm. Then he was struck by a sudden fearful thought. " "He is my batman; what must the men think?" "Yes, " I echoed, "what must they think?" This was almost too much for him to bear, but time and the distractions of war can heal all calamities and his later tribulations must have helped. Lucy, of course, had to be transferred to some less sensitive post.

So far this meditation has left me out, as if I were simply a camera. This, of course, was not the case: I was involved and not involved. My fellow officers who were gay considered, as such persons always do, that I was really one of them, but lacking in the courage to commit myself. I had told them about my adolescent obsessions and that they could therefore, if they wished, regard me as bisexual, but that it was a label I rejected. For different reasons, it was a condition they also rejected and their missionary instincts were aroused. Diana and Nellie were produced but there was no response, and for the time being they were obliged to accept my ambiguities and my betrayal of their cause. Such is the fate of fellow-travelers.

The fact was that the sex part of my erotic life had become wholly sublimated. It was of course still there but its significance was peripheral: whatever anomalies there were would not be resolved in such a manner or in that abnormal environment. Once I foolishly stood in a queue in the boiling sun outside a brothel in Tunis. The man in front of me had a boil on his neck and my interest was extinguished. A more regrettable incident occurred when I was out of the front line in some small town in Italy. My friend Danny Lenihan took me to an amateur establishment where there were very young ladies--in times of peace they would have been innocent and virginal students. We had fried eggs and wine and when the time came to retire to their back room Danny Lenihan was up and away, but I was not. I was, in any event, exhausted from the latest encounters with the enemy. Naturally the ladies were outraged, even though I offered them money. They danced round me chanting and holding up their little fingers, which was meant to indicate the size of my penis. Danny Lenihan was jubilant, but for me it was not an heroic adventure. In later life one comes to regret these lost opportunities--they were not real prostitutes after all; they were casualties of war.

This sublimation was not available to everyone. The usual release was a recount of past sexual exploits and future fantasies. (Not having had a literary education they could not write erotic messages to their wives or girl friends back home. They were aware, in any event, that we, their unfortunate officers, had to "censor" their letters. It was as a result of this experience that I came to appreciate how many marriages broke down in war time because they couldn't express themselves in writing.) I had to recognize, therefore, that my "sublimation" was a consequence of a feminine component and for that I should be grateful.

On at least two occasions this elevated condition was disrupted. These were both simple instances of fellatio. Once it was the platoon sergeant who did this to me when I was half asleep, and he was probably affected by our ration of rum. This was never mentioned thereafter. The other incident was more bizarre. At dawn and dusk we had to go through a ritual called "standing to"--however far away the enemy was. This consisted of standing all dressed up in an alert position outside of our trenches or tents or wherever it might be. (One of our wilder colleagues did this even when on leave in Britain--he "stood to, " he said, in his wardrobe.) The officer's duty consisted of going the rounds to make sure the ritual was observed. On this occasion when I said to Private Adams, "Is there anything to report?" he made this sudden fellative assault and I was too confused to prevent him. Next day he came for an official interview in what passed for the company office, and having saluted and been told to stand at ease, he said that he wished to apologize. Gravely I responded that he could dismiss and that the incident would be forgotten. "Old men forget, " I thought; or I might have thought, "Yet all shall be forgot, " which is why the record has to be set down before it is too late.

7. MY PATROLS

Although it cannot be proven, it is my belief that during that war I spent more of my time on night patrols than anyone else in the western world. Some of them were militarily useful; many were absurd and the rest were impossible in the sense that the instructions couldn't be carried out. If you compare warfare with imaginative literature--a not impossible comparison--then war is a dramatic novel, the campaigns are chapters and infantry patrols are like lyric verse since they have an immediate and brief intensity and they cannot be fully planned.

These ventures fell to my lot, not mainly because of any special abilities--indeed I could never read a compass and had to rely on my companions to find the way--but because there was often no one else suitable to send. The orthodox theory of the higher-ups was that when we were holding front line positions, we should be dispatched on these nocturnal errands to keep up our "fighting spirit, " a state of mind that we knew nothing of. In consequence it was not easy to persuade the men to cooperate and they particularly

objected to being taken out on these walks by officers who
had just arrived. (They were always arriving because their
departures were so frequent.) Such persons were a menace
because, with rigid persistence, they would take their crack-
pot orders <u>literally</u> instead of interpreting them according to
their conscience and the situation on the ground.

When the orders had been transmitted, one had to
ask for "volunteers" in the proverbial army manner, which
is "you--you and you." Then the objections would start.
One would say he could not see in the dark, another that he
had a bad cold and might cough or sneeze and disturb the
enemy, but the most common appeal was that they had wives
and families back home. The implication was that the war
should be carried on entirely by virgin soldiers. This resistance was partly a routine game and usually some kind
of group would eventually emerge. When that happened most
of us would have to rush to whatever passed for a latrine--
it was the kind of anticipatory fear which affected the bowels.

When the time came the experience could be less
daunting than our imaginings. A constant dread was that
we would run into some other patrol from our own side, and
then there might be a panic shoot-out with each other--an
ironic indication of our "fighting spirit." Inspired by their
tensions, the men would be "trigger happy" and such incidents did occur. Indeed, they might fire at moonlight shadows or peculiar shapes in the dark or even a wandering cow.
At least one wily and unscrupulous officer took advantage of
these realities and would travel a little way and then dramatically locate "the enemy" lurking behind a looming bush.
When they had all blazed away and the bush was destroyed,
this officer would return to base, his mission accomplished.
His men would be none the wiser or would pretend they were
not. It was a possible strategy and did no one any harm--
except the bush. A similar event happened when I was instructed to take out, in addition to our men, three Canadians
--i.e., two colonels, and one brigadier--who were on a
"familiarization" tour of the battle front. If this is a tour-
ist show, I thought, we must do our best. They must be
treated as private soldiers, I was told, so we went forth as
usual and arrived at a place where the enemy <u>could</u> have
been--it was no burning bush. Then they were <u>all</u> told to
fire everything they had so that we might provide a splendid
demonstration of the fighting spirit, and a worthwhile excur-
sion. I have liked and respected Canadians ever since.

What kind of missions did we have? I must content myself with three examples only. The first one was a kind of post-mortem on another patrol which had been dispatched to "examine" some enemy positions in a farm house. Most of them had been "wiped out" and the bodies were out there in "no man's land"--this was not a term we used in our war because we were not static long enough. I was ordered to take out another patrol to find out what had happened and to bring back the bodies. This involved taking stretcher bearers, a nerve-racking possibility because of the noise such a large contingent would make. The men were exhausted and realized the unfairness of the mission. Our comrades were dead anyway--did they want to add to their number? I sympathized with them, but orders were orders, I said.

Then came perhaps the most difficult moment in my war when they refused to cooperate. I said, "Well, anyway, I shall go, ' and started off. The difficult bit was not to look back, and one by one they reluctantly straggled along and I gave thanks to whatever gods might be. Having crossed the river (in the last part of our war rivers took the place of mountains) we proceeded to the spot making a most appalling noise. One imagined that the entire opposing army would have been alerted. We located the pitiful remains of the lost patrol in a narrow gully. They had been "ambushed" by a booby trap consisting of a bicycle chain stretched across the ditch and this had triggered off a mine.

The stretcher bearers did their job and collected the bodies, and we set off on the return journey to our lines beyond the river. There was sporadic firing but they could not see us in the dark. Then I made an almost fatal mistake. At such times we always craved a cigarette, which could not be lit in the open, so, just when the dawn was breaking, we entered an empty farm to smoke and collect our wits. It takes roughly ten minutes to smoke a cigarette and during that time the enemy patrol, which had followed us, surrounded the building. When, without taking proper precautions, we came out, all hell was let loose and we had to run wildly toward the dividing river. Miraculously everyone survived including the dead men: they, alas, were beyond all rejoicing. Back at the unit they congratulated us: jolly good show, the colonel said.

The second example is less somber. Somewhere in one of our interminable "advances" our battalion was approaching a town where some rearguard elements of the enemy were still thought to be. They sent our platoon there to find out, so that if all was clear the remainder of the force would proceed. We expected to arrive at dawn and simply walked up the road. At that time our platoon was blessed with an imaginative sergeant who called himself Tiger Braden. He was at the rear of the platoon with his radio transmitter, reporting back to the waiting battalion, and I later discovered that his fantasies had overcome him and he had described lurid incidents of non-existent opposition. At the height of these mythical encounters his transmitter went dead, so the forces behind us assumed the worst: we had been overwhelmed and they must expect resistance. In fact the enemy had withdrawn a few hours since and when we reached the town a wholly different kind of pandemonium broke out. The church bells rang and our small unit was taken over by celebrating citizens. The men were dragged off by wild ladies and the wine began to flow. We were casualties all, and when much later I eventually came to, I was alone in a church belfry. The higher-ups, confused by grotesque messages and the sound of bells, were not pleased at all and the colonel said, "Poor show, lieutenant, poor show." Meanwhile, the sergeant had finally gone off his head. "Tiger Braden will return," he cried as they took him away. One could only hope that he never did.

My third example brought about more fatal consequences. This time our mission was simply to go to a house to see if it was occupied. For once it seemed a feasible mission and there was no preparatory alarm. We crossed the mandatory river by holding on to a rope which stretched across. Without losing our way we located the house, which looked sinister enough to be occupied by all manner of evil presences. As it seemed foolish to take the whole blundering lot of us to investigate, I positioned them at a crossroads with a corporal in charge and their bren gun covering the path to the house. It was all very still and peaceful and, together with my temporary batman, a slow-witted farming man from Yeovil, Somerset, proceeded in what we hoped was a stealthy manner towards the object of the exercise. (This man was very tall--really much too large to be in our war--it was safer to be little.) We had gone about two hundred yards when there was a fearful commotion back at the crossroads, the sound of shots and explosions of grenades and frantic shouting. It lasted only a few minutes and I had reason to fear the worst. We had been observed and our men had been taken by surprise.

I never knew the casualties, but they were all taken prisoner and I heard a voice say, "Vair are you vounded." What was I supposed to do? The question was immediately answered because at that point I stood on a mine--S mines they were called, and normally the thing would shoot in the air and blow off one's head. This one mercifully did not reach that height and the explosion literally shredded my trousers. There followed a desperately anxious moment as I gingerly groped about to find where the damage was. (Naturally we all dreaded being shot in the balls--when evolution made him upright, Homo sapiens was left very vulnerable.) Dazed as I was, relief came when I located some kind of wounds in the backside. It subsequently emerged that they were surface wounds caused by various bits of old iron. I was too confused then to know quite what had happened and thought the explosion was a bomb. My temporary batman had gone and for all I know spent the rest of the war wandering witless over the indifferent hills. Before dawn came, all that remained was to stagger out of the mine field and back over the river clutching the redeeming rope.

The incident had to be reported at Battalion Headquarters. For an officer to return without the men was of course wholly against military etiquette, rather like a captain of a ship surviving when the ship goes down with all hands lost. This time the colonel said nothing, as he wasn't there, but the duty officer expressed a disapproval only slightly modified by my condition. How could he even know that my story was true? I pointed out wryly that at least the object of the mission had been realized. (I did not know him then, but years later he became a "lodger" in our ramshackle boarding house in West Kensington. He was to become well known as a theatrical designer under the name of Tony Waller.)

The old iron had to be removed from my backside, so I was sent miles away to the South to the military hospital at Taranto. Strangely enough, Mussolini's trains, famous for running on time, still ran, if sporadically, and, suitably drugged, I was put on a kind of rack. It is the only time I can remember enjoying being really "high" and the long journey was a pleasant and timeless interval. The remainder of that story is irrelevant here. For the time being there was physical security and a soft bed and no more patrolling.

8. THE PEOPLE OF ITALY

Whether I am accurate or not in noting a degree of
innocence in our Tunisian experience, there can be no doubt
that my Italy dispelled it and made any kind of simplicity or
purity forever impossible.   It was bad enough that the war
came crashing down on people trying to lead ordinary lives.
Even worst was the fact that the Italians were never really
the enemy.   There were Italian soldiers opposing us in
Tunisia and our troops, with their inherent Anglo-Saxon prejudices, regarded them as hopeless soldiers who fired off
hundreds of rounds of ammunition at the slightest provocation,
or none at all, and then ran away or surrendered.   Certainly
this sometimes happened, simply because they wanted to get
out of the war, and they eventually did.   Later, in their own
country, the partisans who fought with us against the Germans displayed different qualities altogether, and earned the
grudging respect of the British soldiery.   True, they were
still "wops" and only marginally distinguishable from "wogs, "
but at least they were our wops and often braver than we
were, as guerrillas have to be.

However, what screwed us up was not the soldiers
but the impact of the war on the ordinary people in the villages.   General Montgomery had earned the gratitude of his
men because he would not send us into the attack unless we
had really massive artillery support.   There was none of the
terrible bitterness felt by Sassoon's "lions led by donkeys" in
the first world war:

> He's a cheery old card, grunted Harry to Jack
> As they slogged up to Arras with rifle and pack
> But he did for them both by his plan of attack.

Montgomery was not a "cheery old card"; he was eccentric,
even freakish, and made his wife run round the garden
every morning.   He didn't smoke or drink and he believed
in a primitive Old Testament God.   Even so we trusted
absolutely that he would not throw us into the conflict like
Wilfred Owen's cattle.

All that was fine and we now moved up the hills
behind a storm of steel, often to discover that the enemy
had withdrawn several days ago.   But instead we came
upon battered hill-top villages where the people still

were, staying put with incredible peasant obstinacy. (At a later stage in the campaign they were often forcibly moved out for their safety, and also because we wanted their houses: by then it was a different kind of war.) Desperately poor, they would rush out to welcome us when their homes were half ruined, sometimes with wounded women and children inside. It was an agonizing business, often repeated. Sometimes we would get intelligence from the villages that the Germans had withdrawn, but we were not allowed to trust their information. Under such circumstances there was neither triumph nor satisfaction in "capturing" or "liberating" their villages--only grief and even shame. True it was a total war and the gap between soldier and civilian had been closed, but when one encounters the uncomprehending eyes of a bandaged child such formulations are blotted out. "What about the blitz?" someone will say. No doubt for the civilian under fire, the experience may be similar, but not--emphatically not--for the man in the bomber plane; if he is fortunate, he flies back home through the impersonal sky to his own distant and hearty breakfast. Whereas we had to witness what our guns had done and listen to primordial lamentations.

There were happier times, of course, and scenes of genuine rejoicing, some of which I shall describe.

Already I felt at home. With my temperament it was inevitable that I should love Italy; consequently, I soon picked up a rough knowledge of the language, although I never trusted the emotion--or indeed any other. This place, I considered, is where I belong, and here is where I want to be. Such responses were reinforced by encounters throughout the campaign.

9. CASSINO

I suppose Cassino is the one name out of my war which is familiar to most people: they know about the monastery which was both a fortress and a weird symbol of German resistance. In our memories it has a special place because it was the only time that conditions, in any way at all, began to approach the static quality of the 1914-18 Western front. There was a great deal of "heroism" on both sides, all largely wasted since the results produced were out of proportion to the vast efforts involved--or so it seemed to us.

Our bit of the battle was entirely a holding operation: we sat there while a cosmopolitan army, which included Poles, Indians and Gurkhas, made their dramatic assaults on that symbolic mountain. All this came about because, when the flat part of Cassino was bombed into rubble, our tanks couldn't get through. One supposes therefore that the hold-up was not anticipated, except in the sense that strategists have to foresee all possible consequences, including the end of the world. All we had to do was to grub about in the rubble for as long as possible and this turned out to be more trying than any number of attacks. Also we were agonized spectators watching others making their doomed frontal assaults on those treacherous slopes, tiny figures clinging to the mountain sides in hopeless positions. In fact, most of the time we couldn't see anything because of the smoke. Like gods from Olympus, the enemy looked down and in daylight the only way to protect us was to put down a barrage of smoke shells all the time. The acrid white vapor got into one's nostrils and eyes but it was better than accurate fire.

Once when I was shaving out of a mess tin, one of these shells came down and made a direct hit on the tin, which reminded me of that other incident of the withered sausage long ago, back in the Nissen huts of Scotland. This shaving operation was a gesture designed to help maintain morale, my own included, but a hazardous one since at such times one tends to shake. Little strategies of this kind had to be devised. For example, one day when the wind had blown the smoke about--we dreaded the wind rising--we saw over to our left that some of our soldiers had climbed out of their pits in order to remove rubble and dust which had fallen about them. They piled it onto a blanket and emptied it all out into neat heaps in a straight row. This was all part of the Guards' tradition of keeping calm and everything tidy. They were watched without interference by the enemy, who were probably too surprised to take action against them.

There were times when we were temporarily taken out of our forward positions and at least once, when relatively in the rear, we were on higher ground and I was able to survey that bleak scene more fully. The smoke floated low over large stretches of water and wreathed around ruined buildings. As a background to the intermittent percussions of the warfare, bull frogs kept up their hoarse chorus and, to complete the classical associations, out of that desolation a nightingale sang. Viewing this primeval panorama, I said to my companion, a regular army major, "Look at all that, and not a single space for a cricket pitch. " He dolefully agreed and launched into his cricketing reminiscences, which I knew by heart. He was one of those stylist cricketers whose every stroke is perfect, even though he couldn't hit the ball. It was this same man who said to me indignantly that he didn't join the army to fight in a war: there must have been a mistake somewhere.

Back in the line--not that there was a line--our nerves began to get seriously strained. Our company commander was one of those dashing officers who looked like Jimmy Edwards* at his most preposterous. He had been a commando and rushed about like the mad duchess, screaming at his batman whom he called his "servant. " Because of what followed, I can make that unkind reference only with a twinge of remorse. The enemy must have located our headquarters, which was, of course, a few holes like the others. One night a particularly heavy mortar barrage came down on that area and he decided that he and the other occupants would have to get out. As they emerged, another salvo arrived and he was killed instantly. The man carrying the radio equipment was blown down a kind of well, but was otherwise unharmed. What happened to the much abused batman was not recorded. The sergeant major, who was slightly wounded, sent for me to take over the "company, " which consisted of a handful of shaking men and two other officers. The only thing to do was to go back into those same positions and hope for the best. Somehow we got the radio going again so that we could report on the night's toll.

All that remained was to go on staying and try to keep ourselves together until we were relieved. Nobody could run away anyhow, because there was nowhere to go.

There was one personal episode which must be recorded. Once again it was a patrol, this time to be taken seriously. The higher-ups were contemplating a direct attack across the river which ran between us and the mountain, but they didn't know whether the river was fordable. My brief, therefore, was to go to the river to see how deep it was. The short distance between us and the water was brightly lit at night by flares--a real no man's land where shells came down constantly from both sides. There was

---
*An English comedian.

nothing to be done about their barrage, but it was arranged
that our own should stop at midnight so that I could reach
the river. (Part of the way I was accompanied by one corporal.) All I had to do was to dodge from one hole to another until I got to the water.

Amid wailing shells I started off, and when midnight
came there was no let up of our barrage because the message
had never got through. The scene was like one of those first
world war paintings by Paul Nash, and I thought that even
then. (At such times one's mind seems elsewhere.) When
I got to the water I lowered myself in and could not touch
the bottom, so the evidence was conclusive. Inspired by
success so far and the thought of arriving at base again, I
retraced the journey. As soon as the mission was completed,
they rushed me off miles away to the rear to present the
findings. It was clear enough that no attack was possible in
that direction. This patrol at least had been worthwhile.

I was sent back to our few square feet of Cassino,
and after what seemed like years later we were relieved by
"fresh" troops. Such operations were always hazardous and
this one was especially so because of our proximity to the
enemy. (Changeovers were sometimes botched because the
departing troops were in such a hurry to get out that they
failed to show the incoming men where they were supposed
to be.) At first this relief went well but as we went rear-
wards, the men were so exhausted that some of them flopped
down and slept, before we were out of danger. They then
got mixed up with a constant milling of men and material
passing up and down. The worst encounters were with the
mule trains when foot-soldiers were pushed out of the way.
In the midst of this confusion one of the mules lashed out
and I received a proverbial kick, full on the elbow. It felt
as if the arm was broken and it was the most intense pain
I have experienced before or since. Clutching this broken
arm, I then had somehow to drive the remnants of this exhausted company to our destination. Many were beyond caring and simply dropped down where they were; even kicking
wouldn't budge them. However, at last all things must pass
and we arrived at some haven of which I have no recollection.

That was the end of our bit of the Cassino battle and
I was taken off to hospital in some place whose name I have
also forgotten. It emerged that the arm was not broken and
I was not there long. The only incident worthy of note was
an official visit from General Alexander, accompanied by a

battery of photographers and reporters. They gathered around my bed, all prepared to record my story, and when the General asked for details it was with perverse satisfaction that I said, "Just a kick from a mule." Embarrassed, they all hurried on to the next bed.

Yeats foolishly said that passive suffering is not a theme for poetry. If I had been capable of writing during that war, it was this experience which would have provided most inspiration. As it is, one has to be content with this reminiscent prose. My personal contribution was recognized by the award of the Military Cross--the officer rank equivalent of the Military Medal I already had. We were naturally cynical about these "gongs," or pretended to be. "They come up with the rations," we said. However, in this instance, I did not feel that it was undeserved. In the subsequent official citation, the mule was not mentioned. It was that animal I should have written my verses about--or perhaps the nightingale.

10. TAKE MY GUN AWAY

We spent an entire winter in the Apennines, somewhere before Bologna. Long ago the men of our division had ceased to believe that our mountain climbing would ever stop. This exasperated those who dished out our information and they pointed out that this time it must be true because there weren't any more mountains after Bologna. We didn't believe that either; we no longer believed anything, and certainly not their stories about the Germans whose improbable antics included going about in "horse-drawn transport." In fact most of the intelligence we received was as correct as it could ever hope to be. As for the mountains, it didn't matter whether there were any more to come or not, since we stopped "advancing." Perhaps there was too much snow; certainly the cold became the main adversary and we could no longer spend all our nights on the bare mountain. We climbed out of our holes and took refuge in farmers' former homes. When we were outside we were much healthier, but once under shelter men started catching cold. Rum was much in demand and there were a few cases of men who fell down in the snow and never got up again: it was a pleasant death, as they felt nothing at all.

Our only exercise consisted of night patrols, wander-

ing from peak to peak, rarely meeting anything or anyone.
With us were representatives of the partisans and sometimes
during our nocturnal rambles they were guides. The hospitality we received on these occasions from poor peasants
was beyond belief. There was a lot of bonhomie and examination of their family photographs and our own. Often my
halting Italian wasn't necessary as some of them had spent
years in America. Coming in out of the cold, we would be
given wine and pork or chicken before a blazing fire. There
was little enough we could do in return.

All this was, of course, strictly against orders, but
so far as I know we were never betrayed to the enemy,
whose location we tactfully didn't enquire about. For all we
knew the Germans were also entertained, but by this time
it would have been improbable because of the ferocious treat-
ment they meted out to the partisans and the villages from
which they might have come. The partisans were regarded
as being outside the "rules" of war and were never taken
prisoner. It was naturally not as cozy as this all the time
and there were infrequent, almost accidental, encounters; as,
for example, when one of our patrols, together with some
partisans, was besieged in a church and we could not re-
lieve them in time. Otherwise it was almost a holiday. I
might have described the wooden "roads" which were constructed, and the mule trains bringing our provisions, but
these I prefer to forget.

The Last Resistance

After this lull our advance continued and some of the
resistance was as fierce as anything we had encountered.
Out of the mountains at last, we were now told that there
was probably only one more river to cross and it would be
all over. There was a series of sharp engagements and
some sporadic street fighting, which is the worst of all.
The forces opposite were usually even more exhausted than
us, but we didn't know that and they did not surrender easily.

On one such confrontation a tank drew up near our
platoon and I said, "Take no notice, it is one of ours."
These were famous last words; someone pointed out that
there was a swastika painted on it and it was preparing to
blast us out of existence. Its enormous gun swung around in
our direction but the muzzle stuck in a bank and we were
saved. Incidentally, during that campaign the German tanks

consistently had an advantage over our American Sherman tanks because they were lower on the ground and the gunners could see beneath the boughs of the olive trees. Often our higher tanks were blind and an easy target. How could the designers have foreseen such a predicament?--presumably the advantage was accidental. The crew of this one must have then escaped into the town because we later met them accidentally. A ridiculous shoot-out occurred, like a scene from a bad film. The tank officer fired his automatic weapon into the room which I was supposed to be searching, and with my small revolver--they were really only of symbolic value-- I bobbed up and down and fired out of the window. (There was nobody else around.) This was the first time I had ever fired a pistol and the only time when I knew I had hit a particular person. After he was captured I was relieved to learn that the bullet had only passed through his shoulder. It is pleasant to imagine that he is today a much respected Burgermeister of some town in Upper Bavaria.

It was at the end of this period that I was wounded on patrol, as already described. Although I was not aware of it then, I had come to the end of my days as an officer in an infantry company. "They" had realized that I needed some other employment where I didn't have to lead men up hills or over rivers any more.

After I had become a casualty, almost the entire platoon deserted. They were called the Bermondsey Boys and had been sent to this platoon because no one else could do anything with them. I was already aware that my kind of "leadership" had its own severe limitations; it could not be built upon or followed up. In addition, like most members of the semi-criminal classes, these men were superstitious; if my luck had at last run out, then so might theirs. This "mythical" element in my role had been important. In some of our attacks I went without a steel helmet, and sometimes with no weapons. On one level this was childish and foolish, yet it expressed a correct feeling that I had become largely symbolic. (There were other officers who did the same thing.) In that context, a "leader" was simply someone whom the gods had chosen to protect. Doubtless such unconscious atavistic notions derive from the remotest past.

Back in the hospital, I enjoyed an almost mystical peace. Like all puritans, I find it difficult to accept pleasure unless I have earned it first. As the punctures in my backside soon healed, it was a short stay and not without incident.

Into the ward where I was they brought a number of Norwegian sailors. Their ship had been bombed and they had all been thrown into the sea. The ship--am I betraying a military secret now?--was carrying mustard gas ... just in case. The liquid gas settled on the sea and some of the sailors were severely burned. The gas attacks the armpits and the groin and these huge, barrel-shaped, hairy men were much embarrassed by the attention that had to be paid to their private parts. Also they were like children when faced with pain: there was a perpetual chorus of groans. When the man in the bed next to me was being attended to by a pretty nurse he became, in spite of himself, excited. Being well trained, she rapped his erect penis with her pencil and said, "That's quite enough of that." Inevitably the groans multiplied.

Apart from myself, the other British officers were recovering from hepatitis or yellow jaundice. They had reached the stage when their eyeballs were no longer white. Like yellow spooks, they sat around looking sorry for themselves. Since they were forbidden alcohol one could sympathize: my peppered backside was infinitely preferable to their disordered spleens.

The time came for me to leave and to avoid the tedious procedure of passing through official transit camps, I got on a goods train carrying nothing at all. There must have been an engine driver, but it had no other crew except two Indians who spoke neither Italian nor English. They were puzzled by my presence and put me on a ledge like those used for large cats in the zoo; all I had to do was stay there. Whenever the train clanked to a standstill, which it did frequently, they got down and collected wood and leguminous leaves which they cooked with curry on the floor. This dream-like procedure went on for some days and I was fed on this monotonous but healthy diet. This train was somehow not involved in time or space and I have had occasion to doubt whether it was real. Certainly its journey did not seem to be urgent, but it must have trundled northward until the end of the line, somewhere the right side of the enemy. Somehow I returned to the 5th Buffs, who had apparently forgotten my inglorious departure. I was told to be Intelligence Officer at the Battalion Headquarters. Remembering my position as a private in a similar unit long ago in Britain, I was very conscious of the irony. Then I had wanted to get out--now I was glad to return.

11.   VETERANS' LAMENT

I should explain that the Headquarters of an infantry battalion is just as much in the front line as the rest of the unit and the danger is little less: Command centers are naturally always favorite targets.   However, for everybody except the Colonel, who is directly responsible for the action, responsibilities are supplementary, supportive or indirect. The headquarter units are intermediaries or links in a chain or ganglions in a network.   The main role of an intelligence officer is to know what's happening and to inform everybody else.

I suppose that, after a fashion, I did this job well enough, but it did not require the qualities which had emerged in my former role, qualities which in any event had grown devious and dim.   The dividends had gone and we were living on a diminished capital.   Certainly it was a relief no longer to be in immediate contact with our adversaries and not personally responsible for leading anybody anywhere, but I was growing increasingly weary of it all.   The progress of our allies on other fronts, where the main action had always been, made it clear that the war in Europe, however protracted it might be, was drawing to a close.   At such a time the last days are the worst.   When one has survived so much, there is a tendency not to take so many risks.   Perhaps there was going to be another life, after all, when the lights would come on again all over the world--as Vera Lynn had sung.

Battle exhaustion is a real thing.   Most commanders believed, or professed to believe, in the myth of combat-hardened veterans sweeping all before them.   But we knew that one could draw a graph which operates for everyone, and the line of our graph was declining irreversibly.   Although our division had naturally been reinforced by new officers and men, there remained a core which had landed in Algiers three years before.   Most of them were in a worn-out condition-- "bomb happy" we called it--which could be compared with the physiological state of a punch-drunk boxer.   We could no longer trust our own well tried responses.   Also in my own case, partly because I was not directly responsible for other people, I began to think more about my own safety, as I had originally done when I was a private.   Now that I was not supporting others, I found it more difficult to support myself. In short, the demands made on me at Headquarters required different responses, which I didn't want to make.   My "heroic" role was over and I didn't like the new one.

Nevertheless the guns went on sounding and some of them were still firing at us. There were occasional disasters, the worst of which was at a place called Aquino, where we found ourselves on an open airfield. It may (or may not) have been before this particular engagement that I was present at a briefing of our three Battalion commanders by the Brigadier about "the next show." During this session, at some lonely farm house, all three of the colonels were more than half asleep from exhaustion most of the time. I tried to remember what our orders were so that I could prompt our colonel. He was a much loved man and still quite young. During the operation next day he was killed by a shell which scored a direct hit on our headquarters out on the airfield: his head was blown off. The signals officer was wounded and I was left alone, confused and dazed. Unable to remember codes, I passed garbled and nonsensical messages over the air, so that they thought it must be the enemy calling. One imagines that this attack must have been a temporary failure, but of course the advance went on. Other colonels came and went and I seemed to be still there waiting for the end.

The end, however, was a long way off and there were other trying incidents--my memories are episodic. During an engagement, one of our company commanders became a casualty and there was no one suitable on the spot to take over. I said to the colonel, "I shall have to go: I am going." Maybe there was an almost suicidal element in this proposal, but it was, in any event, normal procedure that someone from Headquarters should be sent. There followed a violent confrontation with the colonel, who said I must obey orders and was to stay at my post. Instead he sent the signals officer, who led a dawn attack and was killed by a sniper; he was the only casualty. This man, Paddy O'Brien, was a friend who had been with us all the time. He had been promoted "in the field" like me, and had never said an unkind word to anyone. At such a time one can find little satisfaction in survival and my depressions deepened. How long, O Lord, how long?

Gloom or no gloom, there was always light relief; in fact, some of the most farcical episodes of my war took place during this final phase. Many of them were connected with the use of codes. (We had long been familiar with password muddles and when sentries challenged, "Halt, who goes there?" our answer as often as not was, "What is the password?") Even at our headquarters level we were always too

muddled to use them properly.   At one place we received a
bizarre order that we were to send six padres to point such
and such immediately.   In anguished tones, the colonel, a
most conscientious man, cried "What are we to do?--there
are not six padres in the whole of the Middle East." I suggested that another of the higher-ups must have gone off his
nut.   Maybe we should send six of our men in clerical dis-
guise?   Later it emerged that for the time being "padre" was
a code word for machine gun, but they had forgotten to tell
us.

Another time, after a triumphant and unopposed entry
into a town called Castiglione del Largo, we were being entertained as usual by the populace when a coded message
came through.   The colonel at once assumed that it must be
an order to push on to our next objective.   But I had celebrated only too well and was quite incapable of decoding that
or any other message.   They must know that we wouldn't be
in our right minds.   I thickly insisted, "It can't possibly be
important or they wouldn't have sent it in code." The colonel,
however, was sober and angry, but nothing could be done until next morning.   Then I discovered that the mobile bath
unit had moved from one map reference to another: the
colonel was still not amused.

During these latter days, several of our colonels were
elderly regular soldiers who had spent most of the war in
some staff capacity.   Invariably they had complicated names
like Affleck Graves or Odling Smee.   In spite of my penchant
for the absurd, I came to respect them as representing what
was most admirable in the old army which had passed away.
These were persons of a category wholly uncorrupted by the
capitalist values of the civilian world, and they had often
spent many years without promotion in some appalling out-
post of the Empire.   They had a peculiar innocence which
Kipling would have understood.   Indeed, one of them was fond
of quoting Kipling's lines:

> O its Tommy this an' Tommy that, an' Tommy go
>   away:
> But its thank you, Mister Atkins when the band be-
>   gins to play--
> The band begins to play, my boys, the band begins
>   to play.
> O its thank you Mister Atkins when the band begins
>   to play.

Although they were courageous soldiers, they were often not really at home in our war. They had done their time in a less complicated world and easily became bewildered and confused. One of them lost the confidence of our Brigadier, who would give his orders to me to pass on: "Tell Joe such and such. " The climax came when the Colonel, because of his concern for the men, refused to carry out an impossible assignment. Having disobeyed orders he was prematurely "retired" in the middle of an engagement. It was the one time when he was wholly in the right.

Another of my duties which I found irksome was the compilation of the "war diary, " which was supposed to be done after each engagement. At such times one was either exhausted or not quite sober. (I hasten to add that our liquor ration was quite small.) I often wondered whether the records of other units were more accurate than ours. Ten years later some solemn war historian must have marveled at our extraordinary tactics; sometimes the wind would blow half a battle away.

An appropriate anecdote with which to end this weary section is that of Brigadier bum-on--Barnstaple Bewdley. He saw himself as the dynamic commander who went ahead with his most forward troops. On this occasion he charged into our headquarters, where I was vainly trying to locate where everybody was. He was carrying a rifle the wrong way round over his shoulder and demanded to be shown the complete "picture. " Somewhat intimidated, I peered at the arcane marks on my talc-covered map. As we tried to make it out, great blobs of sweat fell from his overheated brow and washed away half our positions and those of the enemy too. Wild with impatience, he said we must bum on to the next hill. Timidly I suggested that the enemy might be there, but he said, "Nonsense, bum on, " and jumped into his jeep and raced down the road. That was the last time we saw him.

12. LAST DAYS

Most of the last months of our war were spent on the plains and there were still rivers ahead, the last one being the Po. It was a bewildering phase and it had become clear to me, if not to my superiors, that my resolution was beginning to falter. (If this had not been observed by them it

would have been because they were in the same condition
themselves.) My morale was not helped by a minor motorcycle accident. Unlike Colonel Lawrence, I experience no
affinity for these machines and cannot empathize with them.
This one would never go where I wanted and finally went
over a small cliff. The injuries were slight, largely consisting of a cracked rib or ribs, but it was an ominous portent. Had I survived all manner of blasts and bombinations
only to fall victim to mules and motorbikes? Fortunately,
I was forbidden to ride again but this meant that, in pursuit
of my military intelligence, I had to go all over the battle
arena on foot.

It must have been about this time that, during one prolonged and desultory engagement, I got "lost" for the first
time. It was one of those fluid situations when many people
on both sides stopped knowing where they were. One encountered other stray persons whose rank and identity were
not apparent, and inconsequential dialogues would ensue. For
instance, I found myself sheltering temporarily in a hole
with an unknown soldier who glared at me and said, not
"Who are you?" as one might have expected, but "What
were you?" He then informed me that he had been an archi-
tect, so I said, "Well, I was a librarian once, but it doesn't
help us much now, does it?" Oblivious to such considerations, he was dreaming of future monuments. He was going
to be a town planner, he said, and I agreed that there would
be plenty of towns to rebuild.

Wandering further through this same confused wonder-
land, I came upon a sentry guarding a cave in the hillside,
a kind of troll or troglodyte sentinel, I thought. I began another polite conversation and, as one might expect from a
cave dweller, he replied in a strange tongue. Belatedly, I
became aware that he was somehow attached to the enemy and
that I was in their part of the landscape. Too astonished to
take action, he allowed me to steal away as slowly as I
could. Like me, he must have been dreaming of things to
come.

When I located our headquarters at last, I had to admit that my contribution to this battle had been less than substantial. My official war-diary accounts became more disordered and festooned with wild surrealist detail: the enemy,
I wrote, had retired into caves within the hillside, there to
await the end of the war. (This, of course, is what Hitler
eventually did, but it had not happened yet.) What was to

be done? I could not, in all honesty, arrange to be certified as a casualty since my cracked rib or ribs were apparently healing themselves, and furthermore, my "bomb-happy" condition was relatively mild. (Such symptoms were often violent and could take the form of shooting at hostile hallucinations. The nearest I came to this was when I ordered a man to fire at the full moon--a command probably inspired more by whiskey than by madness.) No doubt there was some loss of nerve, but it was mainly a failure of the will. All I could say to the colonel was that I seemed to be suffering from "exhaustion," which was not fair to him as he was exhausted also. However, a solution was found and he announced that I would be sent into Egypt, there to undergo a course for mortar officers. I duly found myself, therefore, in a camp in the desert, somewhere beyond the pyramids at a place called Quassasin.

Inevitably this became an ordeal of a different order and no less depressing than my former state. Most of the other officers on the course were inexperienced: they had just arrived from Britain and to me represented something entirely alien. Had I been awarded the Military Cross and the Military Medal and mentioned in dispatches several times in order to accommodate myself to such persons and to endure this ritual nonsense? Was it not ridiculous that I should be in training for a war that for me was almost over? Somehow I must have passed through this ordeal, but the fact that I remember nothing at all indicates that there was a need to forget. It is possible also that I was bothered by a feeling of failure. Who would be doing the war diary now? And what would he be relating?

On second thoughts, there were two memories which may have some significance. The first was in the desert beyond the camp, where our latrine was situated at an hygienic distance. Out there in the brilliant moonlight, surrounded by hessian (sacking) walls, I sat brooding on destiny and thinking how pleasant it was to be sitting on a real wooden seat, when I heard stealthy footsteps--at least two pairs of them--and long shadows obscured the moon. This time, I thought, there is no way out; what an ignominious end to an unfinished life! "What do you want?" I screamed, and relief came when I heard their steps thundering away over the desert wastes. They were, of course, two members of the deprived fellaheen, most wretched of the wretches of the earth, who had come to steal the hessian.

The other incident was not a military one. As the
Egyptians had no reason to be friendly, at that time we were
not allowed out of the camp and the towns were out of bounds.
I considered that even if this interdiction made some sense,
it should not apply to me. I therefore went into Ismailia, a
town to become well known in later wars. After the desert
it was a green and pleasant place. I wandered blissfully
about and during the afternoon siesta, fell asleep on a seat
in the town square. When dusk came and Ismailia came to
life, I woke up to find what seemed to be a huge crowd sitting around looking at me as if I were an unknown and probably dangerous species. They were not hostile, but curious,
so I tried to be friendly and took out my cigarettes. They
were too puzzled to be hospitable, but I was not molested
and was allowed to proceed back to the camp. There the
alarm had been raised that I was a missing person, probably
of unsound mind. It was, of course, a non-event, but it
was the only oasis that my desert had provided.

Fortunately this interval was quite short and I returned to the battalion to take up once more the military
burden and my new duties as a mortar officer. We were
supposed to be "in the line," but it was a funny kind of war
since we were assembled behind the high, built-up banks of
the Po river and the enemy was literally on the other bank.
Using periscopes, we peered at each other across the river,
but very little happened. We couldn't see anything and neither could the opposition, so that all the firing of machine
guns and mortars was worked out by maps. On both sides
the troops were in farm houses which were marked on the
maps. Some of the shooting was remarkably accurate and
several times a stream of hostile bullets came in through the
window of our otherwise desirable residence. By the time
they reached us, these bullets were spent, but they rico-
cheted around the room in such an alarming manner that we
had to take refuge under the table.

From our experience of the last days, there was one
positive gain for me. As mortar officer I had to work out
accurately the range and direction for the firing of the bombs.
At school I had found that any kind of mathematics was beyond my understanding. But now it was a matter of life and
death that no errors should be made, since an incorrect cal-
culation could result in the bombs dropping on our own troops.
As far as I knew, this never happened and I was encouraged:
evidently anyone can do sums when they have to.

We were all looking forward to the last push of all, beyond the Po, but when it finally came about I was not there. I had been sent on leave and spent V. E. (Victory in Europe) Day celebrating with the good folk of the Royal Borough of Tunbridge Wells. It was a kind of anti-climax and obviously my thoughts were mainly with those with whom I had shared my war. For one of my friends at least, what we had always dreaded had tragically come about. Cecil Bremner, one of our Company Commanders, was killed within days of the end. When we had been stuck in some appalling situation he would conduct entire movements of the better known symphonies and we would try to sing. He would never conduct again; just when a new life should have been dawning, he had gone to join so many of our comrades whom we had survived. Beyond this personal dimension, we were also conscious of unknown millions of lost lives from both sides, now joined in the terrible solidarity of death. Psychologists say that there is such a thing as survival neurosis which generates guilt and distress; it was common among those few who came out alive from the Nazi death camps. We rejoiced that our war was over, but the grief remained.

When I returned from leave to my Battalion, it had moved to Austria, and that remains to be related. Meanwhile, there is an odd footnote to be added to the other oddities of my war. I returned to Italy by sea on a Russian ship which was taking home some of their troops who had been prisoners of war in the Channel Islands. I was the only foreigner on board and how I came to be there is now beyond all conjecture. It must have been some official arrangement because I do remember that I was not a stowaway.

The voyage was boring, as they were not allowed to fraternize with their former allies and there was, in any event, a language barrier. I was segregated and the only relief was an occasional game of chess, which I always lost.

Five years before, I had joined the army and become a detached insider and now it had ended in the same way. My Russian comrades symbolized how I had continued to belong and not belong. As a marginal person I had survived and been accepted with love. Meanwhile I had taken no thought for the morrow, which was now becoming real.

13. AUSTRIA

An Occupation Army

An army of occupation is a special kind of force with a unique role. At the beginning the fighting has stopped but peace has not fully broken out. During that war millions of people had been uprooted, displaced and flung about all over Europe, some never to return. Afterwards they had to sort themselves out in order to start their lives again. In Central Europe we were at the center of a returning process which was not a pleasant one since justice was always rough and often impossible.

Quite apart from these legions of the lost, we had to contend with misplaced property. The British and Americans had become familiar with the problem of migrant property in Italy but since the Italians had officially become our allies, the soldiers could not easily legitimize their predatory inclinations by referring to the wickedness of the inhabitants. All victorious armies go in for looting and I had the impression that our depredations were relatively mild, especially when compared with those of the Russians. In an attempt to gain our sympathy, the Austrians made a great fuss about Russian "barbarity." In the same way they were terrified of the Yugoslavs, whose advance into Austria was only stopped by the cease-fire at the Yugoslav border. The Austrians professed to regard us as their protectors from the advancing Slavic hordes.

To an astonishing degree they seemed unaware of the frightful atrocities their troops had committed against the civilian populations of Eastern Europe. When we pointed out to them that under such circumstances it was unreasonable to expect the enemy armies to be polite, they would retreat to the argument that they were not responsible for what the Germans did. "We have always been more civilized," they said, conveniently ignoring their own Nazi movement, which was almost as old as the German one and equally fanatical. Undoubtedly the Soviet armies went in for rape and pillage on a large scale: they had come hundreds of miles across their own wholly devastated and depopulated land. Also, the higher standard of living which they encountered was officially regarded as the result of exploitation. Furthermore, Stalin had sent into Western Europe, not his best troops, but some divisions from central Asia. These were not likely to feel any sympathy for the Austrians, who in their eyes were capitalists to a man.

Our kind of looting was sporadic, minor and unorganized. Military regulations naturally laid down that such behavior would be severely punished, but the decrees were difficult to enforce since we noticed that our superiors who passed on such orders did not observe them themselves. (After one high-minded address on this theme from a particular commander, we discovered a piano in his baggage.) The more organized rackets, however, were not for us: they were carried on among the bewildering and multiplying supporting units which had formerly been very much in the rear, or even in another country. This seemed most unfair since, according to our view, such licensed layabouts were not really part of our war at all.

Vienna

Whatever opportunities for gain there might have been for some, for most of us the early occupation was a most distressing experience. Our first assignment was to proceed to Vienna, there to be the vanguard of our contingent which was to join the representatives of the American, French and Russians in a quadripartite force. (At that time the territory around Vienna was occupied by the Russians.) The people were starving and we were affluent and well fed. To obtain food, therefore, they would offer us anything, including themselves, and when we left the Schonbrunn Palace or whatever it was, they would be waiting outside for tins of corned beef or spam. Any transaction, with or without a return, was of course verboten and we were not allowed to fraternize with the citizens at all. Some women made themselves available in at least three different languages--or in one that was universal.

Most of our time was spent in wearisome ceremonies and parades designed to impress not only the indifferent populace but our victorious allies. Even as early as this, it was apparent that the gulf between the Western powers and the Soviet Union would increase rather than be closed. However, gulf or not, we all met at the State Opera. As cultural agent for the Battalion I distributed tickets; because of an excess of enthusiasm, often at a financial loss. Miraculously the show had continued: night after night the half-starved orchestra played on and the performers sang as if the glory that was old Vienna had never dimmed.

Beyond the footlights there was a spectacle of another order. In the boxes of the auditorium the serried officer ranks of the four powers sat, one nationality on each side, the Russians resplendent in their medals. Below in the stalls and the pit, the natives assembled. Was not this a splendid revival of the shattered European psyche? One would have liked to believe so.

Certainly for me it was like a life stream flowing back through limbs that had been numb. I had always especially enjoyed opera music and here, in addition to the usual repertoire, there was the legacy of light opera in its original home; this was the tradition of Strauss and Offenbach and, above all, Franz Lehar. (My liking for opera had never been fully indulged, although I had once seen real elephants in a production of Aïda in Rome. Doubtless it is the dramatic element which appeals to my divided soul, and the peculiar "impurity" of the medium matches my mixed-up sensibility.)

Fortunately the spell of duty in the capital was not prolonged and we were then transported to the relative tranquility of Kärnten (Karinthia), where the battalion remained until the end of our particular occupation. The vehicles in our convoy which left Vienna were more heavily loaded than when we went in. Beneath the conventional booty a number of ladies were concealed, as it was otherwise impossible for them to get out of the city.

As no more mortars had to be fired, I was intelligence officer again and was responsible for leading the column. This was a role I never liked because of the peculiar way that convoys behave. Anyone who has experienced them will know that for some reason rooted in the logistics of human behavior, the tail end of a convoy can never keep up. When the front is proceeding at a steady pace the rear vehicles have to tear frantically along at anything over 90 miles an hour. (One of our earlier Regimental Sergeant Majors-- famous for the size of his penis--would rush up and down the convoy on his motorcycle, screaming that there was Chaos-- pronounced like Charlie--among the vejicles.) Thus we would arrive alone with the rest of the convoy straggled out for miles back in a most undisciplined and dangerous fashion. This disorderly procedure naturally invited official disapproval, and on this occasion especially, as the driver and myself had shared a bottle of whiskey.

The Drau Valley

So it was that our battalion left Vienna forever and settled in the calm Drau Valley, not far from the picture postcard lakes of Villach and Millstadtersee. It was an idyllic setting, but our responsibilities were certainly not. To start with there was the problem of the displaced hordes from beyond the Urals. These armies were to be sent back to the Soviet Union and only their horses were to remain. Among these disaffected legions there were various categories, and not all of them had fought with the Germans. However, they were all lumped together as traitors and our duty was to round them up for transmission to what they knew, even if we did not, was certain death. Since that time this agreement with the Soviet Union has been rightly branded as a crime against humanity.

On television and elsewhere critics have expressed astonished indignation that such a monstrous act had been possible. What many of the commentators overlooked was the state of opinion among the armed forces at the time. Whatever political reservation we may have had about the Soviet Union, our dominant feeling was one of boundless admiration--even gratitude--for their achievements. Because of them our war had been a kind of side-show and the millions dead were theirs, not ours. Given such a state of mind, it was natural that we should wish to cooperate, painful though it was.

Our unit was not directly involved with this enforced exodus, but was left to look after their horses. Most of us were not enthusiastic about these tiresome animals but the Colonel (who confided to me that he would rather talk to his horse than his wife) was in ecstasy. Each morning, oblivious of the language barrier, he would first discuss his problems with his horse; then we would all have to canter round a large field on our own unruly steeds, learning to ride. I had always been afraid of horses and my beast realized this at once. He, or rather she, was wholly uncooperative and had the infuriating habit of making for the nearest grove of fir trees, where I would be swept off by the branches. Inexplicably it, or rather she, became pregnant, which was entirely uncalled for, and I made this an excuse for sending it/her away. Hippophobic in any case, I said I was.

Now that the war was over, some senior regular officers were sent to join us. They were naturally keen on bringing back the abandoned rituals of their former lives. The Headquarters officer's mess, situated in a barn, was expected to replicate the hierophantic banalities of Camberley or Aldershot. Fortunately there were no flat open spaces suitable for parade grounds, so we were spared the ultimate absurdities. Our former informal evening meals became ceremonial dinners and we could not get up until the Colonel rose. Escape was difficult even then, as he would say to the assembled company, "You, you and you will play darts; the Adjutant will play dominoes with the Quartermaster, the remainder will play poker with me and I shall win." Fortunately I still had sufficient independence to opt out of these diversions (as I had never applied for a commission, I saw no reason to join in their charades).

Outside, the real life of the people had to continue and I could in fact escape by retiring to my billet on the mountain side. Officially we were still not "fraternizing," but for me as for everyone else it was difficult to be billeted with a family without any kind of intercourse. The first requirement was, of course, to learn German, as I had none. The daughter of the house, officially a married woman my own age, was a willing voluntary teacher and I made excellent progress. Priggishly, I was determined that this relationship would remain strictly pedagogic and so, to begin with, it was. When I entered the war I had been, in spite of years of emotional involvement, almost virginal: my few sexual experiences had been inconclusive and unsatisfactory. I was afraid of women. Since then, there had naturally been no progress in my education; everything had been retarded. In some of these areas, therefore, I was still about eighteen or less. I disapproved of sex without love, etcetera.

Being a sensible woman, Gucki (that was her name) had other ideas and after a few weeks she simply came downstairs to my room on the ground floor and got into my bed. It was a cold winter's night and even I could not be so unchivalrous as to push her out. Once the ice had been broken, the arrangement, slightly hazardous because of the suspicions of her ferocious mother, naturally continued. Gucki's husband, like so many others, had disappeared long since on the Eastern front. She probably never found out whether he was alive or dead. After that she had consoled herself with a French prisoner-of-war who had been employed to cut wood on their land. But alas, he had been taken away, so destiny had provided me to fill the void. Certainly she helped with my education. She told me that, above a certain altitude, all things were permissible in their valley: it was not very high.

It was then that I realized for the first time how so many Austrians and Germans knew nothing about Dachau or Belsen or Buchenwald. One could only suspect that they didn't want to know; in fact she refused to believe the reports which were then emerging--all this in spite of the fact that the Austrian camp (Mauthausen) was not very far away, and even closer was Linz, where Adolf Eichmann grew up. Like so many others he had joined the National Socialist Party as early as 1932 and entered the S. S. the same year. (In eighteen months after 1938 he organized the deportation of 150, 000 Austrian Jews.)

However, my main task was not political re-education, but learning the language. The pillow-based system was ideal for this purpose. I should have known that the most effective method of learning a foreign language is to find a lover (schools of languages should operate with this system). In underdeveloped countries it took the adult education literacy experts many frustrating years to appreciate that the same principles should operate in learning to read and write one's own language. They call it functional literacy and try to relate the written word to the innermost needs of the people. In their case, the needs are of course not erotic, but political.

However, we were not particularly bothered by such theories then and underdeveloped countries had not been invented. It was a mutually beneficial arrangement made possible because it could only be temporary and involved no ultimate responsibility on either side. That came later with a different consort in another part of the country.

As a solemn sociological footnote to the above, it should be added that within hours of the lifting of the official ban on fraternization, the valley blossomed with celebrating couples. The General responsible must have felt like a fairy godfather waving his magic wand. The ladies were referred to as "frat, " an unpleasant generic word, but the alternatives were even less appropriate.

The Last Assignment

I started this account by noting that any war can be

seen as a confusing mixture of horror and farce. Now the horror had gone and for me what remained (with the exception of one tragic episode) was largely farce. Much to my relief, I was removed elsewhere. It is possible that a recommendation was made that I should be sent as far away as possible, but this is not very likely as, then and always, I have been regarded, much to my chagrin, as essentially harmless. Certainly, short of leaving the divisional orbit altogether, I could not have been sent farther. I was exiled to an isolated mountain village called Gmünd: the purpose was to set up a Divisional School for training NOCs to become weapon instructors. Since I had never been able to use any weapon, the irony was apparent to me, but not to them because they didn't care anyway. (Our caring was for the time being exhausted.) The absurdity did not end there. All the instructors--that is, six sergeants and one officer (a distracted young Irishman called Fitzgerald) and myself--were waiting to be demobilized. None of us therefore was exactly committed to the cause of weapon training. Furthermore, the "students" were in the same boat and had mostly been sent to us to get rid of them, at least temporarily (I have forgotten how long the course lasted).

In view of my grave new responsibilities, I was promoted to major, a move which, when I contemplated my fellow officers, seemed long overdue. (Alas, I was no longer indifferent to such matters and my long preserved innocence had been invaded by the corroding ambitions of a competitive world.) At least, they announced that I had been promoted and I therefore drew out from the Quartermaster's Store the emblematic crowns to put on my shoulder. In fact the translation may never have been recorded, but it didn't matter, the play was the thing.

Leaving the 5th Buffs was not so traumatic as one might have expected because the battalion was already changing and so many of my friends had gone before I left. One other episode merits a note. I had the good fortune to be in our headquarters (in the barn) when the news of the Labour Party's success in the 1945 General Election came through. Never, even after our worst defeats in combat, had I seen my fellow officers so prostrate with grief, rage and apprehension. Certain events are unthinkable and this was one of them: they lay on the floor groaning. Their conviction was that the "bolsheviks" would bring about the end of the world--their world. (How could they have foreseen that thirty years later, that world would still be there?) I enjoyed myself pointing out that all military ranks would soon be abolished, that the political commissars would come and they would be sent down the mines, etcetera. We, I said, had already decided what should be done with them. It was a great day and seemed almost to make my war worthwhile. At that historic moment some of them must have conceived the idea of emigration, which led ultimately to Rhodesia, where they are doubtless still fulminating today.

Gmünd

If I were to revisit Gmünd I suppose I should be disappointed, as one always is in a return to past scenes. However, for me then, it was not only a romantic place, but also represented a kind of bridge to rehabilitation and a normal domestic life. I felt this immediately we passed through the ancient arch into the village.

Our first encounter with the representatives of the people was typical of what was to come. We had, as part of the occupying presence, some vague military responsibilities. No doubt the local authorities, hitherto unmolested, were apprehensive at this unexpected intrusion, which may account for the nature of the meeting with the Burgermeister and his entourage. When we arrived after dark we were taken to his house, but he was unable to greet us in a manner befitting the occasion, as both he and the assembled company were drunk. He sat in a corner of the room with a large lampshade covering his head and face. Under such circumstances, a ceremonial introduction was impossible and the only thing to do was to join them in drinking the ferocious liquor called Arrack (a word which covers a variety of alcoholic poisons). As usual, they expressed great joy at their liberation from the Nazi yoke and had changed their allegiance without too much strain. This first meeting, if somewhat incoherent, was cordial enough, but it was too much to hope for that relations would remain that way.

Whatever the lasses may have felt, the local lads could hardly welcome with enthusiasm an influx of licentious soldiery, most of them posted because they were difficult to control. I soon gave up trying too hard, but we did make some attempt to stop them fighting with the male population. Our men were outnumbered, but their position was strengthened by their military role and by the possession of money and tins of sardines. In the eyes of the village maidens these assets may have made up for any lack of refinement or finesse or ability to communicate any but the most primitive needs.

Every Saturday night there was a dance in the village hall with an accordion band and traditional Viennese waltzes. At these events, Law and Order often broke down since there was nobody except myself and the village policeman to enforce it. (It was not even possible to lock anybody up.) Sometimes, in these weekly encounters, our forces got the worst of it, and on one occasion they took revenge the following week by throwing their rivals out of an upstairs window. It so happened that the Divisional Commander was to pay us an official visit the next day. When the troops were assembled and paraded for his inspection, many of them had black eyes and bandages and other signs of wear and tear. The General asked several of them how they came to be injured and each one replied, "Football, Sir." He showed no surprise that our football should have been so rough. The army taught me that an essential element in good management is officially not to know too much or to inquire too closely into sensitive circumstances.

In view of these and other events to come, I am in danger of forgetting to mention our teaching methods. By this time the Army Education Authorities had developed certain techniques to overcome the invincible ignorance of the ordinary soldier. Not without reason, they had assumed that simple, straightforward talking would have no effect. We cannot, for obvious reasons, communicate with their brains, they said; we must work through all their five senses. (Gone were the days when recruits memorized army manuals; I met Indian officers in Italy who could recite entire volumes of these curious instructions.) These new methods were excellent but they were often carried to absurd lengths and teaching sessions became a series of hilarious charades, with realistic noises and smells of power and shot. It was not always easy to include the senses of touch and taste: one cannot eat bren guns. (My own contribution usually consisted of rambling reminiscences of how I won the war.) It was all good theater and infinitely preferable to my weapon training days in the Park at Maidstone.

This light-hearted existence was rudely shattered by a fatal accident when four soldiers were drowned. They had gone for a night out to Villach, about 30 miles away, and on the return journey their truck ran into the river.

This mountain stream was quite shallow, but the swift-flowing water swept them away. The girls who were with them got out of the vehicle and survived--no doubt the men had been celebrating too well. When I reached the scene the truck was upright in the water, facing upstream with its lights still full on. About a week later the bodies, black and swollen beyond recognition, were recovered from a deeper river miles away. There was an inquiry but the facts were clear enough. Nobody was censured but I was well aware that as the person in charge of the unit I was officially responsible. It is a memory one would not wish to have.

Transition

Although at Gmünd we were still in uniform our mental state was such that the army receded into the background: as old soldiers we were beginning to fade away. The collective life was losing its meaning and long-forgotten tides of personal feeling returned. With almost unseemly haste I set up a domestic ménage with the Polish displaced person who later became my first wife. She and her daughter eventually managed to reach Britain at least a year after I had left. This non-military development is described elsewhere but it has to be recorded here because it was the most lasting consequence of my war and could not have happened otherwise. It is appropriate therefore that this account of my military service should end there.

14. DEMOBILIZATION

It is significant that apart from my personal life, I remember nothing of the last days in Austria, nor anything of my departure from the training school, nor any details of the sea voyage home, with one exception. We had dropped anchor at Gibraltar and when it was time to continue, the anchor was stuck fast on the ocean floor. The remedy was to cut the anchor, which they did, and the severed chain was left with a little man in a boat--who may well be sitting there still. I was later informed that such an incident was impossible, but who would want to dream up a man at the end of an anchor?

On a drear dark day the ship nosed into Liverpool amid the haunting sound of the fog horns. I felt empty, exhausted and alone. Proceeding to Aldershot via London, I met at the station two very young second lieutenants from the Buffs. I was taken aback when they saluted and showed signs of regarding me with considerable awe. The rows of ribbons were there, but already it was as if the events they symbolized had never been. As I was issued at Aldershot with my demob striped suit, it seemed that the years since I last wore one had removed themselves. As in January 1940, I was once again a new recruit to an alien world. It was some consolation that these were typical reactions for so many. For the time being our identity had been taken away and there was not yet another one.

I tried to dwell on all those things we had dreamed of for so long: the pubs at opening time, people and places to visit, the music that would be heard, the books to be read, but they were not yet real. I sat in the train to Tunbridge Wells and as the familiar landscape swept by I realized that, almost by instinct, I was surveying the physical features to note where we could take cover. Just before Sevenoaks the train emerged from a tunnel and there was revealed a particular pattern of hillside and woodland which had always moved me and dispelled my adolescent gloom. Like an involuntary physical reaction, that mood returned. It would be opening time in the pubs of Tunbridge Wells and I had come home.

PART III: MY COLLEGES

1. LONDON: NORTH WESTERN POLYTECHNIC

My teaching career began in a London polytechnic.
This was inevitable, because most library education was then
conducted in those institutions; in any event I had no university degree. Those years should have been the most produc-
tive of my life, yet what I learned or what I achieved now
seems wholly out of proportion to the efforts involved. (The
long-distance runner rarely notices where he is going.) I
had become embedded in a structure which I knew very little
about. When the polytechnics were first set up they were,
no doubt, a progressive force but by 1950 they had, in many
respects, become the contrary. We had inherited a system
which at that time could be modified but not transformed.

In some respects the technical colleges then represented a peculiar hangover from the industrial revolution.
There was still, for example, a heavy influence which derived from the apprenticeship system. We were expected,
apparently, to teach young people how to do things and the
library profession, along with others, had confused training,
which was their responsibility, with education. The emphasis
was pseudo-practical and our own courses had to be geared
to examinations produced by practicing librarians who were
appointed by the British Library Association. No doubt they
ran their libraries very well but, having been reared as ap-
prentices themselves, they were not familiar with educational principles or processes. They would ask questions which
could only be answered from practical experience in a particular place. If they were lucky, some students might
imagine such circumstances, but they could not be prepared
for them. The processes were incompatible and so were the
partners in that unnatural union. At final level especially,
they were looking for "maturity," by which they seemed to
mean qualities like those of some aged and blinkered nag

87

harnessed to make our alien world go round. They were
proud of this pragmatic, "feet on the ground" approach but
more often than not it was their feet and their ground we
were expected to be interested in.   Inevitably frictions and
misunderstandings arose.   To mediate in this war, "mod-
erating committees" were set up with representatives from
both sides.   Under such circumstances it was remarkable
that we never came to blows.   Our meetings were simply
post-mortem wrangles over each examination paper, and by
that time it made no difference to the students whether we
agreed or not.

Nobody was to blame, of course: these strains were
merely symptoms of an education system in transition.   These
events now represent no more than one phase in the history
of library education in Britain.   I mention them to illustrate
my feeling that (in retrospect) from a personal point of view
I wasted too much time in committees whose work had less
than global significance.   But then I probably did not feel
that way and things always look different from the inside.
We were getting somewhere, it is true, but like any attempt
at social change in Britain it was a slow process.   One
needs to enjoy committee work for its own sake, as if it
were an end in itself.   In the long run that was not my
thing: I was an extroverted introvert and was too conscious
therefore of acting a part.

Other unnecessary burdens were those placed upon us
by the polytechnic system as it then was.   There was an ancient ruling that we should lecture for 22 hours a week.
Not everybody took this literally, but some heads of department did, with results which may be imagined.   Those uncivilized procedures represented a cultural time-lag derived
from a puritan tradition which required that young people, in
their own interest, should be made to suffer, just as their
forebears had done.   It was called "going through the mill,"
a significant industrial metaphor, and like the mills of God
it often ground slowly and exceeding small.   The effect on
teachers could be disastrous; it usually was.   Those who
flourished reminded me of certain corporals in the army
who, inspired by responsibility for the moral welfare of others, would impose mindless and meaningless routines: they
were also under the illusion that facts as such were of primary importance.   But I was not among those who flourished:
I simply survived.

To suggest mere survival, however, implies an odd

kind of retrospective self-pity which distorts the record.
Was there nothing to celebrate? Certainly there was. The
young or inexperienced teacher is necessarily closer to the
students. If he has the right attitudes (I naturally thought I
had) he will rely considerably on student participation, so
that there is a joint or cooperative exploration of whatever
is involved. The lecturer (at least under that system) is
not in a position to deliver his patter from on high since he
has not prepared his lectures and knows little more than his
listeners. This two-way process is stimulating to all concerned and is close to what the flower children of the sixties
called for--mostly in vain. Their ideals were not realized
because such relationships cannot be institutionalized. When
you become an expert in your subject it is inauthentic to pretend that you are not: this is the realm of plays or games,
which students are right in disliking because they suspect
they will lose. (Some lecturers, in order to stimulate discussion, express views which they do not hold: this also is
an irritation.) It is, no doubt, significant that I can remember personally students from those early years and the relationships were closer than at any time since. (An important
contributory factor was that during the fifties library schools
remained relatively small and the student intake was more or
less static: the expansion came later in the post-Robbins
era.)

All worthwhile experiences are dangerous and the
hazard here is that a close involvement with students may
go beyond what the world regards as proper. One eminent
and coarse-minded librarian once said to me, "When are
you going to stop fucking your students?" There was, of
course, no answer to that question. Similarly, many years
later, a Ghanaian ex-student wrote in a learned journal that
my relations with students were "peculiar"--or was it
"queer"? They were outside his usual experience. This
is, however, not the place to explore these non-academic
depths. From the point of view of professional ethics it was
customary in West Africa to defend intimate relationships of
that kind, provided that the students belonged to some other
department (otherwise educationally corrupt practices might
follow). But such statements are beside the point since
these close relations usually arise from the teaching role.
(They were considered normal in Plato's Greece but it would
seem that ladies were not then involved.)

It was also possible to deal with the horrors of the
system by clowning or by evasive tactics, but neither method

is educationally defensible. One possibility was to make fun of the curriculum or those who devised it. Their emphasis on the accumulation of meaningless facts lent itself to parody. (One also has to remember that the textbooks available then were themselves uncivilized and an insult to humanity.) At one time I would close each lecture with the solemn words, "And in days to come, always remember the Gesamtkatalog der Wiegendrucke. " (This was a gigantic union catalog of early printed books.) Years later an ex-student told me how much he had benefited from that advice: most teachers learn eventually that the use of irony is not safe in the classroom. Another unethical tactic was to tell irrelevant funny stories about some of the people, such as bibliographers, who figured in our courses.

From the study of reference materials--as it then was --relief was provided by quoting some of their absurdities. Government publications, for example, were full of surrealist nonsense. In fact, any compilation consisting of isolated data is, by definition, insane. Strictly speaking, none of these devices was permissible but I justified them to myself then on two grounds. One was that the courses themselves were not educationally sound and could not be taken seriously. The other was that such material could be used to throw light on the human condition. This was perhaps a presumption since I had not been appointed for such a purpose. But nobody is perfect.

The factory atmosphere was not without its advantages, one of which was that we were much involved in the world outside. We visited binderies, newspapers, lithographers, paper mills, printing works, publishers, booksellers, and process engravers. The bewildered workers in such places made noble efforts to explain what they thought they were doing to our no less bewildered students. We also visited libraries in national museums, universities, colleges, schools, towns, cities, villages, learned societies, professional bodies, commercial firms, factories, government departments, hospitals, prisons and mental homes. As for me, these events were annual, and there were times when my attitude to libraries and librarians bordered on horror, if not hatred. At a superficial encounter one library looks exactly like another and the same applies to their custodians--even their sex becoming indeterminate. However, my personal reactions were not important--except to myself. The main thing was that we were in touch with realities not our own. (I also toured the Midlands and the North of England and understood for the first time how those places had made possible the egregious gentility of the Home Counties around London where I was brought up.)

Our wish to be part of the world went further yet. Once every week all the students assembled to hear somebody from "out there" deliver an address on matters of professional concern. This was an excellent idea and one of the lessons which emerged was that the more eminent the person was, the less he had to say. The implication perhaps was that he was paid for being there. Or was it that all his energies had been used up in doing what he had done?

My recollections of that place naturally go far beyond those pedagogic problems. I have mentioned a nineteenth-century mental atmosphere; the physical environment produced the same impression. Although the College was built as late as 1933, owing to the weird procedures of local government the plan which they used had been submitted at least 30 years earlier. Dickens would have felt at home. The inmates of the College were to be found in layers and one rarely ventured beyond one's own stratum. The women's department was on the top floor; there were library and commercial people in the middle, while the printers were in the basement where their machines couldn't fall through the floor. Oppressed by this stratification I often took refuge on the roof. This, it will be apparent by now, was no ivory tower, nor was it set in arcadian surroundings; they were Victorian also. It rained a lot, but more obtrusive was the fog. For reasons unknown to meteorology there was more fog in the Prince of Wales Road, N.W. 5 than anywhere else in London. Surrounded by this gloom, we attracted sexual maniacs who would come down from Hampstead Heath during the winter months and breathe their messages to us from neighboring telephone booths.

There was, it should be noted, a great deal of vitality around. Much of this emanated from hundreds of part-time day students and even more hundreds who, after a day's work, came in the evenings, blundering doggedly through the fog. Here was the heroic side of the apprenticeship system: many of them were so tired that lecturers had to go to extreme lengths to keep them awake. (The lecturers were also exhausted but at least they were paid to be so.) A fair proportion of the librarianship students were those who, through no fault of their own, had missed out on full time professional education and could not obtain leave or grants for that purpose. They were mostly no longer young and, year after year, undeterred by their predicament and the evil machinations of examiners, would persist in their studies. In a great metropolis there are innumerable little libraries belonging to organizations devoted to every conceivable cause or interest. In charge of them there are many who perhaps have failed in some other unsuitable vocation. Because of this they tend to be more interesting than "successful" people, and it is fitting that, across the years, I should now salute them: their contribution will be otherwise unnoticed and unsung.

Within the College there was some embryonic political activity of a somewhat bizarre kind. (The later history of the College, after the main part of it moved to Islington and became the Polytechnic of North London, was politically a more serious, even a notorious, national matter.) During the fifties, however, archaic regulations were still in force, one being that no political activities were allowed in the London polytechnics. There was also a curious arrangement that the president of the students' union was a staff member who was elected not by the students but by the staff! On one occasion I was "elected" to this august position, but only after an acrimonious dispute when the opposition right-wing candidate refused to accept the verdict.

There was a dreadful confrontation in the gentlemen's toilet when I was accused of malpractice; some of the voting papers were missing. Fortunately it emerged that several ladies from the top floor had erroneously placed their papers in the refectory suggestions box, and my majority of one increased. Later, during the Suez fiasco, there were riotous scenes when the students held an illegal protest meeting which I refused to stop. Those were stirring times, even if the storms were in a teacup.

Some of us also organized an overseas students' "cultural" society: it had to be called that because of the political ban. This was the beginning of a serious involvement with what is now called the Third World, or more recently the South. The secretary was a Ugandan Asian student called Rajat Neogy, with whom I was closely associated for the remaining time in Britain. Years later he became well known as the editor of Transition, by far the best cultural review that Africa has produced. But it upheld liberal values which are not always welcome in new countries and he was imprisoned by Dr. Milton Obote, then President of Uganda, and

eventually only released after much international agitation.
(The journal is now--1979--edited by Professor Wole Soyinka
of Nigeria.) Our society organized activities outside the
college, including "cultural" weekends in the residential institutions which exist for that purpose. The students were introduced to Beethoven and other eminent manufacturers of
Western culture.

I was also involved with a London unofficial committee
with parliamentary links which concerned itself with accom-
modation problems of overseas students. We worked with
the British Council, which has, of course, considerable experience in that field. The problems are persistent and not
easily solved. It must have been about that time when Wole
Soyinka wrote his well-known poem "Telephone Conversation"
about himself trying to obtain lodgings. Over the telephone
the landlady had asked, "How dark?" His reply included the
lines:

> Facially, I am brunette, but madam
> you should see the rest of me. Palm of
> my hand, soles of my feet are a peroxide
> blond. Friction caused--foolishly madam--
> by sitting down has turned my bottom
> raven black. [etc., etc.]

The Council unofficially had three separate files, one white,
one black, one "coffee. " It also ran orientation courses
(and presumably still does) to help new students absorb the
culture shock. These were practical but ideologically suspect since they sometimes seemed to imply that the British
way was the only one. Outstanding in my memory is its
demonstration of how to eat a boiled egg: the students were
also warned not to put jam on their kippers, although this
was not demonstrated. The rationale behind these sensible
injunctions was the need to mitigate social embarrassment,
and I would be the last person to question activities of this
kind. Britain was not an easy country for foreign students
to be in, and is even less so now. For example, I used to
feel that it was essential to explain that the racist element
in British attitudes is so deep-seated that they are not even
aware of it.

My political education in Third World problems had
begun but there was a long way to go and now I am astonished at the length of time required for me to reach any
real understanding. We should not be surprised, therefore,

if other expatriates experience the same difficulties. It is, of course, not a matter of <u>theoretical</u> comprehension and the attitude which is most difficult to eradicate is one of unconscious condescension. In dealing with the young, teachers develop these traits in any event and exposure to underdeveloped countries is likely to reinforce them. Paternalism and Olympian patronizing tendencies are ultimately more offensive than honest hostility or misplaced contempt.

But I was not fully aware of these matters then. I had come to a mainly political decision which seemed, and still seems, logical and inevitable. When "communism" went wrong in Europe and the light had failed, I transferred my allegiance to the countries of the Third World. That is largely why I went to Trinidad, although there were also personal factors which are not relevant here. As for my career, it seemed to be marking time and I had been a kind of deputy for too long.

2. TROPICAL TRANSFERS

Trinidad

In 1959 Trinidad had not yet achieved full independence; it was still a year or two away. My politics are discussed elsewhere and their only relevance here is that a kind of political commitment influenced my behavior and helped to sustain me during my short time in the West Indies. I was present, I considered, to help the decolonizing process and it largely escaped my notice that this perception of my role was not shared by anyone else. I was aware, it is true, that I would be working within a colonial ambiance but that, I felt, would soon pass. "And I saw a new heaven and a new earth: for the first heaven and the first earth were passed away; and there was no more sea. " (<u>Revelations</u> 21. 1)

But in the West Indies the sea certainly remained and was largely responsible for the collapse of the ill-fated Federation (1962). When I went, though, this embryonic union was still in existence and a close friend, Phyllis Shand Allfrey, was Minister of Labour and Social Affairs. Her novel, <u>The Orchid House,</u> first published in 1953, has been reissued by Virago Press (1982). It seemed logical that ultimately my even more embryonic school would become a Federal responsibility. But, alas, History is indifferent to that kind of logic and there was a certain amount of fantasy around. In retrospect, and to some extent even then, it seemed fitting that our address in Port of Spain was 4 (or perhaps 19) La Fantaisie Gardens (the correct number was never established), and the British governor's peacocks wandered in our garden: they at least were real.

This section is entitled "My Colleges" but in Trinidad then there was no college of librarianship--only me. But that is not quite accurate either, since I had inherited a system pioneered by the British Council, whose contributions were then drawing to a close. I was a wandering tutor attached to the Regional Public Library in Port of Spain. The region in question constituted the former British islands of the Eastern Caribbean and we also provided courses for some students from Jamaica, a very different kind of island. The library service had been set up by able and dedicated people, notably by Sidney Hockey, who had been responsible for my recruitment: he has produced more blueprints for public libraries in new countries than anybody else. Both the library and the teaching tradition therefore already existed. There were hopes that the teaching unit would develop but the entire project was to be reduced in scope. However, while the vision lasted it enabled me to visit the smaller islands which were part of the library scheme. It was an exciting but deeply disturbing experience which happened when I was still trying to absorb the shock of a tropical environment ("I am trying to be underwhelmed, " I used to say). I was sent to talk to the little islanders about the importance of libraries but the contrast between some of the most beautiful scenery in the world and the condition of the people filled me with a mixture of horror and embarrassment. Somehow, over the island radios, I put out my patter urging everyone to read more books and improve the public libraries which had already been set up. Perhaps to preserve myself, I never stopped to inquire how many people were literate or what they would do with their literacy if they had it.

Most of the young people, in any event, would escape to Britain: they had few prospects otherwise. Since then there have been those familiar strident voices prophesying Doom and demanding that they should all be sent "home" again. A ruling class which brought them there from Africa, and whose modern representatives had inherited vast fortunes from sugar plantations and the slave trade, was now refusing responsibility for the consequences. What I was witnessing in the Caribbean was the fag-end of that Imperial endeavor--

not an inspiring experience.   One of the islands I visited was
Dominica (not the Dominican Republic), where the joke is
still current that if Columbus were to rediscover it now there
would be a shock of recognition, as nothing has changed.   In
fact the people would look different because the Caribs were
all exterminated, to be replaced by Africans--but that is all.
A few Caribs survive in a special reservation or human zoo.

In uttering these lamentations it should not be supposed
that I considered the libraries to be premature or irrelevant
--not at all.   My reactions at the time are best illustrated
by quoting some impressions which were published in a professional journal in Britain (Assistant Librarian, 53, December 1960: 243-44).   The second of those two accounts refers
to St. Vincent and ends as follows:

> The point then is that in this place it is sufficient-
> ly remarkable that there is a library at all.   We
> need not care what kind of library it is.   All over
> the world, in neglected areas, a few individuals
> have recognised--long before it became a fashion-
> able cry--that civilisation is indivisible (if we can-
> not bear witness to this concept what else can we
> do?).   The libraries in the West Indies were es-
> tablished by individuals of this kind.   I am con-
> tent to note their achievements.
>
> And so one returns, as to a symbol of our times,
> to the breadfruit tree (long since introduced by Cap-
> tain Bligh) and beneath it a small building where
> glassless windows look out across the unending seas
> whose distances the vision of one small boy, read-
> ing his two months old Children's Newspaper, can
> utterly transcend.

In that passage both the sentiments and the expression
are inflated and overblown.   If I were to visit St. Vincent
now in search of "symbols of our times," it would doubtless
be a symbol of quite another kind and I would not be content
with that concept of indivisibility, which may mean anything
or nothing.   But then, I suppose I was encouraged by the
thought that with the help of that library, the child had become part of One World.   I wonder where he is now: most
likely he is unemployed and lives in Brixton, a largely black
settlement in London.   Now we have become less certain that
the unified world is worth belonging to.   It is likely that at
this moment another child of a later generation is sitting in
that same place, but I would not venture to stress his sym-

bolic role. Instead, I would prefer to record that an ability to read might help him to struggle with his own environment. Even so, it is significant perhaps that I paid most attention to the children, and thirty years later, while trying to analyze library objectives in Africa, I ended on the same note. When former expectations have not materialized, hope or faith in the future becomes a moral imperative. There are still those who believe in "scientific" predictions, but for the rest of us that child is the only future we can be sure about.

Apart from Phyllis Allfrey I suppose that Dominica's most famous child is the novelist Jean Rhys, author of that powerful work, The Wide Sargasso Sea. More than anyone else she captured--in the picture of Dominica--the haunting, evil qualities of that island paradise. Yet it is characteristic of her limitations that there was no historical or political perspective. In her autobiographical fragment, Smile Please (p. 63), she does, as part of her childhood recollections, mention the library.

> The old Victoria Memorial Library had been pulled down and there was a new Carnegie Library in its place. It was very pleasant, usually empty. Sitting in a rocking chair on the verandah, lost in what I thought was the real world, no one could have been happier than I was.

Those were the days when Carnegie benefactions helped to provide reading matter for colonial servants and to civilize the old West Indian white bourgeoisie, which included both Rhys and Allfrey. Many years later, when the sun was setting on the Empire, Rhys visited Dominica briefly and (in the same passage) noted "a long queue, before the librarian's desk. I thought it was a very touching sight, all the black hands, eagerly stretched out, holding books." But, she went on, they seemed to think that the librarian was a machine and didn't notice her as, robot-like, she stamped the books. "I wasn't at all surprised when I heard, a few days later that she was dead." Jean Rhys, inevitably, identified only with an individual who seemed to be a victim like herself. There was no further mention of "black hands," although she does refer to "two sides of the question" without indicating what the question was.

Meanwhile, back in Trinidad I struggled with my "lectures." There were no other full-time lecturers, although an essential contribution was made by Trinidadian librarians, lecturing part-time. The library was--and is--housed in one of those delightful old colonial buildings of assorted ornate styles which surround the "savannah"--a central park--in Port of Spain. It was open to the wind and--where the lecturing was done--to torrential rain which during the wet season swept over our classroom at the same time every day. Because of that we usually referred to the building in nautical terms: "We shall have to move starboard now." Large stones were required to keep our papers from blowing away and these were irreverently referred to by the girls as Mr. Benge's balls. In spite of all that, or maybe because of it, they learned what they had to learn.

I was responsible not only for these three-month cram courses but also for a correspondence course which was distributed to the smaller islands. These were out of date and had to be rewritten: for that chore I needed more boosting of morale than could be provided by the inflammatory rhetoric of the late Eric Williams, Prime Minister to be. My dreary labors were fueled by Trinidadian rum, and one can only hope that no copies of those productions ever survived. It is possible, even so, that somewhere they assisted some isolated souls.

My life there was mainly pedagogic, not managerial, as the school was officially a sub-unit of the library. I was only partly responsible for administration as policy, a set-up which caused some friction. We were still dealing with the British examinations and a tradition had grown up that one of the main functions of the tutor was to "spot" what questions the examiners might ask: one was expected to become a soothsayer.

There was also the complication that the courses could not deal with indigenous realities except as an afterthought. In Trinidad there was still a colonial, as distinct from a neo-colonial, atmosphere. They were studying the library scene in Britain, which seemed odd to me but not to them because they thought of themselves as British. The streets of London, if not precisely paved with gold, were strewn with good intentions: it took me a long time to appreciate all this and I could not fully comprehend the psychology of the students. Taking up attitudes which can only be described as arrogant, I decided that they must be dragged into the twentieth century. For example, in their choice of English literature papers, they had usually chosen one of the early periods because the Eng Lit text books have tidied all

that up. I decided that this wouldn't do and they were required to study modern literature. This meant that I found
myself desperately trying to explain Iris Murdoch and all the
rest to young people whose society was not "modern" at all.
(There were, of course, some very fine West Indian writers
but we couldn't deal with them.) It was still an ethnocentric
approach and I deserved to suffer the consequences. In spite
of all that they usually passed those faraway examinations
and it was a success story of sorts.

Those events were over thirty years ago and there is
now full-time library education established in the University
of the West Indies in Jamaica. After I left Trinidad, no
doubt some of the senior staff helped any remaining students
as much as they could, and some years later the same scheme
was revived when John Linford, who had been with us in
Ghana, went to Trinidad. We were involved in a transitional
enterprise which now has only historical interest. Its main
significance was that it enabled students who had been caught
up in rapid political and social transformation to obtain a
basic qualification. Now most of them who have survived
occupy senior professional posts and their recollections of
those brief courses are probably very different from mine,
but for them--as for me--it was a necessary rite of passage.

In spite of this professional scene, which was more
than faintly ridiculous, it was a rewarding experience. There
were not many students--usually less than a dozen--and they
were all, with one or two downtrodden exceptions, female.
It would be foolish to deny that teaching semi-technical subjects to attractive young ladies is more stimulating than working with moronic hordes. They were, for obvious reasons,
highly motivated and characterized by an almost cynical
sophistication which their society had engendered. In addition to the British connection, their history included African,
French, Spanish, Indian, Chinese and Portuguese ethnic influences. Perhaps because of this they do not go in for heavy
attitudes. As a solemn approach was part of my Anglo-
Saxon heritage, this was good for my education. The Long-
fellow parody says, "Life is real and life is earnest and the
end is not the gaol. " But Yeats, the Anglo-Irishman, knew
better:

> For the good are always the merry,
> Save by an evil chance,
> And the merry love the fiddle
> And the merry love to dance.
>> (The Fiddler of Dooney)

Trinidadians have always appreciated this, although what they
love is not the fiddle but the steel drum and theirs is a land
of carnival. I learned more from them than they did from
me.

Ghana

In 1961 Ghana had been independent for four years.
During the colonial period there had been built up a pioneer
public library service which had become an inspiration to other countries in the Third World. This had been possible because the British Council had provided the foundations and
because its first and only British director, Eve Evans, was
an able and far-seeing person who could see the possibilities
in a country which was then the most advanced in black Africa. Insofar as there was a "model" (I am sure she would
not have thought in those terms) it was the British County
Library system reproduced, with necessary modifications, on
a national scale. (To point this out is not to criticize, since
nothing can begin with a tabula rasa.)

The parallel extends to the personality of the Director
herself. After 1919, when rural library services were set
up in Britain for the first time, a number of dedicated wom-
en were appointed to take charge of the new County Libraries.
This tradition was continued and it is not irrelevant to mention that they were mostly unmarried and conscious that in
Britain the senior posts in libraries had hitherto been reserved for men. They were therefore pioneers in more than
one sense, and latter-day feminists in the profession owe
them a debt. What they had in common was a no-nonsense
approach: they did not, like so many of their male equivalents, go in for histrionic gestures and ego trips. It is not
too fanciful to suggest that Eve Evans possessed these same
cool qualities--and she certainly needed them.

When independence came President Nkrumah himself
recognized the value of the library service and of its directors. Bearing in mind that until that date, staff had obtained
their qualifications overseas, he suggested that an indigenous
library school should be set up. It was at this point that
Eve Evans wrote to me in Trinidad to discover whether I
would be interested in this project. I replied that I was,
since it had become clear by then that there was no possibility of establishing a library school in Port of Spain. The
ship was not sinking; it had never really been afloat. It was

possible, therefore, to leave it without feeling too much of a rat.

In setting up the Ghana Library School we tried to learn from my Trinidad experience. This time there would be a purpose-made building and sufficient full-time staff and the courses would be one year, not three months. There would also be an adequate library with multiple copies of textbooks and a librarian. All these things came to pass because at that time money for such purposes was still available. There were the usual difficulties to begin with: at first I was the only full-time lecturer and the school was not built and the only students were employees of the Ghana Library Board. But later we recruited two lecturers from Britain (John Roe and John Linford) and one from home (Kwesi Villars) and a part-time Ghanaian, Sam Kotei, who is now Professor of Library Studies in Botswana. Students were recruited straight from school and from other countries in West Africa. Then we found that they had nowhere suitable to live. A hostel was set up with a lecturer warden and a bus was purchased to take them to and fro. In short, the foundations were successfully put down and it was a far cry from the improvisations of Trinidad.

I was in the fortunate and unusual position that we did not have to bother with bureaucratic impediments, first because the Ghana Library Board was an independent body, and second because the School itself was allowed a measure of independence. From the beginning the Director of the Library Board understood that I should be left alone to get on with the job, even though the necessary support had to come from her. This kind of understanding was then not common among practicing librarians, who frequently have not appreciated that professional education is a separate enterprise requiring quite other perceptions and abilities. We could proceed unburdened by the dead weight of settled procedures: there were no stultifying precedents. Cynics have often said that many individuals went to Africa and similar places because they preferred to become large frogs in small ponds as distinct from the opposite back home. This may have been so at an earlier time when the Colonial Administration was still in place. But for us there was no "pond." The beaver, who makes his own pool, would be a more suitable analogy. However, we must not pursue these watery metaphors too far, and we have nothing against real frogs, who often provided a background chorus to our lives.

When all this had been done and the school was established, the time had come, it might have been supposed,
to congratulate ourselves and settle down. But, alas, this
was only one of the stations on the way. Our examinations
were still British and we could prepare our students successfully only because we were familiar with that alien scene.
These were the requirements I had already struggled with in
Trinidad and even, to some degree, in London. Once again
the students prospered because their examinations had always been like that: it did not occur to most of them that
"education" should relate to their own lives or circumstances.
Happily they answered questions about the weird workings of
the British Museum or the complicated scheme of library
cooperation between kinds of institutions they did not have.
Cheerfully they studied technical book production processes
which they would never encounter. Avidly they absorbed
details of reference sources which would be of no use to
them. Sometimes, it is true, they went astray, as for example when they reported that there were special books--
such as Debrett--which provide information about peculiar
people whose blood, it seemed, was blue. Fortunately the
syllabus allowed for some choice and, profiting from my
Trinidadian experience, we did not "do" English Literature
but the history of political theory instead. That at least was
a universal theme which could be seen to affect them all

They were, in short, still in a semi-colonial ambiance.
I had always appreciated that the next stage would be to set
up national courses and qualifications. But this could be
done only in a university and the University of Ghana would
never recognize an institution such as ours. The only alternative therefore was somehow to transfer our school, and
that is what, after much toil and stress, was eventually done.
It was the most difficult task imaginable and it succeeded
only because close cooperation was established between myself and Eve Evans and John Dean, who was then the librarian
of the university and is now (1982) Professor of Library
Studies at Dublin. (Formerly the senior people had spent
most of the time disagreeing or not speaking to each other:
this always happens in the early days of professional life.
In Britain leading members of the Library Association were
possessed by lifelong antipathies which can only be described
as violent and virulent.) We also received indispensable support from Conor Cruse O'Brien, who was then Vice Chancellor of the University. He seemed slightly bemused by the
entire procedure, as well he might have been. The university was--and possibly still is--an élitist institution, very

conscious of its Oxbridge origins and connections. Most of
its senior people, Ghanaians and foreigners alike, were therefore hostile to the establishment of professional courses within the ivory tower. The Department was accepted largely by
default; its arrival went almost unnoticed since there were
many other urgent political issues to worry about, notably a
decision made by President Nkrumah to remove--without con-
sulting the university--the Institute of Education to another
place.

In an ideal world the Ghana Library School would have
survived and would have established itself in relation to the
University in a role similar to that which developed in the
College of Librarianship, Wales. But the circumstances
were not ideal nor--as it turned out--even favorable, since
the Department could only thrive in an expanding economy
which would include an expanding profession. That was not
to be; indeed, as all the world knows, the economy thereafter was afflicted by what the economists quaintly describe
as "negative growth." Meanwhile, some of us from elsewhere were able to strut--if that is the right term--upon a
stage established long since by Imperial forebears. Were it
not for this symbolic role that enterprise would not be worthy
of quite so many words.

The subsequent history of the Department of Library
Studies is not part of this story. The most significant thing,
perhaps, is that it was established and, against all the odds,
it has survived. It is clear now that my own main contribution was to get it set up. At the time--to continue with
our aquatic metaphors--it seemed that having fitted out the
ship and embarked, I then abandoned it. Rudderless, it began to drift, etcetera. There were, initially, several ad-
verse factors: one was that the undergraduate program we
devised was not really acceptable to the university or the
profession or my successors; they wanted the basic qualification to be post-graduate. Another difficulty was that my own
position was anomalous: I had entered the university by the
back door, as it were, having been "transferred" in a manner which remained a mystery to most of my new colleagues.
I was acting head of a department which did not fully exist,
since my former colleagues at the Ghana Library School remained with the Ghana Library Board or went away, their
historic mission accomplished. Like the school in Trinidad
it could only be a transitional phenomenon whose purpose was
to round off the British connection. Furthermore, as I did
not have a university degree but a professional equivalent,

my standing within the university was too weak for me to
make the kind of impact that a new department requires: I
would have remained an acting head for at least another ten
years, or perhaps forever. On a personal level there would
have been that premature decline into pathos and moral turpitude which has been the fate of so many expatriates in Africa.
In the long run, therefore, it was perhaps fortunate that the
department was taken over by the late John Harris, the veteran father figure of West African libraries, and afterwards
by Sam Kotei, now in Botswana. At the time none of this
was very clear and I did not leave for these professional
reasons. Yet, in retrospect, that is how it was.

3. COLLEGE OF LIBRARIANSHIP WALES

    In 1967 I returned to Britain and went to Aberystwyth
to the College of Librarianship Wales (referred to hereafter
as CLW). At the time this return seemed accidental and
disastrous; from a career point of view it could lead nowhere.
For domestic reasons, however, it became essential that I
should put my scattered family together again and this was
one way of doing it; that was the priority. To my Ghanaian
colleagues this motive was suspect--even incomprehensible--
and most of them did not accept it. If my wife had gone
away, why didn't I get another one? If two of the children
lacked a mother, what was wrong with the baby nurse?
There was in fact an indigenous wife or concubine; there was
also a baby nurse, but that was not the point. I gave up
trying to explain since I was aware that professionally they
felt betrayed. I had been largely responsible for setting up
a Department of Library Studies in the university and was
now apparently determined to abandon it. I had let them
down and was not forgiven either then or since. It was therefore a melancholy departure: psychologically I had prepared
myself for this exit but the effort involved left me with no
energies to look forward to anything else. I was expecting
to go to Maryland, USA, but the arrangement fell through:
it appeared that the place was unsuitable for colored children.
I was, in consequence, grateful to those responsible for my
appointment in Wales. Evidently they had overcome their
misgivings about my respectability, moral and intellectual.
They suspected that a colonial type degeneration had set in
and that I would arrive brandishing my brandy bottle and
shaking with malarial ague and delirium tremens.

Insofar as there was any trembling, it derived from consternation. However much one may pretend otherwise, a sudden gross reduction in one's worldly importance is not easy to sustain. For the previous seven years or so I had been running my own show and making my unique contribution to the growth of nations. Now, overnight, I had become a minor figure in a large institution and the head of my department was one of my former students. Everybody was very kind and helpful but that would make little difference. In addition I was afflicted by a general culture shock in reverse and readjustment took a long time. All these were "negative" factors, although in the long run the experience was salutory and not negative at all. But in the beginning it was grim, and each morning it was difficult to summon up enough will power to enter the building.

My immediate reactions were partly caused by the nature of CLW itself as it then was. By any standards it is a remarkable institution and a success story resulting from a combination of favorable circumstances, the most important being the appointment at its inception of a dynamic Principal, Frank Hogg. There were, however, peculiarities which had arisen both from the environment and from the way the College had developed. In the first place it was--and is--a unique organization, since it obtains most of its funds not from the local education authority but from the central government. There was therefore more money than is usually found in departments which are part of larger units and a degree of autonomy which enabled that money to be spent. Consequently the college library, for example, is one of the best and largest of its kind in the world.

However, I am not writing an evaluation of CLW, nor advertising its merits, since it does this very well itself. No, I am simply recording my own responses at that time. The first thing that impressed me was that CLW is a monotechnic, so that you have to envisage sixty or more staff who were not only teaching in the same field but were all ex-librarians--hybrid creatures every one--as teachers in professional subjects must be. The academic community at the University of Ghana were naturally specialists in the usual variety of disciplines and it was also, then, very cosmopolitan. Nkrumah, his enemies said, had surrounded himself with a wild collection of alien ideological crackpots and intellectual adventurers. Be that as it may, the university was a diverse and turbulent place, whereas CLW was the exact opposite. My new colleagues were mostly conscientious and able people (as the testimonials say), but their abilities had been channeled, willy-nilly, along identical lines; they were all going in the same direction, which suggested certain common assumptions. What these assumptions were or where the directions led could not easily be determined. Contacts with the university were also slight, not necessarily a bad thing as that institution was ingrown and self absorbed. (The negative side of cultural nationalism is a kind of exclusive myopia.) Even so, this isolation served to intensify these limited perspectives.

In many respects then, the atmosphere was provincial and some of my bewilderment may have arisen because I had not been exposed to such influences before. I should add that most of the other library schools in Britain would have been even more depressing. In short, for largely fortuitous reasons the intellectual climate was low-key and the place had no soul. How many institutions have? However, it was very effective and dynamic in a factory sort of way and was actively involved in professional life beyond Wales. Indeed this national status later became international and thanks to this expansive and positive policy some members of staff, including myself, later had the opportunity for professional work overseas.

Meanwhile, within that structured emporium, my own teaching had to find new directions. I could no longer pretend that I was as close to students as formerly: I felt somewhat remote from their concerns and somehow not quite all there. However, circumstances were sufficiently absurd to keep total dullness or boredom at bay. There is now a magnificent new building and impressive facilities, but at that time we often had to lecture in ancient structures scattered about Aberystwyth. It was difficult to arrive there on time before the students went away. One was a hillside chapel. Another was a theological college, a building of preternatural gloom redolent of Ronuk* and puritan torments. Other lecture rooms were in the old university which, at the turn of the century, had been erected as a hotel by some mad tycoon, overwhelmed by the arrival of the railway. This splendid neo-Gothic folly, where passages came to a dead end, where spiraling staircases led nowhere and where lecture rooms could not be found, somehow caused one's every utterance to be improbable and ridiculous. Beyond the battle-

---

*A British floor wax

ments and the waterless moat there was the sea and the "endless" pier, so called because part of it had been blown away in a famous storm. Gazing out of the mullioned window one would glimpse the heraldic cormorant sitting on this abbreviated structure and holding out its wings. Afflicted by sudden amnesia, I would then have to ask my students, "What were we talking about?" Few of them would remember either; they were often oppressed by nameless primitive obsessions.

At this point a diversion must be excused. In addition to my teaching chores I had become Warden to the hostel for female students. This position should, one might have thought, have been filled by a woman, but apparently none could be found and the last one had been carried away, never to be seen again. Pantyfedwen is--or rather was--a large impressive building with the sea in front and at the rear the desolate spaces of the Great Bog of Borth. The building was so high that it perceptibly swayed in the wind which howled all winter. There were rooms for at least eighty students and some to spare, particularly on the top floor, which was haunted. (The swaying in the wind produced creaking noises.) At one stage the girls demanded that the ghost should be exorcised, but we pointed out that it was on the establishment and listed in the College Prospectus. Immediately below this haunted floor our family had its flat, scarcely a very private place, and we were surrounded by girlish noises and the pattern of female feet and occasional screams.

With regard to the screams, some of my more prurient and pious colleagues were convinced that I had cloven hooves, so I had to ensure that no breath of scandal should ever reach their flapping ears. None ever did, or not that I knew about. The hostel was managed by a staff appointed by the Welsh League of Youth, which owned the building. Together with my wife, I was responsible only for the students and this division of responsibility caused friction between us and the management. We patrolled the long corridors at midnight and put out the lights and locked the door. We took our evening meal with the students and had inherited a rotating system where they sat at the warden's table. Whatever worthy purpose this custom may have served was nullified in our case because much of the time we couldn't think of anything to talk about to them, and vice versa: their view of the world was constricted and ours was a different one. At that time it was also distorted by frequent marital discords, so that there was a great deal of tension

around and this also contributed to the silences. I often fled
the scene and the supper and went to the Grand Hotel, which
was literally across the road. There one could gaze out to
sea and recover a degree of sanity.

I was also disturbed to discover many antique repressive regulations. I had not, I said, been appointed to preside over a nunnery. Whereas, he had not, the man said,
been appointed to administer a brothel and he had to consider
local opinion. The subsequent liberalizing process was long
and stormy. The existing hypocritical arrangements were
within the best traditions of the chapel, whose hatred of alcohol is total, while fornication is tolerated so long as it is
unseen. There was only one key and no one could stay out
after midnight, nor could the girls receive male visitors in
their rooms at any time. However, when he was in a good
mood, and only then, the manager would leave a basement
window open all night. This clandestine system was arbi-
trary and inefficient.

Eventually all these absurdities were removed and it
was arranged that the girls should run their own affairs.
We were involved only in crisis situations, as when they fell
down the stairs or were reported as missing without trace.
On the whole it was a stimulating experience, but we missed
our garden and eventually returned to a private life where our
conflicts could flourish in a less public environment. This
was in a mortaged bungalow upon the hillside in a place called
Llandre, a few miles inland from Borth. I handed over to
a friend and colleague, Bill Martin from Belfast, who immediately put up a poster-size photograph of Ian Paisley on the
office wall.

Later on the girls were removed to a new hostel on
the College campus; the building was abandoned by the college
and ultimately by everybody else. It was finally pulled down
and all that exists now are some picture postcards and nos-
talgic memories in no longer girlish souls.

In my account of that other college in London, I described our attempts to remain part of the world which was
at least on our doorstep. But in Aberystwyth this was not
so: one had the feeling that the material world, as commonly experienced, had somehow gone away. It was therefore
even more imperative that one should strive to "keep in
touch" with it. If that had not been done the staff--who incidentally are mostly not Welsh--might well have become

mythomaniacs or worse. As it was they were obliged to live in a private realm and the College represented the only public one: it was the College which, from time to time, sent them forth so that they could be reminded that Birmingham and Manchester were still there. Otherwise they rarely left Aberystwyth, since to do so involved a major expedition: on the train it took five hours to get to London, which was also the time required to get there from West Africa. In view of this isolation it became necessary to warn the students when they arrived that they had come to a peculiar place. Aberystwyth is a small market town: buried under a thick layer of tourists in summer and students in winter, the ancestral folk went on with their separate lives. I used to remind them that next to St. Andrews, Scotland, the university had the highest student marriage rate in Britain and the suicide level was also high; it was a place where psychologists were much in demand.

To counteract these hazards the College was highly organized--even over-organized, one sometimes thought--and one of its major administrative achievements was regularly to send staff and students out into the library world on study tours. (These extraordinary journeys reminded me of those high-powered expeditions which were sent out to explore Africa from Victorian Britain.) Admittedly the parallel is a little far-fetched and most of our students returned sooner or later, but what happened at their destinations naturally did not necessarily correspond with the intentions of those who sent them there. It was the same with the staff, and I for one encountered alarming incidents on the way. In the railway station buffet in Manchester (or was it Birmingham?) I was attacked by a drunken Irishman for no reason at all and the police had to be called. In Holland Park, Kensington I was attacked again and robbed by a gang of youths armed with nail-studded clubs. Such things had never happened in Africa. The students were also sent to work in libraries and staff members were sent out to visit them. This in itself was a difficult operation and I sometimes failed. It was all very paternalistic but inter alia it made it possible for staff and students to fraternize: in professional terms the experience was worthwhile.

But this was not all. The Principal was acute enough to appreciate that in addition to the British ambiance there was another world elsewhere. Out there existed tropical governments who were prepared--with the assistance sometimes of the British Council--to send their citizens to summer schools. From the ends of the earth they were attracted by this idyllic setting and by the expertise available. Also, special arrangements were made to send some of our staff to Third World countries. There they undoubtedly contributed more professionally than they would have done in their own country, where they were not always appreciated.

The staff wives were naturally left behind on these occasions: as usual theirs was not an easy lot since they had to find work which happened to be available locally and nobody sent them out anywhere. Their interactions could only be local and sometimes there was not much to "interact" with. Some of them learned Welsh; in view of the difficulties of that language a most praiseworthy endeavor. But it could not easily be used and the Welsh themselves were not enthusiastic about foreigners learning their language. Once again marital strains became endemic: some of us became entangled and obsessed as if our beings had been invaded by some pagan Celtic force. The College itself was immune from such influences as it was not a Celtic institution at all--quite the contrary. There was a Welsh department, it is true, which looked after a minority of students who had come down from the hills, but their preoccupations were often nationalist and untypical. They belonged there in a way which most of us did not.

In spite of all these emanations, and partly because of them, it became possible for me to write two books (discussed elsewhere) and to obtain a degree from London university (our professional qualification was accepted as a first degree equivalent). In this manner many of us had become academically respectable at last and the College had made this possible by giving us study leave. During that year as I sat brooding on the hillside it seemed that I might stay there forever and the picturesque graveyard in the wooded hillside at Llandre would become my final resting place. To some extent I was involved with Britain once more and it was a kind of home. Yet to the College I had never really belonged and there were still some years left to go. I had cultivated my garden and studied the Beasts but they were not enough, and when the College sent me for a one-term stint in Nigeria, I had the opportunity to return to West Africa, which I subsequently did. That destination evidently corresponded with my proper Destiny. I had been saved and preserved by CLW and was now professionally qualified enough and sufficiently rehabilitated to return and start again. Before leaving I received an anonymous letter and there was one "word" only: WAWA, i.e., West Africa Wins Again.

4. POSTSCRIPT

The account of College life has not been about an academic career but about the teaching of adults. I use this word deliberately because lecturers may or may not be teachers. Lecturers as such are more concerned with their presentation: it is an impersonal activity.

Persons with pedagogic urges often have this tendency to interfere with the human race. That is probably the root from which their teaching endeavors spring. That is how I was. Leaving aside other motives, such as that which prompts some of us to indulge in self-dramatization, there is usually present a kind of cultural imperialism, a tendency to invade other people's minds. (Conservatives feel that this should be one of God's prerogatives.) This impulse may spend itself on social welfare, commonly dismissed as "do-goodery, " or it may be linked with power drives (as in politics) or it may concentrate on the alleged needs--as distinct from wants--of individuals. This, of course, is a priestly function and as a small child I used to dress up in what I hoped were clerical robes and, because of shyness, stood behind the door of the servants' quarters to deliver my sermons.

There was, of course, in later years no chance for such a role. There are, it seems, many priests whose beliefs--if any--do not correspond with those of their church, but I could not have been one of them. Given the opportunity I might have been a heretic psychoanalyst or probation officer. I was not a politician but a guru manqué. Such drives are often expressed in activities outside people's careers: some people become, for example, boy scouts. True, I was a boy scout and a wolf cub, and even--briefly-- a cubmaster. But in these imitation jungles I never felt wholly at home and lacked an interest in little boys. No, this redemptive impulse moved along other channels; it began with the beasts, continued with infantry soldiers and ended with the teaching of young adults. It was a maternal instinct rather than the opposite. Patriarchal or authoritarian attitudes were, of course, an abomination. A life style like that produces an involvement with the immature, the undeveloped, the neurotic and the mentally dispossessed. So it was also in my personal relations, including the most intimate. I attracted people who felt inadequate. Fortunately, such persons are both more sensitive and more aware than most: they have to be. They were nevertheless psychologically dependent on me and when that dependence passes, resentment takes its place. I have presented this role, so far, as a kind of strength, and so it may be. But it also constitutes a severe limitation, since one's relations with "mature" people are rarely satisfactory and are dogged by misunderstanding.

When I left NWP in 1959, the students drew up a special issue of their annual journal called Allover (it was normally called Hangover). There was a kind of satirical festschrift to mark the end of my indigenous career. There were a number of poems and a mock agony column called dear Auntie Benj--a perceptive tribute. If I had failed to emphasize this missionary element this record would have been both incomplete and misleading. Here I have tried to go beyond special pleading or presenting myself in too favorable a light, yet that temptation can never be wholly resisted and so far I have not mentioned a destructive element which is always present in the type of personality I have described. "Demonic" is too strong and too flattering a word, yet one has to admit that positive (missionary) tendency cannot exist without its opposite. One of our students who had a degree in Theology became temporarily deranged and put it about in Scotland (where such things are credible) that it had been revealed to her that I was Beelzebub, reincarnated. I thought this perception was inaccurate then, but now I can see what she meant. The most senior Hindu gods are Brahma, the creator; Vishnu, the preserver, and Shiva, the destroyer. They are present in us all. I shall pursue such matters elsewhere, but meanwhile, out there in the dark, the mysteries remain. "Of what we cannot speak, thereof we must be silent"--but unlike Wittgenstein we must go on trying.

PART IV: MY AFRICA

1. CAMPUS EXPATRIATES

My life as a Professor in Nigeria was a new kind of experience. For the first time I became a key member of an Establishment (the war years were something else). It seemed advisable to become more respectable and wear short hair and even sometimes a suit and a borrowed tie, as I had to attend unfamiliar rituals. These were often condemned as medieval European survivals--as indeed they were--but formal ceremony plays an important role in that culture and they were far less incongruous than might have been supposed. As for my own part in the proceedings, it was, of course, an act since I am not essentially a public person. However, even as a teacher I felt that situations should be dramatized. This is not a political trait, still less a theatrical one: it could be defined as a literary instinct but it is also a product of a temperamental affinity with high-camp attitudes. This self-dramatization, noticeable also among poets, priests, drunkards, egotists and homosexuals, adds an essential something to an existence which might otherwise be without significance. These are dangerous tendencies and I am well aware that the other kinds of people who play everything down instead of up--who reduce life to a manageable low key and successfully turn mountains into molehills --are also required, especially for the conducting of affairs in a modern state.

What, it may well be asked, has all this to do with expatriate life in an African university? The answer must be that it is relevant because universities in developing countries are, willy-nilly, closed communities. Town and gown do not interact since there may be no town to hassle with-- only, figuratively speaking, a howling wilderness. It is therefore possible to live in such a way that one rarely leaves the campus. (Educationally, this is far from ideal,

113

but few would now suppose that there is a self-evident connection between universities and education.) In these isolated
social units individuals are unhinged and disconnected from
any base. Free-floating agencies, they are overtaken by
fantasies which inject themselves into their daily round and
common task. Relationships then develop which could never
happen in a more normal environment.

One learns to respond to challenges and stimuli which
are not present and which have had to be invented. Somehow, to deal with bizarre events, the creative imagination
must be summoned from the deep. This does not mean that
we have any cause to repine; our existence is neither boring
nor unrewarding. On the contrary, life consists of a series
of bizarre incidents and encounters which have few parallels
in the fixed and settled structures of overdeveloped countries.
Each day brings its own variation on certain basic patterns
and modes. Our preoccupations are such that one feels that
the people back there spend most of their time fretting about
dreary trivialities.

I have merely isolated a significant factor which is the
special dimension produced by impermanence or lack of a
recognizable future. The consciousness of settlers or immigrants is naturally different altogether: they have migrated
forever, but we are birds of passage and sing a different
song. Our world is fleeting and we are set down in transitional societies where the linear laws of cause and effect are
not yet fully established. When the sun is overhead, the
shadows are short and quite ordinary people become eccentric and eremitical or turn into unacknowledged warlocks
and witches who have--so it is alleged--no shadows either.
Meanwhile, in gross contrast, there is the alternative world
of academic labor where courses are mechanistic, pseudo-
scientific and educationally primitive. The ancient modes
have been replaced by the new magic of modernization and
the deadly repetitions of the knowledge industry.

Contributing to this situation is the cosmopolitan com-
position of the community. The non-African members include people from America, Britain, India, Ireland, Pakistan,
Poland, the Philippines, Scandinavia and Singapore. They
are not present because anybody loves them, but as necessary evils until there is a sufficient number of indigenous
products to replace them. It is an illusion to imagine that
foreigners are more interesting than other people, although
I used to think so when I was young; I even married one.

They are simply different and therefore have to be cultivated
as if they were sensitive plants belonging to the cactus family.   They can be divided and sub-divided by race, creed,
language and, above all, by value systems, especially those
reflected by political attitudes and drinking habits.   Most important and most symptomatic of these indicators is the last.
Some of the other chasms can be bridged but between the
drinking and non-drinking classes there is a great gulf fixed.
This class war is conducted on many fronts and each side is
rent by its own internal conflicts.   Some variations arise
from the gaps between private and public behavior.   Religious
taboos and fear of exposure cause many Muslims and some
Christians to tipple half their lives away at home.

This distinction is more important than elsewhere because the assorted foreign inmates of these institutions have
only three main channels of social intercourse.   The first
is provided by work contacts; the second is their own little
coterie, usually a national one, and the third consists of social clubs.   The only pervasive or general meeting places
are therefore the last.   Since the main activity is drinking,
those who abstain from alcohol do not frequent them and to
their colleagues outside their Department they may remain
unknown for many years.   Indeed it is often difficult to establish whether they continue to exist or not--they become
non-persons.

This taxonomy is of course a simplification since
there are occasional accidental contacts, for example, during
the long waiting times in banks and similar establishments.
Or there are official gatherings; but the cocktail party, as
invented by the British, is no longer what it was in colonial
times.   Then, formidable hostesses moved people around to
forestall intimacy and to provide for official contacts with
important persons.   In addition, there exist various esoteric
groupings, mainly religious sects--for example, adventists,
anglicans, anabaptists, armadiyahs, catholics, calvinists,
cherabims, hindus, methodists, mennonites, seekers, sera-
phims, shiites, sikhs, sunnis, witnesses and wailers--all of
whom gather at least once a week.   There are also those
with a common interest such as bridge or poker or horses
or some special kind of fornication.   Finally, there are some
who share intellectual or political interests.   But all these
are ingrown, even secretive, minorities which are too exclusive to leaven the lump.

Contemplating these artificial conglomerations one is

bound from time to time to ask, why do they leave home?
The reasons are not far to seek. Ideological motivation such
as my own has already been mentioned. There are also political exiles or those out of tune with their own national
regimes--an increasing number since late twentieth-century
man is essentially a displaced person. (Those who are not
geographically elsewhere are mentally homeless.) We shall
not discuss them. In more recent years many have come to
Africa because they fail to find employment in their own countries. This is the worst of all reasons, since such persons
have no particular motive for being where they find themselves. Indeed they may know nothing about their new place
beforehand and some degree of culture shock is inevitable;
usually they do not last long. Or they may fret their lives
away trying to keep up with foreign businessmen for whom a
financial base is established in their own countries and whose
umbilical chord is securely tied: they are not expatriates.
Obviously, the most rewarding academic posts are those
where teaching or research is concerned with something indigenous and important, as for example, agriculture or
health or veterinary medicine. Whatever the subject area,
unless there is a firm commitment either to the people or to
the job, or preferably to both, the expatriate academic starts
off on his long road to ruin. He may become one of those
familiar types, so often satirized: inauthentic persons who
slowly but surely crumble away. It would be too distressing
to dwell upon their dismal attributes and tedious beyond
measure to analyze their semi-colonial attitudes, which are
not compensated for by the dedication which the real colonialists once had.

Practical considerations apart, there is, of course,
that tradition which requires people to leave their own country for emotional reasons. Beyond the frontiers, in order
to forget, one bears away a broken heart so that time and
remoteness may put it back together again. Or, as in my
own case, when I came to Nigeria certain conflicting relationships become so intolerable that they have to be left--
if only temporarily--behind. Such phenomena are well documented. Less attention, however, has been paid to those
who have no heart at all, the emotionally dispossessed. A
surprising number of academics have mother fixations: they
leave home to escape from mum, naturally a vain endeavor
since she has long since been internalized. She sits toad-
like inside them always, monitoring their responses--a simple
case of psychic possession. There are also some expatriate
women who share this predicament (naturally in reverse) but

they are more likely to go to Spain or Guatemala. As for the men, all that can be hoped is that Mother Africa will somehow replace the original womb. In some ways she does, since such persons are, as the naturalists say, widely distributed. They are to be found under almost every baobab tree, or pursuing brilliant birds or butterflies, or alternatively sitting in some dreadful bar desperately trying to shed an innocence they will never outgrow. No doubt it is a more realistic strategy than waiting for a wife to turn into mum, and their contribution to African development is welcome.

Intensified by all this social confusion, the sound of breaking marriages is constantly heard in the land: it calls for no more social comment than the noise of the laughing dove. The only comment worth making is to note the unfortunate predicament of expatriate women who accompany their husbands and have no job. Their lot is a dismal one because there is no good reason why they should exist: there are stewards and baby nurses and gardeners and concubines enough to meet all domestic requirements and they are cheaper than wives or washing machines. It is a pathetic role and it is most unfortunate that the novelists have depicted these ladies in such an unfavorable light. It has been claimed that their presence hastened the end of the Empire by at least thirty years--surely an excellent development. One result of the marital fluidity is that the alternate arrangements that are made are improbable, impermanent, and often not viable when the partners return to their own environment. In this respect they are like ship-board romances except that nobody expects them to last, which is their special appeal. The people on board ship are also part of a closed community but it is only a temporary one. Campus society is a little more permanent, but only relatively so. Among expatriates, who are usually on contract, there is inevitably a high rate of turnover, so that people who become intimate and see each other every day then go their several ways and never meet again. Even more extraordinary, after a few months, those who remain cannot even remember the names of those who have left.

Political instability often gives a sudden added impetus to this mobility. Some recalcitrant individuals have been deported from several countries and at least one academic was deported twice by different regimes in the same country (Ghana). This forcible removal has been the lot of a number of my friends and it is a measure of my own lack of impact that I was never granted this distinction. Threats,

of course, have been made, but usually they were withdrawn
next morning. There remain many who are not actually deported but become aware that a new regime will cast a jaun-
diced eye upon them.

Such was the case after Nkrumah fell in Ghana. Most
of us had originally gone there because we thought we could
help Nkrumah in building his African socialism. (Some were
Americans avoiding the Vietnam draft.) We were peculiar
fringe representatives of the typical cultural movements of
the sixties. As such we objected to the elitist conservative
nature of the University of Ghana with its Oxbridge-type
halls. It was all quite magnificent, but was this the real
new Ghana? Perhaps in retrospect it was, but we didn't understand that then: we never ate in the halls or sat at high
table and on the only occasion that two of my wilder friends
did so, it was revealed (amid student applause) that under
their academic robes they were wearing nothing at all. In
moments of euphoria we thought of ourselves--both figuratively and geographically--as members of an avant-garde but,
alas, the army which should have been behind us wasn't
there and the enemies of promise were not to be moved.
We were, initially, enthusiastic supporters of the regime
and our disillusion came later than that of most Ghanaians
because as foreigners we were outside of the political process.

There was an extraordinary gap between the theoretical
superstructure available to us and the underlying social realities, which were less so: the national consequence was a
kind of political schizophrenia. At Winneba the ideological
institute carried on with its valiant attempts to link Marxism
with the African experience, and visiting foreign ideologues
produced their weird and rarely relevant formulations. I
recall a newspaper article by Pat Sloan, the veteran British
communist, which was a learned historical disquisition on the
unsocialist nature of wig wearing, then a common practice
with the ladies. It was not wigs he should have been bothered about.

Because of this hiatus between appearance and reality,
most of us were taken aback when the regime collapsed like
a house of cards within a few hours. The next day all these
hairy creatures sat around dragging at their pot (locally
called wee) and staring gloomily at the map. Where would
they be welcome now? Tanzania? Ethiopia? Tibet? In
fact they were all really only emanations from Europe and
America, since Africa has no sympathy for their kind of
counterculture. Within months they were all gone, mostly to

the U. S. A., where the radicals were still on the march against the Vietnam war.

Those expatriates who successfully return to their own countries have usually been away not more than four or five years. Beyond that period a mysterious process sets in which alienates them forever both from their old environment and their new one. Back there they have no opportunity to make new friends and the former ones have developed in other directions. Not only this, but their perceptions no longer correspond with those of their compatriots at home. Then they start to develop stock prejudices against their African context and begin to abominate their surroundings. Because of these epistemological transformations which they do not understand, their instability grows. Like all those who suffer from rejection, they experience alternating emotions of love and hate (mild schizophrenia) and attacks of suspicion (incipient paranoia). Such is the well known psychology of all those who have chosen exile and expatriation.

However, a move must be made; the process is inexorable. In the old days colonialists were rightly regarded as unfit for domestic consumption except when they retired (tottering along some cold and windy shore). That was fair enough but those who have taken up the white man's burden in a world he no longer controls or comprehends must move on long before one particular service is ended. Where are they to go? Their ultimate stations are to be found in extreme places, each one more remote from settled ways: at the fringe of various deserts such as those of the Sahara or the Kalahari or that of Arabia, or in cold Canadian outposts like Halifax or Calgary, or amid the ruins of some stone age culture as in Papua New Guinea. Their exile is redeemed by one feature only: they are not alone. Indeed, as the twentieth century proceeds they gather together in these last redoubts. Just as the locals who have been abroad are called "bintus," so these survivors are commonly referred to as "wheneyes" ("When I was in Tunapoona or Bangalore," etcetera), and they will remind each other dolefully how in 1959 in Bulawayo a bottle of whiskey cost only two pounds.

2. MARIE

First Impact

This account is not about Africa, merely my reactions

to it. One cannot write about African countries without being
dishonest or foolish or simply wrong. Coming from Trinidad,
that was the first thing that impressed me. After a while,
on an island, even a fairly large one like Trinidad, one begins to feel that the place can be understood and known.
This feeling may be partly an illusion fostered by the absence
of a language barrier or any marked cultural differences, but
it is roughly correct. In Africa, on the contrary, one soon
realizes that the longer one stays the less it is possible to
comprehend anything at all. Anyone who somehow manages
to keep an open mind can do no more than evaluate, more or
less accurately, his own fluctuating reactions. Is this an
exaggeration or a re-creation of the old "Heart of Darkness"
myth? I don't think so, because we are not dealing with
Conrad's mystical darkness but with societies in a state of
flux. (Sociological investigations are misleading because
they have to freeze a moving flood.) All that I am relating,
therefore, is the development, within a new environment, of
my own fantasies and perceptions.

Return to Lost Innocence?

Beasts and the pursuit of the elemental have figured
elsewhere in this record. No doubt most people experience
the wish to return to Eden even though they are realistic
enough not to try to go there. Or the urge may be disguised
and take forms such as the cultivation of uneconomic allot-
ments in Britain or fishing in the polluted Seine, or the need
may be expressed as simple fantasy. (I heard of a foreign
legionary stationed in the Sahara desert who, every evening,
an hour before sundown, would sit with his fishing rod and
line over a bucket of water, and when he went to the bar
afterwards they would ask about his catch.) My own fantasies were mixed up with at least some kind of reality, and
naturally the most persistent was associated with sex.

Sexual Imperialism?

Sooner or later, anyone traveling alone must decide
whether to accept sexual offers as part of local hospitality.
My own experience is described elsewhere. When I went to
Ghana I was only vaguely aware of the many sociological implications arising from the exploitation of women in underdeveloped countries, and it was not until later that all these
things came together. Technically the women one encounters

are usually "prostitutes" but the variations of this universal
condition are infinite. The Africans often still use the bib-
lical term harlot, or they are called "free" women, which
may simply mean that for the time being they have no husband to lock them up. The terminology is misleading and
in the Third World a large proportion of young girls who
leave their villages have no other possible occupation. Nearly all of them hope to find a protector or a steady relationship, but except for short periods these hopes are usually
vain. They are, in consequence, to begin with at least,
semi-amateurs and quite lacking in the bleak professionalism
of their present-day Western counterparts. In Britain the
parallel, if it exists at all, can only be found in the past,
for example among the social conditions of nineteenth-century
London. Travelers like myself tend to be frightened by the
hard-faced phantoms who lurk in European city doorways and
when accosted hurry on, not without feelings of guilt. But
in less developed lands no such difficulties arise, as both
men and women have to supplement their pitiful income somehow.

At that time I was too much absorbed in my own
predicaments to give these matters due consideration. I
was still at the stage when such encounters are romanticized,
even idealized. An important element in these situations was
that the ladies were black. I came to believe that I could
not really be interested again in white women--a not uncommon disorder of the perceptions, which lasted for some
years. It colored my attitudes about Africa and was part of
my wish to stay there.

Settling Down

Living in a place is obviously a wholly different matter from traveling through. Brief encounters have their own
irresponsible and limited attractions but they are not possible
as part of a settled existence. In West Africa I was involved in an environment which, for the expatriate worker,
is still colonial. Sexual imperialism, except in novels like
those of Somerset Maugham, is a neglected subject. Since
all types of imperialism are just as demoralizing to the op-
pressor as to the oppressed, I became fascinated by the various possible forms of moral turpitude which can develop: it
was useful to compare them with my own. Characteristic
Maugham situations are primitive and banal, vulgar affairs
conducted by persons such as contractors and makers of

roads. A not untypical sight in Ghana was the return of the local young lady bearing household items on her head (for instance a gas cylinder) half an hour after the man had seen off his hard-faced wife at the airport. One wondered whether she had always been bitter like that, but nobody cared: she only came for a visit once a year. Such arrangements are practical and viable: there is no fantasy and no illusion. They are a necessary part of the scheme of things.

I was more interested in those who wrecked their lives by ignoring reality altogether. One such was a university colleague, whose deliberate illusions far outstripped those of Don Quixote with his Dulcinea. He used to tell us that next weekend he would be visited by the Goddess of the North, whereas last week it was the Goddess of the East, and so on through a range of ladies modeled on those of the Nordic Sagas. It was impossible for outsiders to connect these majestic deities with the nondescript little girls who came in from some outlying village. All that was needed for him to be financially ruined was one to be more cunning and rapacious than the rest, and that is what eventually happened. One imagines that he had no regrets.

My own case was similar, except that I eventually recovered and was not ruined, at least not financially. It takes the average European a long time fully to appreciate that in Africa human relations of any kind, including sexual affairs, have to be regulated by money. The financial transaction is an indication of affection, even love. I recall an eminent European visiting librarian sitting aloof in a Kano night club, puffing on his pipe and saying, "I've never paid for it yet and I won't start now." He was a married man and I refrained from pointing out that if that was the case, his marriage must be very odd.

That was one hang-up which had to go. Another which took much longer was a tendency to overload all my relationships with an amount of emotional baggage which they couldn't sustain. It was, of course, all part of the quest for the Grail. Like the man with his Nordic Goddesses, I tended to idealize the young ladies I picked up, or who picked me up, at the Lido, an excellent establishment in Accra, which probably no longer exists. This often led to ludicrous misunderstandings. It also caused some alarm among my Ghanaian friends, who thought I didn't know what I was doing: perhaps they were right. They had seen so many expatriates go down this road, and were wholly unable to understand.

Why not find a respectable woman, etc. ?--they were conscious of their responsibilities as members of an embryonic
bourgeoisie. As for their own needs, there was usually a
servant girl who didn't have to be paid and was expected to
be grateful. There was an absurd incident when an eminent
Ghanaian was involved in trying to pull me away from a
young woman who was pulling the other way. As I was half
clad the struggle was neither edifying nor dignified and the
man won because it all became too ridiculous.

It should not be imagined that this was a full-time
occupation and that I had become a collector of fallen women.
In fact, apart from odd encounters, there were never more
than three, originally not at the same time. The trouble was
that once these ladies had become regular visitors to the
house, I was completely incapable of getting rid of any of
them, or of arranging that they didn't come at the same time.
I was saved from this predicament by resolute action by one
more devoted than the rest. Marie was a Fulani girl from
Northern Nigeria and disposed of her rivals by the simple
expedient of threatening them with a knife. That was the
end of my polygamous existence and I was grateful. Polyg-
amy is only possible if it is highly regulated and institutionalized. There followed one of the most pleasant years
of my life.

Marie was not her real name; I doubt whether she
had ever had one, nor did she know how old she was. I
later discovered that she was very much younger than I
imagined. Some unknown convulsion had brought her parents
to Ghana and they had long since disappeared. The arrangement originally was light-hearted enough and started by my
locking her up for several days to indicate my "serious" intentions, which she wouldn't believe. This failure of communication became less frequent as time went on but the relationship made me appreciate fully what an alien and terrify-
ing world illiterates live in. This becomes quite crippling
as soon as they are in contact with literate people, who tend
to exploit them. There were many minor misunderstandings,
mostly caused by language or cultural differences. She was
a Muslim and held me personally responsible for what seemed
to her the absurd doctrine of the Trinity. She refused to accept that I was not a Christian and when I protested that I
had my own god, she said that was juju--a perceptive remark.
At that time I was subject to fits of choleric rage, often
brought on by alcohol, and these produced equally violent reactions of mirth and amazement, which made me even angrier.

People who have lived at subsistence level don't get excited about unimportant matters.

In matters of sex she was matter of fact and in this respect fairly representative. Many of these girls had acquired practices from their European friends, but otherwise their responses were uncomplicated, even pre-erotic: they did not have sex in the head. There is a fairly common belief in Africa, mainly among the men, that the sexual behavior of white people is depraved and unnatural. In particular, they claim to object to oral sex. (In her case she was very happy if it was done to her, but not the other way around.) She also retained traces of her puritanical background in a Muslim village. She didn't like kissing and in moments of climax her face had to be covered, a curious survival of the veil perhaps--or merely that women shouldn't show emotion?

Many of the men, incidentally, are also totally opposed to women being "on top, " presumably a natural response in a patriarchal society. (One remembers how Lilith, the other wife of Adam, was expelled for behaving in this unsubmissive manner and had to become the female equivalent of the wandering Jew.)

Marie naturally did not share this prejudice and was typical in declaring that she preferred non-African men because they were more considerate. She also repeated the theory that black men are more "virile, " in the sense that they "bothered you too much, " i. e. , too often and only with reference to their own satisfaction. It is not possible to establish the truth in this area, a serious matter because in racially mixed societies this sex myth is tied up with class conflicts and is therefore partly responsible for prejudice, fear and discrimination. Even in colonial-type communities, many of the more repressed white women are obsessed by rape fears and fantasies. It is not accidental that pornographic films often feature black men with white women, but not vice-versa.

As for me, I became a martyr to her imperious demands. Possibly because of some anatomical peculiarity, she insisted on positions unknown to the Kama Sutra and left me almost dismembered. I was also required to squeeze her nipples in a vice-like grip, which was possible only because I have double-jointed thumbs. Permanently I had bruised knees from making love in the bath and was after-

wards subject to a violent washing of all orifices, including
nose and ears. (Muslims believe, not without reason, that
all infidels are unclean.) It was an exacting regimen, but
in the interests of dramatic effect, I have perhaps exaggerated
the masochistic element.   I have never shared the tastes of
those gentlemen who like to be bonded or whipped.   It would
be more appropriate to regard such behavior as evidence of
my chivalrous instincts.   Much of our life was spent in an
air-conditioned shuttered room, which had nothing but artificial light.   It thus became possible not to know whether it
was day or night.   Most of the time I have the unfortunate
Western habit of living partly in the future, but for once I
had forgotten about linear time.   I would wake up and look
at her sleeping form and think, this is enough, this is all:
it was being instead of becoming, but of course it was only
done by a kind of conjuring trick, possibly the influence of
indigenous magic.   These, after all, were only moments.

In such a manner a year passed and then we were
overtaken by an inevitable Nemesis.   For reasons which are
irrelevant here, I had, at the beginning of that year, arranged to return to Britain.   When the time came we discovered that the bond had become very close and the parting
was quite terrible.   The nature of her feelings was different
from mine but that didn't make anything any better.   For me,
however, much as I might have preferred it to be otherwise,
this was the end of an idyllic interlude; for her it was the
end of a life she might never find again.   I can now see that
the relationship had been so satisfactory because I knew it
would have to end, but it didn't seem like that then.

By all the laws of probability, that should have been
the end of the matter, but there was a sequel.   About two
years later I was in a pub in a small village in Wales when
a man whom I didn't then know came up and handed me a
battered photograph: it was of her.   Always susceptible to
signs, I regarded this as a miraculous portent.   How could
it have come about?   The answer was straightforward.   By
that time she had gone to Lagos and met a man who came
from the village where I was then living.   In this manner
she had discovered where I was, but at that time nothing
more could be done about it.   All that happened was that I
now knew where she was.

Two or three years passed and then the time came to
return to Africa, and in 1972 I went to Northern Nigeria.
From the same friend in Lagos I received a message that

Marie was still there and frequented the Can Can night club.
If that was her base it could mean only one thing. However,
I felt impelled to go and faced the horrors of Nigerian Airways in order to find out. (At the time there was also a
conference of Commonwealth librarians, which provided an
excuse: it could be no more as I was not a delegate.) This
night club, which could be anywhere in the Third World, is
now closed down. There were soft lights and loud music and
it was well set up for its purpose, but such places for anyone with a sociological imagination are infinitely sad--gay
certainly, but sad. Not all of the girls came from a background without hope. Some were ex-Secondary School with
0 levels who had chosen the bright lights and the easy life.
However, I was not conducting a social survey, but looking
for Marie.

When she came in after her nightly visit to the cine-
ma, my impression was that she was little changed: one
could not see very well. Her story was predictable. After
I left Ghana she went to Lagos in search of her fortune.
(The oil boom was beginning to make the wicked city a lucra-
tive place--for some.) She found another "protector," a
German businessman, and for a time all was well. She began to collect household items: a radio, an electric fan, a
tin lock-up trunk--this last item was always thought of as
the first step on the road to affluence. (Somebody must have
made a fortune making these mottled iodized containers, which
are to be found all over Africa.) The next item would usually have been a sewing machine. It is interesting that the
seamstress has had the same social significance in all societies at a certain stage of development--witness Thomas
Hood's Song of the Shirt: the price of respectability is grim
drudgery.

But the inevitable happened and the man went away,
a characteristic feature of sexual imperialism. Another is
that once girls take up with foreign partners, it becomes a
fixed pattern, one of the reasons for the existence of so
many people who are not black but colored. After that her
small properties were all stolen or she may have sold them
and her only real home was the Can Can.

I hired a room there, a tomb-like cell where the stut-
tering air conditioner could not redeem the drab furnishings
or the cracked and spotted mirrors or the soft porn illustrations on the wall. Nor could it drown the deafening noise of
the music. She wanted to come back with me to Northern

Nigeria: it was after all her original home, but I was realistic enough to appreciate the impossibility. What would
she do on the edge of the Sahara? For too long now she had
been part of a way of life which could not be abandoned.
One tell-tale sign was that during the night she made regular
journeys to collect more beer. Also her sexual responses
were muted and perfunctory; she was now somebody else.

I had known already that one can revisit the past but
not recapture it. Even so, it was a melancholy and heart-
rending occasion. She had become one among millions of
women whose only hope lies in making enough money to return to "normal" life, but meanwhile they develop a taste for
expensive luxuries, including copious quantities of liquor, and
saving, therefore, is rarely possible. Most likely she will
simply "disappear." For me, on the other hand, this event
marked the end of my exposure to feminine black power, an
experience begun so light-heartedly ten years before.

3. RACIAL INTERACTIONS

Cosmopolis

The ideological preoccupations I have described were
reflected and influenced by my personal relationships mostly
within the university: they went through many fluctuations
which I now scarcely remember, but present always I suppose
was a wish (which in retrospect seems rather pathetic) to be
accepted. This urge has always been at war with my no less
persistent "radical" impulses, which demand that I should
not be accepted, at least not on Their terms. But this predicament is discussed in another place and I must first deal
with my Nigerian colleagues who have to get on not only
with their fellow countrymen of different ethnic persuasions--
a difficult enough proposition--but also with a variety of foreign nationals.

Except when race is used for political or career pur-
poses--which it often is--the Nigerians are remarkably tolerant, especially when one considers the racism which has been
directed against them, either collectively or individually in
other countries or in their own. What prejudices they have
are well-founded. For instance, Asians are accepted but
without enthusiasm, since many of them make no attempt to
"belong" and they send all their money home and may be

otherwise quite indifferent to their new environment. With
notable exceptions, the Poles are regarded in the same way--
their economic motivations are similar. (Middle class values are nowhere more apparent than among our colleagues
from Eastern Europe. If Marxist doctrines officially exist
in their countries, it is clear that for them at least they are
irrelevant.) As for the few remaining British, the Nigerians
are bound to be ambivalent. In most English-speaking African countries there are a few outstanding expatriates, including some academics, who have chosen to identify themselves wholly with the new regimes whatever their politics
might be. Cynics have seen this as a form of opportunism,
one which is more often associated with businessmen such as
those famous gentlemen who acted as bearers to Idi Amin.
However, this strategy is logical enough for those who may
well have always held the same values as those of the new
élites. Such persons make an important contribution and
often receive official honors, not only from the British Government but also from the new countries they have served.
They are Establishment figures and are regarded by the indigenous people with respect, qualified by certain reserva-
tions which they would find difficult to define. Sometimes a
sycophantic element is present which, in the more extreme
cases, takes the form of a liberal distribution of sexual
favors.

The new rulers understand them well enough but they
may be puzzled by the wilder representatives of the political
left. In the days before independence, such persons were
not allowed and they do not know them well. (In the francophone countries of Africa, for instance the Cameroons, there
was a much closer link between liberation movements and the
communist party in France.) But in Nigeria they feel more
at home with expatriate semi-colonial attitudes and some of
these survivors are figures of fun, who can even be patron-
ized or regarded as historical monuments. Sometimes in
bars they are egged on and goaded to make wild, blimpish
and apocalyptic utterances, for example in favor of the South
African whites. It is a special kind of tolerance, since these
old hands are no longer a threat.

To return to the European radicals, one would not,
after all, expect the members of an aspiring bourgeoisie to
appreciate those who apparently reject the values and the
status symbols they are striving to acquire. One finds an
ironic contrast when expatriate domestic interiors are filled
with African artifacts--often "airport art"--while those of the

Africans remind one of pictures of the homes of the European middle classes in former times.   The important difference is that prominent among the copious bric-a-brac, there
will be the color television set and masses of stereo equipment including stroboscopic lights.   The co-existence of old
and new are always bizarre and sometimes sinister.   For
example, when alleged traitors were shot on bar beach,
Lagos, the spectacle was watched by television viewers in
a slot between advertisements for detergents and pomade.
Machine guns were used because there is a popular belief
that certain criminal or political offenders are immune from
bullets.   (Meanwhile, above the rattle of the guns, one could
hear the insistent rhythm of somebody pounding yam.)

Radicals from the United States are also suspect and
likely to be thought of as agents for the C. L A.   Otherwise
Americans are approved of as White Nigerians who understand the importance of the market place and the social obli-
gation to make money.   (In many African traditional religions,
for instance among the Yoruba, an indifference to material
goods is regarded as criminal.)   As for black Americans and
West Indians, they are naturally wholly inexplicable.

National Traits

However, for the Nigerians the main problem is how
to get on with each other, as is illustrated by the well known
pamphlet, "How to Be a Nigerian" by Peter Enaharo.   Among
other Africans they have a reputation for being noisy, abrasive, quarrelsome, arrogant and rude.   Natural stereotypes
are never wholly fair and obviously there are many quiet Nigerians.   Nevertheless, behind the considerable smokescreen
some fires are always burning.   To change the metaphor, it
is as if the atmosphere were charged with pervasive electricity.   On crossing the border, for example from Ghana (in
earlier times at least an orderly friendly place), one notices
the contrast at once.   Even during entry formalities an up-
roar erupts, if not because of you, then over some hapless
fellow traveler.   Such incidents are by turn infuriating, depressing or hilarious, according to one's mental state.   These
things happen even at the most trivial level.

For instance, the buying of a box of matches may
cause altercations of almost cosmic proportions.   Once when
proceeding from Lagos to Ibadan (that word recalls the way
we "proceeded" when going into action in the second world

war), I stopped my taxi to buy a box of matches. Ten kilometers further on, I discovered that the box was empty, whereupon the taxi man, ignoring my protests, insisted on driving back to engage in a tremendous shouting match with the no less indignant vendor. If this can occur because of a little box, what monumental muddles must develop from matters of greater moment? Describing this pervasive atmosphere, journalists have usually concentrated on the terrors of the road. I shall not therefore dwell upon them, except to note that in my view the astronomical casualty rate is a direct consequence of national psychology. (When I remonstrated with a Fulani driver for going too fast, he said it wouldn't matter if he were to be killed because he would turn into a grasshopper. The same man, when we were passing bodies strewn on the road after an accident, said never mind, they are only Yorubas.)

This characteristic effervescence has been described as "social exuberance," a favorite description by themselves, or as "dynamic chaos," and it is not without positive features. For one thing, it means that Nigeria, being also a very large country--one can scarcely call it a nation--is largely ungovernable. Because of this, even the military regimes have been relatively benign; they could not have otherwise survived. (An Idi Amin or a Bokassa would be unthinkable.) The relevant term is, of course, "volatile," which can be used either as approval or otherwise. In a European context, one thinks of the Italians, who also make a great deal of noise. This kind of aggro or machismo may give way at any minute to convulsive laughter. And that is how it is--a switch which more phlegmatic souls are utterly baffled by.

Imagine then, after a month or two in Britain, where the natives are decent, formal and correct, returning to Nigerian Airways at London Airport. Immediately the brouhaha begins: there are no queues and at the departure desk a great battle ensues to secure the passage of persons and vast quantities of bags, boxes, bundles, cartons, trunks, electronic contraptions and miscellaneous other loot which, taken together, would prevent, one would think, any plane from ever leaving the ground. The concept of excess baggage is unknown and during the struggle, bags have to be used as weapons. Only the fittest survive and opulent businessmen have been known to drop down dead. Assuming that one has rested for some time in Britain's quiet lanes, it is an exhilarating experience. One knows one has come home.

Race and Politics

But, of course, it is a curious "home" and one's relationships are mainly those of an artificial campus life which
goes on almost independently of the outside world. Social
relations between expatriates have already been discussed.
Interaction between Nigerians and white expatriates is complex
and variable because of different individual attitudes. Everybody, at some time, may get caught in the many possible
traps. Leaving aside job connections, one can illustrate by
reference to social clubs.

For instance, at the A. B. U. (Ahmadu Bello University)
staff club there have been periods when, at certain times of
day, the regulars became almost entirely segregated and
some people on either side felt no discomfort. There would
be an ostentious "white" table and the two sides were friendly but separate: if an honest apartheid could ever have had
any reality, this might have been it. Similar groupings used
to exist in Ghana, at Legon in the halls when I was there:
this seemed quite natural because Ghanaians often conversed
in one of their own languages, whereas in Nigeria this rarely happens because of linguistic diversity.

However, to return to A. B. U., some individuals, including myself, disliked this semi-separation and it could be
broken down so long as one was careful not to sit in the
wrong place. Interracial interactions were then cordial but
not particularly significant. Late in the day, drunken encounters were often more revealing, but these hardly qualify
for serious consideration since next day they are forgotten.
It was therefore all hail-fellow-well-met and hearty, with an
accompaniment of loud laughter. Superficial? Certainly, as
all pub contacts tend to be. There may also be some special
local factors.

To the external observer, social relations among the
Nigerians themselves rarely seem very intimate. It has often been surmised that the lack of intense involvement with
other individuals, as distinct from a community, springs
from childhood experience in the extended family. The
European-type domestic nuclear unit produces people whose
relations--or entanglements--with each other may reach ob-
sessive and claustrophobic proportions. The oedipus complex is so rampant that monsters arise, and emotional crip-
ples. The African alternative strikes the outsider as so
much more healthy but at the same time relationships seem

to be casual, as if they will surely lapse when somebody goes away. One consequence is a curious combination of considerable subtlety on a practical level and a lack of internal sophistication: the complexities are social, not subjective. There is a built-in nexus with their ethnic brothers that Europeans no longer have. Otherwise friendship, like sexual contacts, rests on a basis of material mutual aid. A friend is someone who can help you: that is what he is for. (In a hierarchical society the disadvantage of such a system is that those who succeed have too many friends and those who do not have none.) I suspect that even in Europe, most people, as they grow older, come to value most those who are there in time of need. Common interests are all-important but they do not last.

It is public life we have been discussing. As for the home, it is a place for the family, with all its ramifications, and there is not much room for anyone else, except sometimes visitors from one's own ethnic group. (As far as expatriates go, the differences, or assumed differences, in feeding habits may limit hospitality.) The communal life of the villages then has given way to the community of the family shut off from the neighbors. Campus life is a bit like suburbia without commuters and at night the scene is a cemetery with lights.

Dogs

Apart from the presence of servants or serfs (also housed nearby), a marked difference that can be discerned is the prevalence of dogs. These beasts, like dogs elsewhere, have a strong territorial sense but within their territory they include their part of the road running by, so that they harass everyone that passes along it. Unfortunate peasants traveling back to their villages are driven off their bicycles. Everybody else has a car but the creatures still jangle the nerves by running and barking alongside. Just as in the olden days in other places the largest and fiercest dogs belonged to the lords of the land, so the numbers and size of the dogs represents status. A professor is expected to display at least one large house with an "upstairs," as it is called, two personal large cars and one official vehicle, and six large barking dogs. When the dark comes, at intervals they howl in unison all night long and the small children whimper in their sleep.

These animals are a curious and infallible symptom or sign of underdevelopment which the economists never mention. (Cocks are perhaps more often thought of in this connection. I recall that in Roseau, the capital of Dominica in the West Indies, the crowing of cocks was so troublesome to tourists that the townsmen, who are still peasants really, were ordered to put them in low coops so that they could not rear up to crow.) To conclude this digression, I should mention in fairness that the people who own the dogs believe that they keep them to frighten away the robbers or their enemies.

Women

Within this strange non-community, the more or less educated wives, when they are not at work, are expected to stay indoors to look after the children (a process which includes the supervision of the servant girls or serfs) and the cooking of food for their men. When he has eaten and watched the T. V. news--a boring restatement of official pronouncements--the husband is likely to go out. There is a gap between domestic and social life and beyond that gap the men can play and what they do, or with whom, is no concern of their wives. (I am of course discussing only the habits of the new élite.)

In such a context sexual relations outside marriage, whether monogamous or polygamous, need not be clandestine, whereas, even now, in permissive Europe, fearful stresses may attend the married condition. It is the difference between a mistress and a concubine, a matter of different property relations. In fact, in African transitional society, many women are a strange amalgamation of the two, and so much more. One eminent professional lady told me cheerfully that her husband prefers her to work because he then has more money for his girl friends. The alien concept of women's lib., often thought of as a colonial imposition, takes on a new form. It is the burdens that must be shared, and little else. It is still a man's world.

Interracial Alliances

As this account is meant to be about myself, I must include two brief encounters which perhaps illustrate the expatriate predicament. When I first went to Ghana, Doris

used to appear almost daily in my office. She was about
eighteen and quite presentable but I couldn't make out what
she was doing there. When I asked the secretary, he just
giggled, so I said at least she might sit down. It was, perhaps, I told myself, some peculiar local custom where girls
were employed to sit in offices to keep them out of trouble
and out of the sun. Subsequently, I realized that the hospitable Ghanaians had encouraged her to present herself in
this manner but she was too shy to be very articulate. (She
was supposed to be, I gathered, a clerk in some other place.)

Foreseeing that I might otherwise get tangled up with
more glamorous, but less innocent, ladies, they were doing
their best to help. As usual I made rather heavy weather
of all this but after an extended and confusing interlude, the
relationship settled down. It was all a bit low key and
apart from representing some small irregular addition to her
meager income, its main value, I suppose, for both of us,
was as an education in race relations. In an intermittent
and desultory way, the liaison, or whatever it was, continued
until it was brought abruptly to an end by the alternative lady,
Marie, described elsewhere. What merits Doris's inclusion
here is the way she took revenge after the break. It could
have been an episode from The Canterbury Tales. She managed to get into my house in Legon very early one morning
and got into my bed when I was asleep. She then proceeded
to arouse my half-sleeping instincts by all known devices.
When I was fully excited and very much awake she laughed
and ran away. It was a simple strategy, but painfully effective.

The other episode was also educational, but mainly in
a sociological sense. Mercy was a student at a teacher-
training college in Zaria. I met her late at night when I
was driving home with an English friend (who was later
killed in an accident) after a party. She was wandering about
in a vague way on a deserted street and neither of us took
any notice until some minutes and five kilometers later,
when the thought struck us simultaneously that we couldn't
leave her there. So we went back and she got in the car in
the same abstracted fashion and came home. She said she
was looking for milk from a kiosk, and I thought she must
be a bit high from drugs. Later, I found that she was always like this, a little fey perhaps. She spoke rapidly in
hushed conspiratorial tones as if she were anticipating some
impending Doom.

She followed up this episode with considerable enthusiasm and was the only lady I encountered in Africa who resolutely refused all financial assistance. On the contrary, she used to bring gifts on her weekly visits; for example, large quantities of potatoes. She was not, however, at all popular with James, the one-eyed steward, because of her voracious appetite, which made inroads into our scanty store of tins.

More worthy of note were her peculiar sexual habits, which I found disquieting. I discovered that she was most interested in any kind of foreplay (especially oral) but that the final act, although permitted, meant nothing at all. It was a kind of frigidity and it took some time for me to appreciate that this was yet another contribution by the missionaries. She had formerly been at a convent boarding school and every night the Roman Catholic Irish reverend father would go on his rounds. Certain intimacies then took place (as the newspapers say) and, apparently, these usually took the form of oral sex on her behalf, while she was not expected to do anything in return. When I said that really this was not a good thing at all, she said, of course it was alright, because he was not allowed to do it with his prick. She also declared that similar incidents took place in other boarding schools. Unfortunately, I forgot to ask her whether the man performed this service to all the girls in the convent. Sociologically, therefore, this information is not statistically of much use, but I offer it for what it is worth to any properly accredited historian of the missions.

The consequence, of course, was that I was put off by this lack of total response and the relationship waned. In earlier days my own missionary instincts might have been aroused in order to assist her liberation. But my missionary days were over.

Wedlock

Some educated Africans marry more or less educated white women. Often these marriages are a consequence of almost accidental propinquity (the presence of African students in Europe and so on). To discuss the original sexual link would take us too far into the treacherous waters of black-white associations and it is more appropriate that novelists should wallow in them. That black gentlemen should prefer blondes need now surprise no one. Many women have accordingly dyed their hair, and in Italy during the war it was

alleged that they even wore curious fair pubic wigs for the
benefit of their black American consorts. When an English
friend went to bed with a Ghanaian he said afterwards, now
you know what it is like to go with a black man, and he was
put out when she replied that she hadn't noticed any differences. As this example indicates, there are so many overtones beyond the realm of simple sex. (Perhaps there always are.)

What is more relevant here is the marital condition.
Alas it is rarely a satisfactory one and the relationship is
even more dire and associated with grief than is the case with
monoracial unions. Often a marriage which seems to work
in Europe, where the man is away from his own environment,
begins to break when the partners return to Africa. It is a
painful process, especially for the woman, and it is a matter
for surprise that some of these arrangements survive. (One
cannot but lament that popular wisdom on such matters is so
often well founded.)

More significant for us are those expatriates who have
fled from mum. Some such as those we have already described become neuter; others marry African ladies from the
bush or the bordello (as it were), and the remainder embrace
their own sex. Mum, therefore, is responsible for a great
deal; as somebody said, "The hand that rocks the cradle
wrecks the world. " (Perhaps I should add, as is later made
plain, that I do not feel that I belong among her victims, although the possibilities were there.) However, we need not
repine since many of these relationships--I mean the married hetero ones--survive at least temporarily and somehow
these incongruous couples dredge some grim satisfaction out
of their lives--a positive achievement which must be respected.

When they marry the local uneducated girls it is
usually because their demands and expections seem to be
less than those of the castrating white females they have
known or fled from. That is the beginning, but more than
this is naturally required to sustain the union and in many
cases a firmer foundation emerges; somehow common interests grow, the most binding being the brown children. In
other cases the Pygmalion syndrome operates (just as it often does with the adoption of African children). The man
then attempts, usually in vain, to "educate" the lady and mold
her to his own dubious image. She is instructed in ethnocentric arts, such as the cooking of bacon and eggs, or sur-

realist painting or the history of the first World War.   Mostly she is bored but not rebellious.   Nevertheless there are the total disasters when the internalized Mum is wholly triumphant and the couple spend most of their time fighting and the neighbors have to be called in.   (During these sessions the furniture is destroyed, windows are broken and standing structures smashed--but it is after all not personal, but university property.)   The final separation has to come, but it takes a long time.

Gay Opportunities

As for homosexual activities, about myself there is nothing to report.   I am obliged therefore to rely on the experience of others and they are included because they have been my friends: to that extent there has been a vicarious involvement.   Mostly they are attracted to Africa for one reason, namely that the boys are attractive and seem to be perhaps more available than elsewhere.   How well they succeed will naturally depend on their particular requirements and personalities.   The gay revolution has not yet reached Africa and even now there are many respectable white academics who quietly go about their official business and preserve their tendencies in the private closet.   This is a possible way of life but we cannot discuss it because they don't.   Among the colonialists there were many such--indeed I discovered in Ghana that in certain circles, for instance among those who served in bars or petrol stations or as stewards, all Englishmen were considered homosexual, whether they had wives or not.   Such misconceptions must have arisen out of their experience, which was something to be accepted as part of the structure of the world.

In any event the boys do not consciously think about such basic physical matters; hence it is possible to claim, as many Africans do, that homosexuality does not exist in their society.   It is only the concept that is absent, not the reality: practice without theory, a phenomenon puzzling to the Western mind.   (In local languages, I have been told, there are no words to describe such matters.)

Because of these epistemological problems, several of our compatriots have found themselves out of their depth. There are, of course, gay bars, or the equivalent, in the larger cities, as there are anywhere in the world, but outside these oases the unhappy wanderers may encounter puz-

zling predicaments. There are always desirable young men
around who apparently respond to their advances and are happy to take advantage of their hospitality; they are also flat-
tered by the unexpected attention paid to them by these weird
white wealthy creatures. All this is most encouraging but
after the initial acceptance of invitations, social discrepancies
develop. (Alas, there are no underground etiquette primers
as there are in San Francisco.) It rapidly becomes clear
that the young men don't know what they are expected to do,
and their benefactors are not always capable or tough enough
to show them.

At this point somebody will remonstrate that such
problems are not confined to Africa, especially for those
who can only relate to young men from the working class,
or worse, who go out in search of "rough trade." Are we
not all familiar with the sagas of Christopher Isherwood,
Tom Driberg, Ackerley, E. M. Forster and Terence Ratti-
gan, to mention only the most prominent and articulate?
Certainly this is so, but the guardsmen of Knightsbridge, for
example, know very well what they are doing, even if it is
only for money. But in illiterate communities there are no
printed words to help, nor even classical pictures. The
misunderstandings, therefore, are more frequent, and sometimes disastrous.

However, in most places, there are some suitable
partners who do not have these hangups and are both willing
and aware of their responsibilities; usually they have been
initiated by former foreign friends. When these consumma-
tions are arrived at, one might venture to predict happiness
ever after, but human joys are never so unconfined. Being
the products of an exotic erotic culture, our colleagues are
driven beyond these sensible arrangements. Not content with
these simple satisfactions, they long for the boys to love
them and great waves of pent-up emotion flood over the scene.
When this happens, the indigenous participant naturally fails
to respond--how can he be expected to cope with the well-
known madness of the white man? As for the latter, he may
keep on trying, or settle for so much less, or take to drink
or the consolations of religion. But whatever the way, Mother has won again.

Meanwhile, there are the respected establishment figures who organize their lives by sublimation and good works:
priests, missionaries, welfare workers, United Nations experts, teachers and doctors--all make their contribution as

they always and everywhere do. On an individual, personal level they may pay for the education of African boys or take them into their households. (Adoption is rarely possible since among Africans it is not a permanent condition.) It is a beneficial process provided that it can be sustained and followed through to university level. When it is not, these unfortunate children, already alienated from their own people, then fail to find a new identity or a job: they become cultural freaks, monuments to faltering and confused idealisms. The line between good works and self-indulgence is not easily drawn.

A Silent Minority

Now that catalog of racial interaction is over, it occurs to me that in concentrating on somewhat "way out" relationships I may have neglected what sociologists call the norm (a ridiculous word). Certainly their silent lives have been passed over because their interactions, after all, are mainly with each other and we are not familiar with them. Furthermore, they do not represent a proper norm since it is a normless community. They would have belonged to one back home and that is a theme more suited to the analysts of suburbia. (They endeavor to keep up standards and arrange musical soirées and recorder sessions, while Rotarians have their picnics, and paper chases are organized for those who ride horses.) Their presence among us suggests that something may have gone slightly wrong with their lives, but what skeletons are or were in their cupboards will have to remain there since they have not been exposed. One can suitably leave the last word with Lytton Strachey (as reported by his biographer):

> We are all cupboards, with obvious outsides which may be either beautiful or ugly, simple or elaborate, interesting or unamusing--but with insides mysteriously the same, the abodes of darkness, terror and skeletons.

Darkness and terror are universal but skeletons were once individuals in a particular environment. It is simply these that I have been discussing.

4. THE OTHER EIGHTY PER CENT

Beyond our isolated academic communities the "masses" subsist. Most universities spawn a vast number of campus followers and employees and traders who live mostly around the boundaries. They are a link between us and the remoter world elsewhere. Our campus life could be described as "unreal"--not so much an ivory tower as a multicolored bubble. What kind of reality can the world outside be said to have? We cannot know since it is a question we would have to ask them and no one would be so foolish. All one can record is personal interactions with the nearby intermediaries.

We encounter non-academic Nigerians in clubs and bars and shops and banks, or in queues at the post office and petrol stations, or in the market, or possibly the Church. Even they can be avoided, since both expatriates and Nigerians in more exalted positions do without these time-wasting transactions and send their minions to make the arrangements, a process which is bad for the soul but soothes the nerves. Some people never leave the campus at all. Naturally there are academics who have to do research or advisory work in the bush (agriculture, sociology, medicine) and may experience temporarily the traditional or "real" Africa that is still somehow there. (Against all the odds it was always there, even before the Europeans "discovered" it.) Such work is more rewarding than teaching out of textbooks but the peasants remain remote and immune from outside understanding, part of an inaccessible past. None of these contacts therefore are total enough to be truly personal and the time has gone when anthropologists would imagine they had been admitted to the tribe. Western anthropology was part of the colonial enterprise. Any outsider rash enough to investigate village life may be fed with exotic and lurid lies, and the tables are turned when the villagers ask earthy questions. "No wonder you have no power when you were never circumcised. " (Exit anthropologist amid laughter, uncircumcised tail between his legs.)

The only place where interaction is prolonged and in a peculiar sense intimate is in the house, where the Africans work as stewards and baby nurses and house boys and gardeners. (The new élite still use the colonial word "boy" without embarrassment.) It is a "real" contact but very odd, much less straightforward then in the colonial past. The colonialists (some of whom survive) felt no inhibitions about incorporating their servants into their way of life: they were organized and trained and disciplined and looked after in a paternalist way, just as they do in South Africa and did in the former Rhodesia. Each night at sundown, in an exchange of gossip over the drinks, their antics are described with amused solicitude: "Our James is a gem, " or "You have to save their money for them or they will spend it, " or "Of course they all have worms"--always They. (When you find yourself using that tell-tale word, it is time to go.)

In short, the native minds were thoroughly colonized-- no "black is beautiful" nonsense for them. To suggest that they became alienated from or despised their own culture is too facile. What they came to accept was a kind of apartheid, with the assumption that the white man's way of life is not only different but superior. For example, one-eyed William, a hangover from colonial times, refused point blank to cook indigenous food and if asked to do so, would chatter with rage in pidgin English. Waving a piece of unbleached tripe which we had bought, he would shout, "Me no cook African food. " His doctrine was that European stomachs are different. Eventually, because of these attitudes, he had to go, having, with our assistance, built a house, acquired an extra wife and added three more children, bringing the total to eleven, half of whom in former times would have died.

Faced with all this, what is the modern liberal-minded foreigner with egalitarian attitudes to do? My parents were domestic servants, so for me there was an extra dimension. I didn't want to go through all that again, this time from the other side of the bread line. That was my feeling when I went to Trinidad, but I soon understood that trying to do without servants (like not having a car) is next to impossible. Those who persist in these ethnocentric attitudes become unpopular, because they deprive people of much-needed jobs. Since official aid is not available one becomes a substitute for a modern welfare state, and at times of crisis (births, betrothal, marriage, burial, sickness, housing, transporting and the provision of status symbols like clothes, watches and radios) assistance has to be provided. Yet we are not really equipped for these peculiar relationships and the retainer becomes bewildered by our inexplicable ambiguities. Instead of being told what to do, he is asked what he would like to do, a burden he does not want.

Apart from all this, the employees retain their function as intermediaries between their masters and the world

outside. Through them the employer may arrive at some
dim understanding of how the other eighty per cent have to
live. Among the folk even now there are two pervasive features from which the privileged are partially exempt. These
are: first, the prevalence of "corruption, " and second, the
persistence of traditional magic. Both surround them like
the air they breathe. The bribery system is not a social
aberration or malfunction as it is in some parts of the developed world, but a way of life. It is indispensable for
survival, a method for preserving and reinforcing the existing social structure; it is a central, not a peripheral, cultural reality. Contrary to what so many pundits and preach-
ers profess to believe, it cannot profitably be discussed in
moral terms. (All "problems" have a moral component but
the solution is beyond personal morality.) So long as the environment remains underdeveloped, there can be no solution,
since "corruption" is a necessary economic characteristic
of the societies we have lived in. This is the argument I
have always used to justify my willing participation in the
system. When in "trouble" (a condition which recurs), I
have always happily offered various amounts to anyone in
sight. They have accepted them not just because they are
mercenary, as everyone has to be, but because they are
pleased that I am one of them. When policemen in Ghana
hailed me as their friend, that is what they meant: it was
a privilege I was grateful for.

However, I knew well enough, even then, that it was
my privileged status which gave me protection. I could afford to offer the something required to make their lives sup-
portable. But for the poor who cannot pay out these large
amounts, there are no friends and they can obtain next to
nothing, sometimes neither medical attention nor a job nor a
house, nor a driving license nor a passport nor a place in
school for their children. The system is rendered tolerable
by the other side of the same coin, the "godfather" principle,
which is mostly a reflection of the extended family and of
ethnic affinities. African reactionary traditionalists tend to
claim that there is no need for state intervention for welfare
purposes because the poor are looked after by their richer
relatives and "brothers. " In addition, beggardom as an institution is at least as old as the other oldest profession, and
in Muslim areas is reinforced and preserved by the religious
duty to give alms, one of the seven pillars of Islam.

As for the almost universal survival of magic (in West
African coastal regions commonly called "juju"), there is a

belief prevalent among outsiders that its influence can operate only if you "believe" in its power.   This is a gross
over-simplification: most educated or half-educated people
no longer adhere to the kind of animist faith which their
forebears held.   However, this does not amount to a positive
disbelief.   For example, they will accept without difficulty
that scientific reasons can be found for the causation of disease, death or disaster, but such reasons are not regarded
as adequate because they do not explain why it should happen
to one person and not another.   Some other external forces
must be at work: it is advisable therefore to consult a magic
man even if only as a kind of insurance policy.   In the West,
many people go to church for the same reason and offer up
prayers just in case Somebody is there.

It is better not to pursue these arguments but to quote
some of our own experiences.   Our baby nurse, Justina, had
an unpleasant, aggressive husband who believed in the rights
of men.   She was trying to escape from him and we seemed
to provide for that possibility.   As she had an assured income and somewhere to live we thought that with our help
she would be capable of resisting his demands that she should
return to share the miseries of his other less desirable wife
and children.   Our missionary instincts on behalf of oppressed women were aroused and a war ensued which lasted
for several years.   We were prepared for a long siege but
ultimately it was an unequal struggle because although we had
money and could continue to pay both the juju man and the
police more than their usual amounts, this process could
not continue forever.   Moreover the existing social mores
did not provide for female emancipation.   There were, nevertheless, temporary triumphs, as when our counter-juju
caused Clements to fall off the kitchen table when fixing a
light bulb or when Justina was rescued after being kidnapped
by the police and locked up.   Or when one weekend he appeared in the guise of a large sinister black cat, Justina and
the neighbors beat the animal to death.   If this act had any
deleterious effect on Clements it was not apparent.   Naturally
his juju frightened her more than it did us (good Christian
though she was).   The arcane objects which we found around
the house, like lizards' heads tied up with cotton and match-
sticks, were ceremonially burned.   The police, meanwhile,
were on to a good thing, but like all good things it had to
come to an end and we had to admit defeat.   She was taken
away by a triumphant Clements, albeit the triumph was short-
lived and partial as she subsequently got away by finding another man to protect her.   This was probably always the only
available solution.

Ghana can provide an example of another legal confrontation. At the airport site outside Accra our immediate
neighbor was the ambassador from Upper Volta. Relations
were not good, as it had been alleged that he had eaten our
favorite cat. Also our steward (a Nigerian called Peter) had
offended his domestic staff. Their revenge was well-organized
and thorough: they trussed up a live turkey and placed it outside the door where he was sleeping. Then, in the small
hours of the night, a whistle was blown as a pre-arranged
signal and the suborned police rushed in amid loud commotion and took him--wrapped in his night cloth--away. We
bailed him out and the subsequent court case went on for a
considerable while. The proceedings were conducted in Ga,
but from time to time the counsel for Peter (accused of
turkey theft) would point at me and say in English, "That
white man there," which made us feel relevant and necessary. This time justice was done: Peter was vindicated and
the police were solemnly warned not to do it again.

Neither of these two stories illustrates any particular
cosmic theme but they are quoted to show the kind of involvement that can happen to innocents abroad. The saga of our
Tuareg connections in Nigeria likewise has no general significance except in so far as it may reveal our own mixed-
up attitudes. It was after the Sahelian drought of 1976 and
even before large numbers of Tuaregs fled from the Sahara,
mostly from the new francophone country called Niger--a
model neo-colonial state. As their cattle and camels had
died they came into Nigeria, where the people were at least
not starving. At the university the men came to rest indefinitely and are employed as night watchmen (locally called
watch-night men). They are too dignified to undertake man-
ual labor and are not familiar with the work ethic. Their
way of life is remote from that of the Nigerians, who regard
them with distaste not unmixed with superstitious awe--just
as Europeans are alarmed by the gypsies. Of Semitic or
Berber origin and light skinned, they were the blue-veiled
pirates of the desert who for centuries levied tribute from
or looted the trans-Saharan caravans. Now all that has gone
and their present pastoral peaceful way of life is probably
also doomed by "modernization." It persists only in the
imaginations of the more eccentric historians and popular
fiction writers--a position they share with their former an-
tagonists, the French foreign legion. (Biggles came down at
least twice in the Sahara.)

Their culture includes their own language (Tamashegh)

and a body of literature in their own script (Tifinagh). Like the photogenic Masai of East Africa and other nomadic peoples, they are a problem for their rulers, who would prefer them not to exist. With their theatrical robes, androgynous appearance and long, straight, plaited hair, the veiled men have the kind of appeal which desert dwellers always possess for certain types of European. A favored few provide sexual consolation for white ladies neglected by their husbands or white gentlemen rejected by the world. Beyond the campus, eccentric anthropologists wander about the Sahara and may well be more numerous than the remnants of the doomed tribes they are supposed to be studying. Somebody should investigate them. One formidable university lady went among them measuring their skulls in order to gather evidence about their historical origins. One is reminded of the explorer "Gypsy" Burton, who would measure the penis size of sleeping Arabs in order to buttress his dubious "scientific" theories. (One of these was that although the inert Arab penis was larger than its European equivalent, it could not claim the same superiority when erect. His evidence for this conclusion was not produced; indeed, like many Victorians, he never felt the need to explain himself.)

But, to return to our exiled Tuaregs, we discovered that having employed one, originally as a night watchman, we became unwilling hosts for many more, just as certain biological organisms produce their own parasites. Inevitably this symbiosis was disturbing but it was difficult for us with our bleeding hearts to object, because they had otherwise no visible means of support. They lay about looking decorative in communal heaps and never stole anything except perfume or any unguent or emollient which could be rubbed over themselves. With quantities of expensive cooking oil, they cooked a staple diet of beans on our electric ring and the place became a kind of bean kitchen. Mostly, at least in the dry season, they stayed outside (during the rains many returned home) except when watching T. V. We speculated in vain about their reactions to feature films--for example, Ben Hur --which for them might well have been the news. How could they know whether the creatures of Sesame Street were real or not, or how they got into the box anyway? How should good Muslims react to Miss Piggy? Because of the language barrier we could not ask them.

In the struggle for survival they also resort to magic men. Muslims who require charms or potions are given verses from the Koran which have various uses. His Nigerian

friends alleged that Mohammedu was putting Koranic ink
washed from his charms into our beans, a device designed
to gain our assistance for furthering his plots and projects.
When individuals are smitten by love or passion, their irra-
tional behavior is universally attributed to love potions in the
soup. The weird brews that from time to time we must
have consumed had no noticeable consequence and my own
obsessions at least happened elsewhere, apparently without
these occult aids. But who can blame them for finding tan-
gible reasons for the otherwise inexplicable vagaries of the
human heart?

Meanwhile Mohammedu preserved his dignity as night
watchman: he had in fact never watched but slept. Later
he became a kind of steward, a sort of gardener, a semi-
chauffeur and a quasi-groom for our bad-tempered horse.
In all these capacities he followed no one's instructions but
his own and he eventually had to be accommodated within the
house. Outside, reclining brothers embellished the landscape
like flamboyant flowers. When all this had been done it
could not be undone: we had broken the rules about the
proper place of servants and therefore had to suffer the con-
sequence--a certain lack of privacy. We usually retreated
to our air-conditioned room, where they could be neither
seen nor heard. When things went too far, as they were
bound to, and they were taking various liberties and excessive quantities of tea or milk, or sitting silently in the living room as if it were the Sahara--then, and only then,
overcome by exasperation, we would drive them out. The
process--an insidious escalation would then start again--was
like an undulating graph reflecting the ambivalence of our responses. This was our domestic set-up, a far cry from the
upstairs-downstairs of my childhood, and equally far from
the English concept of home as a castle.

These highly selective instances are meant to illustrate certain relationships within a highly competitive society.
In such a world even your best friends are enemies as well:
they have to be regarded as economic objects. Yet, as
everywhere else, simple human kindness breaks through and
the usual calculus of rewards and penalties is forgotten.
This happened to me several times as an aftermath of driving episodes. In Ghana the police on one occasion went to
extreme lengths to save me from myself--all without any
kind of incentive. It was one of those days, known to all
those who are born under certain constellations, when things
were likely to happen. I had been drinking at the Ambassador

Hotel outside Accra and had there encountered a correspond-
ent from the British newspaper, The Daily Telegraph, who
was busy preparing a hostile report on Nkrumah's Ghana.
Because of this we had a violent argument which was rudely
terminated by a large piece of blue plaster which dislodged
itself from a pillar and crashed onto the table, narrowly
missing our distinguished reporter. Still fuming with choleric indignation, I drove off in my Beetle and went over a wall
in front of the police station.

When I was making a statement the policeman said,
"Write down that a big black dog ran across the road in
front of the car." At this my rage returned and I insisted
that I would not invent a dog, and they could see I was drunk
and why didn't I put that down? After that I returned home
and onto our highly decorative grass mat wept maudlin tears
arising from some current grief. Later there was an official encounter with a senior police officer who shouted that
people like me abused the hospitality of the country and disgraced the white part of the human race and so on. Then he
sent the sergeant who was there out of the room and switched
to a quiet manner and a smile and said, I hope it won't happen again, especially in front of the police station. So we
shook hands.

On another occasion in the same black Beetle I woke
up in the early morning and found that I had somehow driven
it far off the road into the bush, miraculously not hitting
any major trees. Peering through the half light I then saw
a number of young men emerge from the undergrowth; they
lifted up the car with me in it, as if I were a baby in a
pram, and carried it back to the road facing in the right
direction. They said nothing and refused all remuneration,
as if this procedure were a part of their daily routine and
displaced expatriates were regularly to be found at dawn
scattered about the bush in battered cars.

Episodes like this naturally go a long way to wipe out
less fortunate memories. It is perhaps because of this that
so many foreigners who leave West Africa eventually return
--as I did myself after six years.

5. IDEOLOGICAL DILEMMAS: THE CALL OF THE WILD

In "My Colleges" I described my first official contacts

with students from the Third World. No doubt an analyst
would trace the origins of that development back to my earli-
est infancy when hideous upper-class white ladies peered into
my pram in Hyde Park. Could anything be more traumatic?
Or, in order to explain an interest in the exotic, one could
use an old-fashioned esthetic interpretation. For instance,
when we return to Britain so many of the natives there seem
to be malformed in the way that some potatoes are; or is it
only their spiritual condition, a consequence of mounting
mortgages or constant commuting or too much television?
Like all rational explanations, these won't do, and the reasons must be sought in psychological variations.

We can be classified by our attitudes to foreigners:
a healthy reaction is supposed to be that we can't abide them
--any of them. As a Kingsley Amis anti-hero said, doubtless reflecting the insularity of his creator, "I like it here"
--meaning Britain--and he went on to insist that Abroad was
a tiresome place. This view was characteristic of the fifties
when a group of writers, notably Philip Larkin, reacted
against exoticism of any kind. His poem, "Poetry of Departures" is a subtle example of that reaction and he always
vowed never to visit Abroad except under duress. This was,
of course, a literary movement, but there were other more
sinister manifestations. The "silent majority" (which later
became far from silent) was originally not bothered by such
matters since nobody minded if it stayed at home. However,
in recent years severe problems have arisen because foreigners have not remained Abroad where they belong but
have invaded other countries either as tourists or guest
workers, or worst of all, as immigrants. When and where
this happens, the majority strategy is to pretend they are not
there: this is the infallible indicator of passive racism.
(The extreme lunacies of the National Front are too obvious
to be discussed here.)

But I was naturally never a member of this establishment and we have, on the contrary, to consider the others
who don't like home, the professional lovers of the unknown
who either reject or are rejected by their tribe (whose mores
are by definition exclusive). Usually such persons are re-
sponding to a sexual configuration which is somehow para-
normal. Perhaps because of the public school system the
English representatives have been relatively numerous.
These foreigner lovers--xenophiles?--can be easily classified. First, there are those with Nordic inclinations, sometimes brought on by studying Beowulf at an impressionable

age. In our time these were exemplified by W. H. Auden
and Christopher Isherwood, whose lovers were all Germanic.
The Nordic choice naturally has its own special disaster
areas: consider the awful influences of German nineteenth-
century Idealism on Coleridge or Carlyle. The political pit-
falls are plain enough but even on an emotional level those
who succumb to these savage gods develop obsessions about
Valhalla and Matthew Arnold's "vasty halls of Death." I was
not wholly immune from the teutonic syndrome and spent
several years struggling with the German language; I even
began to appreciate their poets in a debased kind of way.

But it was not a lasting condition, perhaps for lack
of opportunity. For the same reason I never became caught
up, as I might otherwise have done, with the Mediterranean
mania which has been the other characteristic British tendency. No doubt it is less endemic than it was: the Italian
graveyards may be littered with expatriate bones but the
grand tour is no longer mandatory for English milords, who
now entertain in their draughty stately homes the tourists in
reverse. Even the monster Norman Douglas has been laid
to rest and others, like Lawrence Durrell or E. M. Forster,
moved on to Alexandria, there to follow Cavafy's example
within a more decadent Hellenic ambiance. Were I permitted
to live another life, not as a grasshopper, but in some human form, I might wish to join the Mediterranean club.

L'existence Tropicale

Instead one was almost caught up in the other version
of the malady which is one of the tropical diseases now almost eliminated. A learned French doctor has described the
symptoms very well: he refers to the victims as "psycho-
pathes volontaires" and notes how

> L'existence tropicale les attire comme un aimant;
> elle satisfait toutes leurs tendances psychiques ou
> passionelles: nouveauté, mystère, authorité, liber-
> té, actions d'éclat randonnées dans l'espace, as-
> pirations sexuelles vers des rites inconnu, rêv-
> eries des ivresses de l'opium ou du haschich....
> Elle réalise tous les mirages de leur esprit.

I must have been influenced by that nineteenth-century
motif, especially in its literary form, and perhaps it was
uppermost in the first stages of my exile, especially in the

West Indies. Yet in contemporary urban Africa the disease
is bound to wane. A modern African city is too squalid to
be exotic in this way. The aroma of piss and groundnut oil
replaces that of the olive, and the scavenging vultures hop
around like bedraggled poultry. Only a vision bordering on
the perverse can romanticize this scene.

No, any urges in this direction ultimately became
secondary. Even so there were times when these arcadian
dreams were temporarily real, usually in isolated places in
the hills or on the coast of Trinidad; also less frequently in
remote traditional villages in Ghana and finally, in Nigeria,
scarcely at all. The alternative attitudes were more political
and I tried to participate in nationalist movements. As self-
appointed decolonizing agent and champion of the black oppressed I went to Trinidad. The first shock came when I
was made to realize that the Trinidadians did not need and
were not interested in my assistance. Indeed, they were
positively hostile to such endeavors; evidently my attitudes
were a little too simple. If we could not help in their struggles, what were we supposed to do? Their answer, of course,
was that we should get on with the job we had been appointed
to do.

For a time this satisfied me and after reaching Ghana
I was content to make my professional contribution; indeed I
was wholly preoccupied with these exacting labors. Furthermore, my family responsibilities were absorbing enough and
at different times my remaining propensities as a "psycho-
pathe volontaire" were expressed in the subterranean activities
I described in an earlier section of this chapter. Finally,
for some long time I was embroiled in one of those total
emotional involvements which blotted out the world. That
represented another dominant motif in my life and had nothing to do with Africa as such: we simply happened to be
there.

It is therefore scarcely surprising that my political
consciousness remained at a low level. I must have been
an intellectual zombie at that time and have no recollection
that I read anything significant beyond my professional chores.
(This can't be true.) Certainly my relations with Ghanaian
colleagues were excellent: "student contact" was rewarding
because we had the challenge of getting them all through the
British examinations, and the policemen were sympathetic,
sometimes even without bribes. What else could one ask
for? On one level, nothing at all, but I had not pursued the

matter in any depth. I was probably still at the stage when I congratulated myself about my African friends without considering certain ineradicable cultural differences. I was preserving the liberal illusion that we were really all alike, an attitude which falsifies relationships since they know otherwise. I was merely reacting against racist attitudes which could still be detected among some other expatriates. Beyond that my explorations were superficial. (How easy it is to disapprove of one's self in retrospect!)

Domestic Interlude

When, after six years in Ghana, I returned to Britain, I began to suspect a certain amount of intellectual disgrace. I had somehow been wallowing like some African buffalo in the warm mud. Were these not the symptoms which some expatriates develop when they have been in Africa too long? The Colonialists used to ostracize or, if possible, transfer any of their officers who "went bush" and consorted too exclusively with the natives. (Standards must be maintained.) Without fully appreciating the dangers, perhaps I had become the modern equivalent. However, I had escaped and there the matter might have rested. In my new environment I could hardly involve myself in Welsh nationalism, sympathetic to their aspirations though I was. For them the struggle was between the English Welsh and the Welsh Welsh, and I was neither. However, as a result of the work required for the preparation of two books, some degree of mental rigor returned. I began to be re-radicalized, or re-politicized, perhaps an anomalous condition for one who might otherwise have passed into the tranquilities of middle age. In this state of mind I returned to Africa.

Political Speculations

Nigeria was the best possible place for me to continue my political education. My arrival (1972) coincided with the oil boom--there was of course no connection--and this meant that certain characteristics endemic in the new African states were already exhibiting themselves in an extreme form. External commentators from all political quarters had been deploring the attitudes of the new élite who succeeded the colonialists. On the right it was lamented that they were not proper capitalists because they were greedy and irresponsible and had no interest in saving or long-term investment. As Achebe observed (A Man of the People):

Then a handful of us--the smart and the lucky and
hardly ever the best--had scrambled for the one
shelter our former rulers left and had taken it
over and barricaded themselves in.

But these outside business observers had no one else to deal
with and, against all the evidence, still believed that international capitalism might have a human face. On the left it
was noted that the new entrepreneurs were linked to their
big brothers overseas: this was the reality of neo-colonialism.
Also the failures of conventional economic analysis and international "aid" were only too evident. At the same time, the
left could not easily explain why "class formation" was so
fluid, nor account for the absence of indigenous radicalism.

Among the Nigerians themselves, attention had been
concentrated on wickedness and corruption, so much so that
a new circulation of élites had come into being according to
whose turn it was to be probed. The system was bound to
produce "bad eggs, " as they called them, and when these
were thrown out, others would take their place. Meanwhile,
those who were discarded could go into dishonorable retire-
ment, a position not without prestige. While this went on,
the peasantry existed as they have always done, except for
the addition of some more middlemen and moneylenders, together with bicycles, transistor radios and a few tin roofs.
True, the great highways went through their villages bearing
the Big Men on their important Affairs, but the villagers
were left almost as isolated as before. Many of the younger
ones drifted to the exploding cities. (Other people migrate,
but peasants "drift" like wind-blown dust.) There, against
all the odds, they struggle and hope with extraordinary ten-
acity. It was left for a few indigenous radicals--voices cry-
ing in the wilderness--to ask themselves how the dominance
of this new pseudo-bourgeoisie could be broken. Why is it
that the people are more interested in ethnic personalities
than in ideologies which they do not have?

These were the questions which I had not sufficiently
considered when in Ghana. The troubled history of that attractive country suggests that the Ghanaians themselves had
never properly analyzed these circumstances. Aborted socialism (Nkrumah) was followed, after a military interlude,
by phoney liberalism (Busia), and then the military returned
and simply froze the situation as it was. Finally there was
the extraordinary phenomenon of Flight Lieutenant Jerry
Rawlings, surely one of the most bizarre and appealing heads

of state ever known. His level of political awareness was such that he was intent on making a "revolution" without ideology or revolutionaries. He then concentrated entirely on cleaning up corruption as if it were a <u>cause</u> rather than a symptom of the national predicament.

Sitting in my air-conditioned room in Zaria, with the dust whirling outside, I brooded on these insoluble problems and worked on my book. A persistent difficulty was that I was not in a position to produce any evidence for a thorough analysis. If I had been able to speak Hausa it would have helped. People who live in countries where investigative journalism has reached a high level cannot imagine what is is like to live in an atmosphere where all the channels of "communication" are mystification agencies. For most people most of the time it is impossible to know what is really happening. "News" does not have to be suppressed; it doesn't exist in the first place.

At the time I was writing this, a significant development in Nigeria was the creation of large-scale agricultural enterprises financed by outside agencies, usually the World Bank. Most of these ventures were irrigation schemes and had been attended by social dislocation, with the peasants ejected from their farms. Serious riots and revolts had occurred, especially in Sokoto State. But these events were neither reported nor investigated, nor interpreted. True, Committees of Enquiry were set up but such bodies tend to be composed of people whose <u>perceptions</u> prevent them discovering anything but the official view: that is the heart of the matter. (The universities are filled with such people.) Meanwhile, the authorities mouth phrases like "Green Revolution, " apparently totally unaware of the social implications and of the injustices which that process has produced in India and elsewhere. (Agricultural technical improvements without a social transformation inexorably favor the richer farmers or "kulaks, " and the majority rarely benefit or may even be expropriated.)

Trying to make sense of all this, I was driven inexorably back to a neo-Marxist position. The central problem then becomes one of <u>political consciousness</u>. European liberals have always objected to the notion that somehow the level of political awareness must be raised. If they had lived in Africa long enough, such objections would have to be abandoned. The alternatives are not stagnation, nor the preservation of "tradition, " but a gross exploitation disguised as development. Some of these preoccupations got into my book. When it was published, critics noted, quite rightly, that although it attempted to dispel so many mystifications, it was noticeably short on solutions. I consoled myself by reflecting that I was in good company, and who could pretend that anyone had yet provided satisfactory strategies? All I had done was to stress potential developments. The last chapter ends: "In most cases the evidence points to the conclusion that these potentialties will be fully realized only when the revolution comes." Could anything be more chiliastic than that?

6. THE STRUGGLE FOR EDUCATION

A Literary Challenge

The foregoing impressions of life in an African university were written while I was there four or five years ago, and on reading through it now I can see that it is not exactly a balanced description of what it is like to work in such an environment. What interested me, I suppose, was the psychological condition of the people who worked there, and the way that they responded to a hermetic way of life. At first sight the social relations I discussed might seem to be an ideal hunting ground for a novelist, yet he or she would have peculiar difficulties, notably a problem of credibility. That scene is remote from the experience of suburban man, and perhaps more appropriate for the anthropologist. (It is notoriously difficult to turn anthropology into literature of the other kind.)

There have been novels about university life in West Africa but none of them is well known. (The East African experience, especially in Kenya and the former Rhodesia, where the colonialists settled, is another world.) There have been successful novels about expatriate life generally--for example William Boyd's recent A Good Man in Africa--but such works, however amusing they may be, inevitably irritate those who live there, whether they are Africans or not. Extreme situations provoke satire, which is not realistic and is not intended to be. (Nobody would go to Evelyn Waugh's Black Mischief for accurate information about Abyssinia as it then was.)

The limiting factor is that such works are not really

about Africa but simply variations on the theme of the innocent abroad. Since the novelist's readers are mostly not
African and are not familiar with conditions there, he can
best appeal to them by presenting farcical situations which
develop from the ignorance or inexperience of expatriate
characters. For this method to be successful, such people
have to be lovable but impossibly stupid, as is the case with
William Boyd's hero, Morgan Leafy ("Splendid rollicking
stuff," said the Spectator). Yet this same theme of innocence could also be treated at a deeper level altogether.
One would have to create characters whose lives are utterly
transformed or destroyed by the inexorable passage of events.
That predicament is not farcical but tragic. We are all
trapped by Fate or by ourselves and the expatriate's traps
have an extra dimension since they are peculiar to his condition. It is that condition, which in Africa has not been
fully explored, and that literary challenge, which has not
been met. If we cannot meet it our criticisms of other's
attempts carry that much less weight. It would be interesting to pursue a significant parallel with Cervantes' Don
Quixote, who could defy and transcend his environment--a
paradigm for the world--because his creator made him not
stupid but "mad." It was only because of this that his innocence prevailed. But alas, this is not our theme and we
must return to a world where innocence gets lost.

The Background

What I wrote also excluded the educational and administrative background. It was, after all, not a psychiatric
retreat but the largest university in black Africa and it had
been created for important historical purposes. Northern
Nigeria, a predominantly Muslim region, had been economically and educationally underdeveloped as compared with the
rest of the country. The literacy rate had been and continued to be very low. Insofar as the Emirs of the past had
been concerned with literacy at all, it was with the traditional Koranic type, whose intentions were not educational in the
Western sense but devotional in the interests of a revealed
religion. For these same religious reasons they had resisted the spread of "modern" education since it was considered (not without good cause) that it would undermine the
Faith as they interpreted it. In the rest of Nigeria, Christian missionaries had been instrumental in developing their
own kind of education, but they were excluded from the North
except where the rulers had specifically asked for them.

This was one of the characteristics of indirect rule invented by Lord Lugard. The indigenous Emirs were allowed to preserve their traditions and their own hegemony provided they cooperated with the colonial power, an excellent arrangement which suited both parties well. The British certainly preferred what they regarded as a dignified and ceremonious culture to the noisy nationalists of the South. (The Yorubas were seen as abrasive and aggressive, while the Ibos were known to be far too clever for their own good.) The Colonial Service contained a high proportion of younger sons who welcomed the pastoral life of the tranquil North. The native code of honor apparently corresponded with the ethos of the public schools, where character training had always been more important than mere learning. Since their outlook did not include the concept of exploitation they could not be expected to object to the injustices of a semi-feudal social system. The message of the Koran is essentially egalitarian, at least as far as men are concerned, but equality was not noticeable in that rigidly hierarchical society. (The original Christian doctrine has, of course, been perverted in the same manner.) Religion, therefore, was and is used by unscrupulous politicians for their own ends, and in still "primitive" communities the mixture which results is explosive.

At the grass roots level in the villages the introduction of schooling had not been particularly welcome and it was against this background that the university was set up to serve a vast area which now consists of the Northern States. (Some of these states--for example Kano--are larger in terms of population and size than some European countries.) The responsibility of the university was to help the North "catch up" with the rest of the country, and it was a national institution only in that sense. (The "catching up" process is doomed to partial failure because the educational "gap," like all sociological gaps, tends to remain: those who are in front do not wait to be caught up with, but tend to push on ahead.)

It followed that in admitting students we had to give priority not simply to "Northern" applicants but to the most "disadvantaged" areas within the North, even when their educational level was low. (Certain qualifications based on the former O- and A-level entrance system were, of course, insisted on, but the grades within those levels were often minimal.) But an educational structure cannot be created or transformed overnight. You may provide for higher education but it does not operate effectively if the primary and secondary levels are insufficiently developed. The "backwardness" of our intake was compounded by language difficulties. Our students were still not really familiar with either spoken or written English; they still <u>thought</u> in their first language and this affected their grammatical constructions. Most of them were "first generation"; that is to say, they came from peasant homes where English wasn't used. This factor is decisive, and the difference between them and those who had "educated" parents was most noticeable--a difference, incidentally, which could be observed among members of staff also. (In Ghana such persons might find themselves abused, when abuse was required, as "bushmen" or even "peasants," the first syllable being pronounced like pea.) In the case of staff the rural background was reflected mainly by a lack of intellectual (as distinct from social) sophistication, and when one remembers the efforts they had made, it would not be expected that they should look ahead. They had exhausted the energies most people spend in a lifetime and the traditional past was still with them. This is a limitation which becomes serious only at a policy-making level or when they undertake postgraduate responsibilities.

These educational characteristics were, of course, rooted in ethnic and religious realities which were inextricably entangled: they influenced the work of the university at every level and, in consequence, educational concerns could not be judged on their merits. (They never are, of course, anywhere, but in that place the covert factors were unusually dominant.) Partly in response to ill-informed criticism about "tribalism," Nigerians are sensitive about such matters, since the word suggests a failure to achieve national identity. Yet the critics--or at least the British ones--are thinking in terms of the Scottish clans or the Wars of the Roses (a Yorkshire/Lancashire rivalry that is not over even now). They fail to appreciate that the real analogy is closer to the differences among British, French, Germans and Italians. If Europe were ever to become unified, at least there would be a religious tradition in common, but in this instance it is not so.

The Last Expatriates

It is only in this context that the role of expatriates can be understood (some of them did not understand it themselves). Our job was not just to hold the line while Nigerian staff were getting their qualifications--which is what most of us originally supposed. We were also there to keep the Southerners out, mainly at the senior level. Such a role eventually imposed serious limitations, one of which was that we should not involve ourselves in university policy. It often seemed to me therefore that I was burdened with responsibility without power. As one Vice-Chancellor (the Muslim one) pointed out to me, we should concern ourselves with expertise and day to day administration: when crises arose we should keep silent. At one of these he said to me, "You must not be so sentimental" (which in West African English means emotional). As "crisis" was almost a permanent condition this was obviously an impossible distinction. Officially some of us held key posts and there was a committee of Deans and Directors of which I was--for two years--a member. This was naturally a policy-making body, subject to final ratification by the Senate, but as individuals we had to pretend we were almost sleeping partners. This was in fact the final phase of the expatriate presence in the running of the university and one which at the older University of Ibadan had happened a decade or so earlier.

We were the last expatriates, in a specific historical sense, and our position was an equivocal one. We could only operate through Nigerian colleagues whose outlook roughly corresponded to our own, or sometimes the relationship was in reverse. These were often in a minority but some of them were among the most remarkable people I have known. They preserved their integrity against overwhelming pressures and I refrain from naming them only because they might prefer it that way. (Certainly praise from this quarter, if it ever became known in Ahmadu Bello University, would not automatically help their careers. In any event, several of them require no such dubious assistance as they hold high positions elsewhere.)

There were, of course, a great many foreigners at lecturer level, perhaps as many as forty per cent. They were of various nationalities but predominantly Indian, Pakistan and Polish, the last being prominent in technical fields. I am not here discussing their contribution, which would require a chapter in itself. With some exceptions they were mostly committed only to their careers and their families, and that is what was mainly required. They often did their jobs well and kept their heads down; bearing in mind that some of them came from countries to which they were in no hurry to return, this was natural and sensible. Having ad-

mitted that, one found it irritating, if no more, when in
faculty meetings many of them would tend to vote with the
majority if and when they knew what it was.   Remaining professors and heads of departments who were not Nigerians
were often happily cynical about their role and content to
keep a low profile in order to serve out their time.   It was,
in most cases, coming to a close; but they had, in most
cases, nowhere else to go.

But some others, including myself, were torn by
dilemmas.   At such a time a political animal feels itself to
be cornered and goes in for futile gestures.   In my case
these took the form of drunken shouting, or just shouting.
My ideological line had naturally always been that our allotted destiny was to fade away like old soldiers (one of
which I was) or like Lewis Carroll's Cheshire cat.   You
may recall that after being just a grin, the cat's head appeared and Alice remarked that a cat may look at a King.
But the King said that the head should be removed and "the
Queen had only one way of settling all difficulties, great or
small.   'Off with his head, ' she said, " and went away.
That was symbolic of our reality, since we had agreed to
hand over our posts to an indigenous incumbent as soon as
possible.   But when is that?   There were of course many
political complexities; it was not, as one might have supposed, simply a matter of handing over to a Nigerian colleague.   As already noted, the social pressures which I encountered reflected not a Nigerian nationalism but divisions
within the body politic.

Radical Nigerian colleagues, whose views I largely
shared, except for the violent controversies which characterize left-wing attitudes everywhere, would insist that it was
time for me to step down from an administrative role.   They
were not really interested in who my successor might be.
The implication was that I might become a kind of symbolic
monument to the past: they were fond of such figures because they were harmless and they were not expected to work
except in a token fashion.   I pointed out that historical monuments are there mainly for the birds to shit upon, but this
was not a very effective response and when the Vice Chancellor (the Muslim one) in his subtle fashion said, "What
are you going to do?" I knew what the answer had to be.   I
had been influenced by my friends and by my own propensities.   It was, of course, an inevitable process but whether
that was quite the right time is a matter for dispute.   Like
all those who, in the last resort, are more affected by princi-

ples (or what they imagine to be such) than by power, I was politically naive. (For the benefit of those who are not familiar with that system, I should explain that we were not being asked to resign our professorships but simply to step down as head of department--a permanent post.) On the face of it this looks quite reasonable, and the theory was that one could concentrate on "research." But for various reasons which may eventually emerge, I could not.

Factional Pressures

At that time in the university the dominant movement was not just nationalist, nor had it ever been. It was not just "Northern" either; within the Muslim majority there were radical elements interested in power ploys, and others who were relatively neutral. In addition, some of them were infected by the fundamentalism which was influenced by political events in the country generally. This faction was hostile not only to expatriates but to Nigerian Christians generally. These forces increased their activity when a Christian military ruler, General Gowon, was ousted by a Muslim, Murtala Mohammed, who later--after he was assassinated--became a national hero and martyr. When he took over, a Christian Vice-Chancellor, who later became foreign minister, was summarily removed and replaced by a Muslim nominee. Because of this and other developments the Muslim factions were in the ascendant and the pressures on other groups, both expatriate and indigenous, increased. Such pressures were often subtle and neither the religious nor the ethnic conflicts could be publicly discussed in those terms. (Nigeria had, after all, miraculously survived as a nation after a terrible civil war, and that lesson had been learned.) The real issues were disguised as educational even though everybody understood that the realities were not. The spirit of irony was all-pervasive.

For example, at one time a Department of Comparative Religion was set up, a Head was appointed and took up his post. But the "Department" never acquired either staff or students and after doing nothing for a year, the man went away. Also, from time to time, within the democratic structures of the university various "progressive" proposals were made. To meet such challenges resort was made to the time-honored device of setting up special committees. For instance, as Dean of the Education Faculty I was commissioned to preside over several committees, including one to make recommendations on a system of student assessment of lecturers, as is common in the USA and Britain. I came to realize that the only way to save time and energy was not to call the committee meetings at all.

I should emphasize that these remarks are not intended to constitute an indictment of the university. It had to function within a particular social and political context: that is all. (One might wish to condemn the context but that is another matter.) Within these limits many Nigerian members of staff made courageous efforts to apply equitable policies, and these efforts had to be heeded even if they were subsequently frustrated by other means. It is only when these non-academic influences are understood that the problems of that university--and others in Africa, or perhaps anywhere--can be understood. The Nigerians are fond of the saying: "There is more to this than meets the eye"--and indeed there always was.

Disorders and Disturbances

These underlying realities broke through with alarming frequency, and then the University would have to be shut down. Sometimes the trouble was mainly internal, as when students or staff went on strike over particular issues. But nearly always these disturbances were linked with political developments in the country. The worst incidents were naturally those when the police or the army or civilian rioters came on to the campus. The worst of all happened at a time when there was political agitation following a Muslim demand that the Shariah law should be introduced in the courts. After a peaceful student demonstration inside and outside of the university, the army entered the campus and there was indiscriminate shooting: many students were injured and at least a dozen were killed. Others were pursued by soldiers into Samaru, the township just outside the campus. The army units were out of control and at the time it was almost impossible to know what was happening or why. (Later it emerged that a largely Christian Brigade was under the mistaken impression that there had been a Muslim uprising within the university.)

On another occasion religious fanatics (probably incited by political forces) invaded the campus chanting their holy war cry, "Allah Akbar," and attacked the Vice-Chancellor's house and administrative buildings. One of his guards was stabbed and he himself was lucky to escape with his life. (As a new non-Muslim appointee he was not acceptable to the Brethren.) At that time Nigerian staff and students who were Christians were threatened and intimidated and some fled the university or went into hiding.

Only on one occasion were foreign lecturers involved and this was a relatively minor incident which followed a party which expatriates had attended. This was a foolish event since it took place on the day when the Head of State, Murtala Mohammed, was assassinated. It was alleged that the foreigners were celebrating because of this, and stones were thrown and their passports were taken away by the police. Some of us who were in a position to do so, tried to intervene to help them.

For me this activity on behalf of our white colleagues was a new role which occasioned some surprise. (It was assumed by hostile observers that some of us were pro-Nigerian in order to curry favor.) From time to time staff members were given twenty-four hours to get out of the country and no reason was given: such matters were at least officially beyond the control of the university. In fact these deportations happened much less frequently than in most other African universities. Allegations were regularly made that certain individuals (especially Americans) were foreign agents. They may have been so, but it was difficult to see what the CIA would have to report upon in such a place.

The saving grace always was that there would be an official inquiry after these riots and disorders. For example, at the time when a number of students were killed the circumstances were thoroughly investigated by a commission which included prominent individuals from outside. There was no cover-up and the report did not hesitate to apportion blame. It was stated, for example, that the Vice-Chancellor had been negligent and irresponsible. Yet on this and other occasions no further action was taken and that Vice-Chancellor later became a Minister in the Federal Government. His personal qualities were less important than the political forces he represented. Under such circumstances, staff morale was often low and the university as a corporate body was severely weakened. Yet it survived as a going concern because its role in the life of the nation was indispensable.

Academic Standards

Because of this need to survive, whatever the cost, examinations were always held somehow and a new crop of undergraduates was released into the world. Obviously, under such circumstances academic "standards" must have been affected. For example, lecturers had to compress a year's course into a much shorter time. There were other built-in negative factors such as the language difficulties mentioned above. These were compounded by the presence of a cosmopolitan staff whose members spoke in varieties of English which were not easily recognizable as such and who could not always make themselves understood. The other important deficiency was a shortage of up-to-date reading material, especially periodicals, and inadequate research resources. It may be because of these difficulties that academics in Britain or the USA are not impressed by the qualifications of African students or by lecturers' experience. Appointment boards in Britain often look askance at British candidates with a record of service in the Third World. I suspect, however, that many of these conventional attitudes arise from insular prejudice and an invincible ignorance. Beneath these responses there lurk primitive resentments against those who have betrayed the tribe by going away. These can be rationalized by taking the line that there might be a risk involved; who can tell what strange practices may have been acquired? Furthermore, there is an inability to comprehend why any sane or stable person would wish to leave Britain for any country other than America.

What these people overlook or do not want to know is that under the circumstances I have described, both staff and students make efforts which are quite unimaginable in more sheltered environments. Precisely because there are so many obstacles to be overcome, they are overcome. The challenge is so much greater that the response has to be the same. African undergraduates, moreover, have certain peculiar advantages. First, to get to the university at all they have often survived extraordinary hardships which have already taxed their abilities to the utmost: they are used to hard work. The women students have special obstacles put in their way: their traditional function was, of course, to work and produce babies, not university degrees. (Their men folk often took the precaution of ensuring that they were pregnant before they started their courses.) In general, both men and women are older and more mature than their counterparts elsewhere. Second, they are still so close to the

oral tradition that they can absorb large quantities of material and reproduce them when required (or sometimes when not
required). Third, they specialize in group study, especially
when doing revision--a most effective method. Critics will
immediately pounce on this kind of learning as mere parrot
reproduction, but if they are honest they must admit that at
an undergraduate level it is this kind of work which is served
up at universities everywhere: that is what the educational
industry is like. And this is not all, since the staff often
go to great lengths to make up for the limitations we have
noted. Finally, the most important factor is probably that of
motivation. Unlike most students in more developed countries,
these students must pass their degree because it is the only
route to a reasonable career. One has to admit that their
education is notoriously not related to their own environment,
but this much-discussed feature is the product of historical
circumstances and is not their fault. It is the only kind of
education they have known.

That is the student part of the equation and their efforts are remarkable when one considers that the university,
as an institution, has to struggle with the difficulties I have
mentioned. It is the staffing problem which is the most important of these difficulties. That kind of indigenization
which involves local candidates whether they are the best
applicants or not is bound to affect teaching standards. There
is also a rapid turnover of staff caused by the social mobility which economic development brings about. Many staff
members leave to join new academic institutions elsewhere,
often in their own states, and others take up political or
diplomatic posts. Inevitably traditions suffer and old battles
are fought all over again because nobody can remember the
past. (Sometimes, as in totalitarian countries, the past is
abolished and those who were in it become non-persons.)
The university as a whole may in consequence lose a sense
of direction, but the potential remains.

At a research level, for reasons already mentioned,
one might detect, in many instances, a falling off from this
mythical international standard. Yet even there the best
work can stand comparison with similar studies elsewhere.
In our particular field of library science, from a career point
of view, it became advisable for library staff--especially if
they intended to work in a university--to take a second degree. Some of them did not have "academic" interests or
abilities and one consequence is that the system of higher degrees can become devalued. It is a trend which I believe

can be observed in other countries besides those in Africa.
It can be defended on the grounds that the original system,
based on a British prototype, was élitist. But it is an alarming process and one wonders where it can stop. If everybody
has a Master's degree, then who will be most qualified?

Partly because of this, many Departments, including
our own, were in a hurry to set up Doctorate programs,
even when the human and material resources were not available: it was a matter of prestige. If the market should
eventually become flooded with Doctors some other distinction
will have to be devised, and already there are persons with
two Doctorates in different fields. (I recall that one such
always designated himself in the plural.) During the Chinese
cultural revolution phase, attempts were made to halt this
process by sending academics to work in the fields, but that
couldn't happen in Africa. (It is true that in Nigeria there is
a system of compulsory national service but most of the ex-
students are assigned to work which corresponds with their
non-manual status.) However, I am not producing yet another treatise on education systems; my main intention here
is to emphasize the extent of the struggle.

Ceremonial Celebrations

After the battle was over, it was entirely appropriate
that the end of the journey should be marked by ritual and
ceremony, in particular by Convocation when degrees were
awarded. Before that great day could come, elaborate,
lengthy and contentious procedures had been undergone.
Great efforts were made to achieve a fair result and, bearing in mind circumstances which are not likely to be found
in more settled places, this was no mean achievement. Such
circumstances may include, for example, the prevalence of
child birth (before, during or after the examinations); the influence of witchcraft; the possibility of ethnic bias; the impact of sexual "corruption"; the incidence of death on the
roads (leading to posthumous awards); the use of varying as-
sessments by staff members from different national back-
grounds; the non-appearance of external examiners; disagree-
ment between one department and another--and so on. Many
of these conflicts naturally relate to grades rather than passing or failing. These procedures are, of course, universal
but in that place they are more melodramatic and traumatic
than elsewhere, if only because so much is at stake. Without that qualification--a passport to affluence in this world--
the failed student has nowhere to go.

But we must return to the Ceremony--probably the most important day in the lives of students, some of whom have come from their mud huts to this almost unimaginable goal. So important is it that some of them feel that they have arrived and no comparable efforts will ever be necessary again. They assemble in some vast temporary structure (bits of which will be blown down during the ceremony) and, together with some of their relatives and many Dignitaries, await the arrival of the Chancellor and his entourage. Meanwhile, those of the staff who choose to "process" dress up in the long-forgotten robes of numerous exotic universities and wait outside in the sun (it is of course very hot). Eventually the great man arrives in his motorcade, surrounded by outriders--on at least one occasion there were machine-gunners on nearby rooftops who were ignored by intrepid spectators perched precariously in every tree. As the Chancellor enters the building we begin our Procession and in an entirely Shakespearean manner there is a fanfare from long Hausa trumpets--a prolonged farting noise of two notes--and the band, a relic of the bad old colonial days, strikes up. It plays some familiar melodies such as "I do like to be beside the sea side" (here on the edge of the Sahara) and "When the Saints come marching in," which somehow seems appropriate as we eventually approach the platform. Then we settle down to the long roll call of names.

At one ceremony an unfortunate incident occurred: as an expatriate Dean of the largest Faculty I could not be expected to read out all those long names, so a Nigerian colleague was allotted this task. But consternation broke out when he--as a Southerner--could not pronounce them either. Having reached what he thought was the end, he turned over the page and discovering that it was not the end, uttered a prolonged amplified groan. This was not, as a stranger might expect, a laughing matter. The audience was angry, and I was indirectly responsible.

A high spot was the award of honorary degrees, sometimes to foreign Heads of State. One such was President Machel of Mozambique. It was a memorable occasion, not least when he concluded his speech by calling for cheers and acclamations--"Viva African freedom," etcetera. The audience, unused to such mass demonstrations, responded well enough until he came to his last call, "Viva the Liberation of Women," and then there was a deathly hush. "Evidently," he said, "You couldn't hear what I said," and repeated the call more emphatically. Finally there was a faint response, but not from the assorted Emirs present.

After the ceremony the time for revelry had come.
Nigerians are very good at pageantry and ritualistic observation and also at enjoying themselves.   Free beer flowed and
always at such times unauthorized gate-crashers managed to
join in its consumption.

Meanwhile, beyond the campus, not more than a mile
away, the immemorial peasants are working in the fields as
they have always done.   In a similar fashion the nomadic Fulani bring their white cattle through the campus along the
fixed routes which they traditionally used.   If the university
is in the way they seem unaware of it.   (On one occasion
when I was in the hospital a herd of these beasts wandered
through the corridors.)

Consolations

The experiences I have described were often tedious
and sometimes painful, but they were neither trivial nor
meaningless.   For those of us who were part of a diminish-
ing British presence, there was an extra dimension since
our predecessors had been agents of a Colonial enterprise
which had left behind--in addition to many other ambiguous
legacies--the English language.   We could not feel responsible
for that, yet we were there because of it.   I stress this historical factor lest it should be thought that my attitudes were
mainly masochistic.   We had, it is true, abandoned the normal rewards which accumulate after a career rooted in a native environment, and in their place there was this special
consolation, not exactly a prize, but a source of satisfaction.
The official recognition, which normally comes from service
to one's own community, had to be replaced by an awareness
that we had been, in however small a capacity, agents of an
important political process, usually called decolonization.
Naturally, many of my colleagues never thought in such terms
and presumably they developed their own consolations.   What
I have been discussing is the transfer of power in that particular institution: they were transitional circumstances and
all social transitions produce tension and confusion.

The Staff Club

During the seven years after my arrival in 1972 I sat
in the staff club (intermittently of course) and from that van-
tage point witnessed the end of the transition as it was re-

flected in that place. Similar manifestations could have been observed in the two clubs on other campuses. (Unfortunately there was no place where staff and students could meet on an equal footing--the social gap was much greater than in some other universities elsewhere.) Eventually that club became for me a symbol, not of progress nor even of survival, but of continuity. At the beginning "the establishment, " meaning departmental and faculty heads and key administrators such as the Registrar, were regularly in attendance--but not for long. As time went on these figures decided to keep a lower profile, because it became politically advisable to do so. After that the club was mainly used by some of the remaining "foreigners, " including Africans who were not from that part of Nigeria. With some exceptions the Poles, Indians and Pakistanis stayed at home, for economic or religious reasons or both. (The social pressures on them came mostly from their own compatriots.)

The institution therefore became not central, but marginal to the life of the university--if "life" is the right word. We became fringe creatures, aware that our presence there was condoned but that was all. In my own case, for instance, representations were made opposing my appointment as Dean on the grounds that I was a "drunkard, " which in strict Muslim parlance means anyone who drinks alcohol at all. (Those, of whatever Faith, who drank spirits in their own homes were not so categorized since their offense was not public.) It became apparent that this issue was being used by a particular faction for political ends. In the university at Kano, as one would expect, the same process became total and their club was shut down.

We should not fail to mention the swimming pool which was on the same site but not part of the club: this too was deplored by the Faithful. Those who used it regularly were mainly white expatriate ladies, especially Poles, who were not important enough to be a political target, but it was naturally considered disgraceful that they were exposing themselves not only to the sun but also to the lustful eyes of drunken males. At one time a wall or partition was considered but the plan was abandoned for economic reasons. It was pointed out that, in any event, the ladies were some way off and--to the short-sighted--only a blur. Swimming, as distinct from bathing in rural pools, was not part of Nigerian traditional culture. (There is a curious myth that when Africans fall into the water they sink to the bottom and do not come up again.)

As we have already noted, the new fundamentalist
politico-religious forces within the university were part of
the wider movement beyond the campus. The brethren out
there, notably in the ancient walled city of Zaria, were inspired by fanatical zeal. Those--the great majority--who
were socially deprived and dispossessed were encouraged to
divert their frustrations into religious channels, and on more
than one occasion when they invaded the campus their targets
included the drinking clubs of both students and staff. Our
club was not exactly burned down because it wouldn't burn,
but the damage was severe. We were attacked with axes and
spears and bows and arrows and the store was broken into
and the contents smashed or removed. Hostile mobs are
frightening but the scene was not without farcical overtones,
as when bikini-clad white ladies from the swimming pool had
to flee through the bush leaving their clothes behind them.
Afterwards one was reminded of minor air raids during the
second world war. I understand that there have been other
attacks since. All of them, however, have been faint echoes
of what had taken place in Khomeini's Iran. (True there was
an association where students were designated Ayatollah and
not Comrade, but they constituted a small, if noisy minority.)

The university remained relatively civilized insofar as
all these violent activities were officially deplored and subsequently investigated. The fragile fabric remained intact because Nigeria is not theocratic, but a secular state. It is
in this respect that the club became significant for me. Between the bar and the swimming pool there is an enormous
tree which was blackened but undestroyed by successive in-
cendiary fires. (It is, I believe, a shea tree, whose oily
seeds are used for making butter and soap.) Rather than the
club it was this tree which for me became symbolic. I came
to think of it as Ygdrasil which, according to old Norse myth-
ology, overshadowed the whole world, binding together with
its roots and branches heaven and earth and hell. This is,
of course, a pagan concept and I like to imagine that this
unifying principle is stronger than all the forces of the "religions of the Book," the institutions whose concept of human solidarity is so restricted that it never goes beyond
their own fraternities. It is important, therefore, that the
university should continue not--for the staff--as an alternative
to some other career in business; nor just as one more institution for national or personal development; nor as an intellectual prison. In this respect the cosmopolitan ambiance
could be neither a distraction nor a liability, but a positive
feature. A university, whatever else it may be, should be

able to transcend immediate circumstances: it must specialize in Hope and some kind of vision for the future. Some
of my Nigerian colleagues in ABU would condemn that last
sentence as "liberal" nonsense, but I am content to let it
stand.

PART V

MY PUBLICATIONS

I have spent a lot of time scribbling--it is an urge which has always puzzled those who do not share it. Typical was King George III of England's response to Edward Gibbon, the historian, "Scribble, scribble, Mr. Gibbon, eh? Scribble, scribble. " Here I propose to discuss what the results have been for me but mainly in relation to professional publications since little else has emerged except the chapters of this book and one can hardly write about them.

Within their limits these publications have been "successful" but it was not the kind of success I sought. This is because I started with literary ambitions--a common enough complaint and most of those afflicted by it in early years are later cured by the struggle for existence. But my profession both as librarian and subsequently as academic permitted-- even required--that I should publish and in consequence these half-buried scribbling drives found a possible and socially legitimate channel.

It seemed likely that whatever "creative" abilities I was blessed with would be used in this way. Yet I have not felt that they were, partly because I was trying to write professional literature which might also have a general appeal. It is probable that the two aims are not only different but incompatible. Some writers--Borges, for example--have been librarians but they do not write about libraries as such. The rest of this chapter is mainly concerned with this dilemma.

A bibliography produced in 1977 by an undergraduate student (as he then was) Mr. O. C. Ande-Muottoh listed some 130 items but many of these were naturally reviews by other people. These offerings started to appear while I was still working in St. Marylebone library in 1950. The first one at-

171

tempted to discover why public libraries in Paris had remained underdeveloped. The theme is significant because it
illustrates preoccupations which have been constant ever since.
I suppose you could call it a search for the reality behind ap-
pearances. This is of course a <u>religious</u> quest but it has expressed itself mainly in a quasi-sociological form. God's
plan for libraries was no more apparent then than it is now.
For examination purposes, I had studied some political and
economic theory (nearly always through secondary sources)
and because of this I began part-time lecturing at London's
North Western Polytechnic (as it then was) in the Literature
of the Social Sciences. The scope of that subject field was
typical of library studies at that time. Thereafter I became
a full-time lecturer but before that there were other minor
contributions relating to information services. Several of us,
including Douglas Foskett were concerned with what we regarded as current deficiencies both in theory and practice.
As another chapter in this book indicates, that theme has also
never gone away. At that time it did not occur to me to ask
what information <u>is</u>: like everybody else we <u>knew</u> what it was
and there was not enough of it.

When I started teaching full-time the wide range of
"subjects" with which I was expected to deal was reflected in
various pieces most of which appeared in the <u>Assistant Li-
brarian</u>, a journal which then, as now, catered in a lively
fashion to the younger members of the profession. These
pieces included a series under the pseudonym <u>Thomas Clear-
water</u> who later became <u>Felltimber.</u> This project was carried out in collaboration with colleagues Edward Dudley and
Harold Smith. As the names suggest there was a left-wing
political component and we were clearing the ground as well
as the water. As far as I can recall they were--at least my
part of them--too "clever" to be serious. We were grieved,
I suppose, that an intellectual approach to life and literature
was not as common among librarians as we would have liked.
At the present time this question does not arise since nobody
expects librarians to read: that expectation was based on a
Humanistic tradition that has passed away and our generation
witnessed its passing. It is not yet clear precisely what has
replaced it but fortunately I no longer have to pronounce upon
such matters.

Later in the fifties I was necessarily wholly involved
in library education. Some of us were painfully aware that
this discipline--insofar as it was one then--was lumbered and
cluttered with dreary, uncivilized relics from the past. Ac-

cordingly we attempted to redesign librarianship courses so that they might conform more closely to generally recognized educational principles instead of simply describing what librarians and libraries did. There was a Standing Committee on Education for Librarians of which I was chairman, and we produced a series of pamphlets called Notes for Tutors--the most important of which (done originally with Edward Dudley) dealt with the study of reference material: its content is commonplace now but it wasn't then. The number of full-time librarianship lecturers at that time was necessarily small and we relied on our part-time colleagues: it was mainly for their benefit that such efforts were made. I am sure we thought that these activities represented Progress and so they did but it was still well within the British amateur tradition and nobody was paid for their work. Professional education was still in its infancy.

Apart from this dominant theme, my dilettante tendencies were reflected in various divergent explorations. But one bonus was that, prodded by a colleague (Philip Sewell), I became aware of the importance of being able to write scientific or technical English. This realization was slow in coming and often I was obliged to remove literary flourishes and pseudo-poetic phraseology. One offering was rejected because it read, the editor said, like a pastiche of T. S. Eliot. It was a satirical account of a professional conference and--inter alia--referred to lonely souls kicking driftwood along the sea shore. Then there was a paper given at a meeting in Croydon, Surrey which analyzed a certain kind of soft- or pseudo-porn characterized by the Anglo-American novels of Hank Janson. During a riotous session students read out typical passages. It was all good clean fun but the editor of the Library Association Record considered that the contents were not suitable for that solemn journal.

I have mentioned these deservedly forgotten items to illustrate a lack of direction which can be explained by the absence of an academic background. For example I embarked on several grandiose and impossible projects. These included a huge bibliographical guide for public libraries on the selection of French, Italian, and German literature. There was also an even more monumental guide to periodicals in all subject fields. Somewhere in some forgotten attic in West Kensington, London, the remains of these efforts must still provide a rest for mice. For these projects I enlisted the aid of students. If any of them should read this account I hope they will feel that their labors were not, after all, in vain:

they were helping with my education.   But I shall be accused
of perversely writing about publications that never were and
I should add that towards the end of that time I did produce a
(commissioned) annotated bibliography for Unesco on technical
education in Britain.   This was a straightforward and more
manageable task, my first and last exercise in systematic
bibliography.

The main published result of that decade of largely
wasted endeavor was a textbook called Bibliography and the
Provision of Books which was published after a long delay by
the Association of Assistant Librarians.   As the book was
about obstacles to recorded information it was appropriate
perhaps that obstacles arose.   First a colleague recommended
that it should not be published: "Gobbledegook, " he said it
was and certainly it was pretentious.   (I had suffered from
that inchoate mass of material for so long that such preten-
sions were perhaps forgiveable.)   Then several of the printers involved became ill or sustained injuries, one of which
was fatal.   Printers (like actors) are a superstitious lot and
they were reluctant to proceed but eventually, about two
years later, it appeared and was well received.   The method
was normative and deduced from principles I thought I had
invented.   Certain requirements were stated and I proceeded
to examine why they were not met.   I no longer "think" in
that way and I cannot recognize the person that wrote it.
The method--it seems to me now--was mechanistic and reductive but it did represent a primitive form of systems
analysis which was of value.   There is also an obsessional
element which may have derived from that polytechnical environment.   My religious instincts had somehow turned into
convictions about the Importance of Bibliography--a not uncommon professional hazard from which I escaped only by
going abroad to countries where bibliography, like sex, is
kept in its proper place.

For a number of years thereafter I was so embroiled
in adjustments to Third World conditions that my published
contributions rarely went beyond brief progress reports.   I
was nevertheless involved with setting up and editing two library journals (in Trinidad and Ghana).   That experience
made me realize what a trap such work can be.   There are,
I suppose, born editors but I was not one of them, certainly
not in those circumstances and probably not at all.

Apart from those activities it is clear to me now that
during those eight years I had nothing to say and for once I

made no attempt to say it. Experience abroad, like active service in war time, may leave one confused, overwhelmed, and dumb. It has often been observed that the best accounts of conditions in foreign countries have been written by those who have stayed a short time only--a few weeks or months maybe. I did, in fact, spend the first three months in Ghana writing about the West Indies. I mention this only in passing since the work did not deal with libraries and in any event was subsequently lost by the publisher. It was not clear for whom it was intended and was probably no great loss to humanity. Nevertheless I have often regretted that I have no copy of the text since it would have revived my fading memory of the West Indies.

From that time on, the later books were hybrid publications: they were not about libraries as such but about the social context in which libraries operate--I hoped because of this that they would reach a wider audience and reviewers (not to mention the publisher) hoped so too. But, except to some minor extent, this was not to be. It is debatable whether it could ever be. Can one envisage a popular response to Leaves from a Librarian's Notebook or Library Lore for the Masses? Why not? There are, after all, those best-selling books about criminal and medical cases or about the teaching of children or even the dubious activities of publishers. And there are those interminable homely works about a Yorkshire vet. If people enjoy reading about sick animals, why should they not read about librarians? On a more serious level there is a universal concern with philosophy, history, politics, psychology, or sex. If the common reader does not resort to library literature to be saved or amused or liberated, is it not possible that he is mistaken? One must continue to doubt and at the time I am writing about the question did not arise, since I had no opportunity to consider it.

After 1967 there followed the Aberystwyth experience, which at least in this context was not unrewarding. The unexpected consequences of my eight years abroad was that, with the assistance of my colleagues, it was possible to produce a book not about Africa but about Britain. This work, Libraries and Cultural Change, was a success and eventually sold about 12,000 copies. It met a professional demand because I was seeing my own country as if for the first time. There was a shock of surprise and I became a child again or at least a student among other students. But as one reviewer (Havard Williams) pointed out, it was too personal to be a safe textbook and "students using the book for examination purposes should do so with caution." Needless to say students are not cautious and over the years examiners, including myself, have often met with alarming parodies of my tentative explorations. The writing of textbooks--for which I am unsuited--is like building construction: the separate components should be pre-fabricated and then carefully fitted together. This is an important process but it is not organic and my tendency is to function more like a vegetable organism. The main value of that book was that I tried to look at the world in order to define what place librarians might have in it. Most library literature is necessarily specialist and takes care not to deal with the world. Like Lewis Carroll's walrus one can deeply sympathize: the oysters however were all consumed.

> 'O Oysters' said the Carpenter
> 'You've had a pleasant run
> Shall we be trotting home again
> But answer came there none
> And this was scarcely odd, because
> They'd eaten every one.

I am tempted to pursue this fishy analogy further but must desist: who wants to be compared to an oyster?

During that time in Wales I also produced a book called Communication and Identity. Insofar as it was reviewed at all, reviewers were either baffled or too kind. The publisher, Clive Bingley, was annoyed by its lack of success since he had apparently expected a greater response. Whether he was irritated with me or the market or himself could not easily be determined. The favorable reception for the previous book had perhaps caused us to overlook the fact that this was a different proposition altogether. The readers were mostly not there and when this became apparent, Clive said (with more hope than conviction) that perhaps it would become a cult book. But the cult was not there either. Now it seems to be little more than a series of annotations on a motley collection of gurus, pundits, sages, charlatans, and academics all gathered together for my own esoteric purposes. The work was an expansion of what I had done for a London Master of Arts degree. But what was acceptable--just about-- for an academic exercise, was less so for general publication, a not uncommon occurrence. The background was that I had become closely involved with the youth culture of the sixties. Being then at least 50 I could hardly claim to belong to that generation but the attitudes of the flower children seemed to correspond with those which some of us had acquired in Africa. We too thought we had rejected the European past and current repressive structures. I examined all the prophets of the counter culture and somehow linked them not only with my experience in the Third World but also with a somewhat vague existentialism which had replaced a Marxist ethos. The various ingredients in that heady mixture--a witches brew?--could not easily have been digested by anyone and the academic level was wrong. But I did not repine. I considered that the experience would help in my personal development even though I knew that such a process may well be imaginary. Certainly I had shed a facile rationalism forever. In a characteristic portentous fashion--a habit which often verges on self parody--I declared that "the reader I have in mind is somebody like myself--a general reader for whom stock responses no longer suffice but who has not yet 'given up'." Evidently the somebodies like myself were not as thick on the ground as I had imagined.

After that it became necessary to return to West Africa. While there I was at first too concerned with administration to indulge in professional scribbling. Yet because of practical involvement within the university and outside the trappings of the European alternative culture became irrelevant and a radical commitment to specifically African political issues reappeared. I began to feel that I had arrived at a realistic understanding of some African circumstances which I had formerly failed to analyze--the result was Cultural Crisis and Libraries in the Third World. The title, of course, is ridiculous and the word "libraries" was inserted by the publisher; once again it was a difficult birth and the gestation period was characterized by tropical fevers and paranoid dissension. The disorder even spilled over into Britain when part of the work was in a bag that was stolen on Paddington Station, London. (The police officer said, you should have been more careful when all these black people are around.) For these and other reasons (which included a loss of confidence in my capacities) the publisher was no longer interested. He was in any event selling the business and Saur, the new temporary publisher, was interested even less. (He was understandably more concerned with his own financial problems and a monumental British Museum library catalog.) Not long afterwards the British Library Association became responsible for the Bingley establishment. In spite of all that the work--more or less intact--did appear and, bearing in mind its limited appeal, was well received.

Inevitably these events marked the end of my association with Clive Bingley. It was, on the whole a rewarding
one for me and it would be ungenerous not to record my appreciation of his encouragement and help over a long period.
I always recognized that publishers are a necessary evil and
some of them, including Clive, are human as well. Because
of this he remains a friend. Eventually somebody will produce a study of his substantial contribution to library studies
in Britain but that is outside my self-imposed terms of reference.

In retrospect it seems fitting that this would be my
last professional work. The political winds of change were
blowing in another direction entirely and most people in the
developed countries had become bored with the interminable
troubles of the Third World. The British, for example,
were now more exclusively concerned with their own and had
elected a right-wing government with similar limited perceptions. That government reverted to simplistic nineteenth-
century notions that if individuals were not rich it was their
own fault and the state should teach them a lesson by leaving
them alone. The same attitudes were adopted towards the
new countries of Africa. Puzzled and dismayed by these bar-
baric developments I found some consolation in the thought
that at least that book had emerged from my last years in
Nigeria. True, it was a hybrid once again, yet it was used
in some universities for development studies: that should
have been enough.

Meanwhile when all that was out of the way I began
to write these meditations. There were not many distractions
--those caused by electricity failures were perhaps the worst
--and shut up in our air-conditioned study bedroom in Nigeria
I would neither see nor hear what went on in the world outside. Cyril Connolly once observed that when the children's
perambulator arrives in the hall there is an end to scribbling.
But in Africa these things are ordered otherwise and somebody else is only too anxious (provided that they are paid)
to take over these domestic duties: one benefits from the
wickedness of the world. To examine what I was writing
then would carry self-analysis to ridiculous limits since this
chapter is part of it: we have come--for the time being--
to the end.

Yet this account if I left it there could not easily be
justified: I was not, after all, Graham Greene nor even
Somerset Maugham and what I set out to explore is from a

literary point of view a marginal experience. I started by
noting that I had hoped to go beyond the purely professional
and this has not been possible. I suppose that most people
who are not insufferable feel that they have never realized
their potentialities and in this view they are correct: the
world is full of wasted abilities. That being so, the question
I must try to answer is why scribblers, including myself,
continue with this kind of endeavor whether they are successful or not. Leaving aside writing which is <u>wholly</u> related to
practical matters such as teaching (textbooks), it seems probable that the reasons people write professional articles or
books are the same as for any other kind of literature.
There is a career element involved of course--we were all
ambitious once--but the rewards are so dubious that this
motivation is not sufficient to explain why some people never
stop. Many successful writers have tried to explain. For
example, George Orwell, whose journalist work rarely failed
to exhibit a kind of inspired common sense, supplied his own
answer in his essay <u>Why I Write.</u> [1] He provided four "great
motives." Firstly: "sheer egoism" which needs no further
comment except that he does not explain why egoism should
take that particular form: it is a universal condition. Second: "aesthetic enthusiasm" by which he means a perception
of beauty in the external world or in the arrangement of
words. Certainly I can subscribe to that. Third: "historical impulse" which is an urge to set the record straight.
This too must be a common factor: Robert Graves in his
prose work has spent his entire life doing just that. Finally
"political purpose": he confesses to a desire to push the
world in a certain direction. This perhaps is the most variable motive but it was, of course, characteristic of my generation. That desire, however, may well result in practical
political activity without any reference to literature.

Like so much that Orwell wrote, that explanation
leaves too many stones unturned and one must conclude that
what we are discussing is a particular kind of temperament.
He was, after all, writing about himself. I am obliged,
therefore, to return to my own predicaments and assume, for
the moment, that for various reasons, which only the psychol-
ogist might unravel, for some people the writing activity is
almost--but not quite--an end in itself.

Anyone who persists must necessarily be involved in
the psychological states which are associated with the problem
of method or style. The question, <u>How</u> do I write, is perhaps more interesting than why. It always seemed to me that

any kind of creative work is concerned with bringing inert material alive. (There are philosophical considerations here which I will not pursue.) This can only be explained by analogy and there are so many. One can think of an illumination like that of the glowworm or an electric filament. Or there are many watery images which may invoke large shadowy fishes emerging from the deep, elusive shapes which may easily disappear again. Or one classical writer referred to enticing birds from a dovecote. Those who retrieve information are familiar with the concept of "free flow" but I suspect that something else is involved there, since this can only happen after the creative process.

Whatever analogies are used, there are barriers to be removed and these are mainly psychological. These are processes similar to that of psychoanalysis: buried material must be released from the deeper levels of the mind. The concept of inspiration is familiar but who can say whence it comes? In most cultures supernatural forces are invoked. As Auden observed "The winds must come from somewhere when they blow. "

Expressed in such a manner the phenomena involved sound most alarming. But this is only because of the metaphors and there are several consoling simplicities. The first is that the creative element is present in almost everyone even though it may be destroyed by formal education or an uncreative world: it is a matter of finding a suitable medium. The second comforting thought is that these things are not comparative. One is not competing with others and certainly not with the Great Masters. If this were not so one might do no more than read Gulliver's Travels and then shut up forever.

What many public persons do not appreciate is that all worthwhile writing is private and personal because one is trying to communicate with other individuals as well as with one's self. That being so, in my own case, I have instinctively preferred what Hazlitt called a familiar style: that is why I have stressed psychological barriers. Many of these can be overcome with long practice--which is essential anyway. Apart from anxiety states the worst of these is self-consciousness, which inhibits spontaneity. Most people have these hangups to begin with and that is why they cannot write letters. Many writers (like Orwell) advocate a plain style but this is not what I mean: that too can be an affectation.

There are of course adventitious aids. I associate
each of my books with particular beverages. At the present
time it is Spanish wine which could explain the benign tone
of this account. On the other hand spirits are not recommended since they induce premature incoherence and futile
rages. I realize that, by such means you may ruin your
health and your personal relationships, but that is of no consequence: the cause is the thing. (The history of literature
would have been quite different if absinthe had not been
banned at the beginning of this century.) Fortunately not
everyone will require drugs and suitable alternatives may be
found, or--as time goes on--they will not be necessary when
the internal blockages are dissolved. Yoga exercises may
help but it is difficult to write at the same time: hot baths
have the same disadvantage. (In Ghana I prepared most of
my lectures in the bath but they would have been more effective if written down.) Finally, to move on to another
plane, the best kind of inspiration derives from the condition
known as being in love. The unrequited variety is preferable
and once again poor Hazlitt comes to mind. But one should
add that he did work very hard.

To return to my own professional writing I should also
mention that the trouble with a familiar style is that it may
become too personal for effective communication. Idiosyn-
crasy is usually condemned: my dictionary defines it as a
quirk, mannerism, or foible. There is the additional problem that some "quirks" are national or culturally determined.
In my own case a tendency to be allusive and an ingrained
dislike of spelling things out cause communication difficulties
ranging from bewilderment to total incomprehension. What,
is to be done? As far as I am concerned, very little: it
is too late. But you have been warned. These are the dilemmas of a "generalist": the specialist will face a different complication. How can one avoid jargon? An alternative
term is "gibberish. " In order to achieve any kind of preci-
sion specialist words have to be used. All that can be hoped
for is that the writer will not use words as if we were all
supposed to know the language.

This last section may suggest to some readers that
this itch to go on scribbling is nothing but a disease which
is tiresome in the way that other people's neuroses tend to
be. This is not the impression I wish to give. Certainly
this trait is not morally to be admired. Thomas Hardy for
example was, in general, not admirable at all but the relevant factor is that he was totally single minded and persisted

in spite of every conceivable obstacle and his own considerable limitations. "An infinite capacity for taking pains" is
quite inadequate as a definition of genius, but it is relevant
in our context. It is something which every scribbler needs.

All this is deliberately subjective and I must conclude
with a wider perspective even though it is still my own.
Orwell, whom I have quoted, was an exile in his own country. In our time we have become more familiar with the
exiles produced by the current transformations in the world.
Such a one is Milan Kundera,[2] a Czech refugee, and his
analysis is perhaps more relevant to my predicament and
that of so many others in discussing "Graphomania" (an ob-
session with writing). He considers that it is likely to reach
epidemic proportions whenever a society develops to the point
when it can satisfy three basic conditions. First: sufficient
social well-being to allow people to devote themselves to useless activities; second: an advanced state of social atomiza-
tion resulting in the isolation of the individual; and third: an
absence of significant social change. I suspect that the last
condition is the most important. All these requirements now
exist in most, if not all, of Western Europe. In the Soviet
Union the second condition may not yet prevail but certainly
there are a lot of scribblers there who have no immediate
hope of publication. For them it is an activity not far removed from prayer except that they are addressing themselves
not to God but to their fellow creatures who are "out there"
and who are almost as inaccessible. In the USA I imagine
that the individual is separate not because society is "atom-
ized" but because he is part of a lonely crowd. The key
factor is isolation, which is naturally greater for the exile
like Kundera or myself, but the psychology is the same.

The main characteristic is that the scribbler is thinking of publication because he needs an audience. As Kundera
notes, graphomania is not a desire to write letters, diaries,
or family chronicles: it is a wish to communicate with unknown readers "out there." The other significant point he
makes is that many of these isolated people are neither literary nor retired. They often belong to the swelling ranks of
the new model army of the unemployed: they scribble because they refuse to accept that they do not exist.

That is not my predicament except possibly at a deeper level (I write, therefore I am) but I have been an exile
most of the time. I used to think that this was why my books
were not "academic" in the usual sense since I have mostly

lived in places where documentary sources are inadequate. But clearly that kind of isolation was not accidental, unless one believes (which I do not) that our lives are totally determined by material circumstances.

One is driven to the conclusion that the personal element has always been paramount. Faced with this characteristic which (outside of imaginative literature) is normally deplored I am consoled by the thought that there have been effective writers who are important because they were personal: they include Pascal and Kierkegaard. As I am in Spain it is fitting that I should refer to one of the greatest of them. In his introduction to Miguel de Unamuno's Tragic Sense of Life, Amalia Elguera noted that his voluminous output was "almost obsessively autobiographical and communicative rather than informative." He also claims that, apart from poetry, autobiography is the only medium which can reflect "the man of flesh and bone" in depth. As Gerald Brenan observes, 4 "He was never a learned man ... and took from books only what he personally needed. He put the same questions to every writer and noted the answers." That is what I--at another level--have, willy nilly, done. I have just mentioned writers who rarely came down from the high mountains whereas I have scrabbled about only among foothills. But that fact is not relevant here. It may well be that the method is not always the most suitable for publications in Library Science and perhaps that is why I am now engaged on an autobiographical exercise. If and when this work is continued it will doubtless emerge that this particular chapter is merely a foundation for further explorations.

References

1. George Orwell, Collective Essays, Journalism and Letters. Secker and Warburg, 1968, Vol. I, p. 3.

2. Milan Kundera, The Book of Laughter and Forgetting. Faber, 1982, p. 92.

3. Amalia Elguera, "Introduction," to Miguel de Unamuno's Tragic Sense of Life. Collins (The Fontana Library), 1962, p. 7.

4. Gerald Brenan, The Literature of the Spanish People. Penguin, 1963, p. 377.

PART VI: PROFESSIONAL CONCERNS

1. THE MYSTIQUES OF INFORMATION

There is a curious gap between the high claims which have been made about the current state of information and our perception of it. For a long time now it has not been easy to understand the exact meaning of such resounding phrases as "Information Revolution" or "Information Society" or a "New World Information Order." A typical harassed librarian, faced with severe budget cuts and restrictions on services, may be forgiven for feeling that there must be a contradiction somewhere. A similar fog surrounds the earlier references to a "post-industrial society," which it is alleged we now inhabit. According to this concept the machines are now extending the human brain, where formerly the industrial revolution had only replaced muscle and brawn. We are given to understand that because of this development, more and more information will be required and used. Highly organized by advanced technological processes, it will, like some life-giving substance, flow around the globe. It is even alleged that the inhabitants of Ouagadugu and Shalimar will benefit as well. For our profession all this sounds most encouraging. Perhaps it might be more so if we could really grasp what is involved. Since I suspect that we do not, I propose to explore the matter further.

In 1981 I wrote a review article (which was fortunately never published) about the MacBride report[1] on global communication problems. It is appropriate now to use that review as a basis for further explorations. The report, published by Unesco in 1980, was produced by an international commission set up in 1976 "to study the totality of communication problems in modern societies": it was called Many Voices, One World. The background, of course, was that at successive Unesco conferences and elsewhere there had been increasing pressure from the Third World (usually supported

185

by the Soviet Union), directed against the domination of the non-communist "Third World" by Western communication and cultural agencies. This conflict continues and, since 1980, there have been further compromise proposals which have satisfied nobody. The general position is still very much as it was then--it could hardly be otherwise--and the central issues remain.

The task set for Chairman MacBride and his team was impossible to begin with. "The totality of communication problems" has defeated attempts at elucidation since Time began. How many of us can communicate effectively, even with ourselves? The report, naturally, could not deal with such matters and concentrated on practical issues. On this level (that of global politics and economics) the remit was impossible for other reasons, the main one being that the members of the Commission (mostly journalists) were drawn from various countries representing the conflicting power blocs in the world, and their views were incompatible in consequence. Under such circumstances it is remarkable that the Commission was able to produce a report at all. As two of the Third World members observed (p. 281), the result was more "a negotiated document than an academic presentation." As a "study," therefore, it has little coherence and, since its recommendations are mostly imprecise generalizations, we need not pursue them here. But certain interlinked issues of quite basic importance are embedded in the pages of the report. In particular the following can be extracted.

1. The theoretical problems concerning the nature of communications: these are partly matters of terminology but the implications go far beyond definitions.

2. The economic conflict between North and South as they appear, for example, in the Brandt report. [2]

3. The political factors which are implicit in the concept of a free flow of information.

In this survey I am concerned with all of these issues, but especially with the first. What we need, claims the Report, is a new communication order and if we can achieve that, "Mankind will ... have made a decisive step forward on the path to freedom, democracy and fellowship." Such high-flown claims are, it appears, mandatory in documents of this kind and I suppose we should not examine them too closely. Yet as human beings we have to consider the real nature of communication since we are involved with it always--trapped, some would say, like flies in a universal web. (But where is the spider?) One recalls Sartre's gloomy dictum that Hell is other people.

In the past the communication system has often been seen as an isolated phenomenon within society, related essentially to technology; divorced more or less "from other aspects of society, its place in the political system, the convergence with social structures and its dependence upon cultural life are seldom given adequate thought." This statement (jaw-breaking officialese though it may be) does get it right. One consequence of this typically reductive consideration of communication "as an isolated phenomenon," or thing in itself, is that we are not sure what it is. (Oh yes, there are innumerable books but that may be partly why we do not understand.) I have quoted one of these by Wilbur Schramm[3] elsewhere, but it is worth repeating: "The more we have outlined and defined what communication is, the less we have been able to talk about it as a separate thing, for communication has no life of its own" (my emphasis).

Can we not say the same about information? To corroborate my answer to that question I examined a Symposium, Information Science: Search for Identity,[4] edited by Anthony Debons, which records the proceedings of the 1972 NATO Advanced Study Institute in Information Science. This remarkable work includes the results of deliberations by over one hundred participants, most of whom are well known as pioneers in that field. Their findings are wholly in tune, if only by implication, with what I am trying to get at here. For example, concerning special issues Walter Stern observes, "The really important issues now to be faced ... are no longer technical, but those of social responsibility" ("An overview ...," p. 285). Bearing in mind the NATO sponsorship, such matters could not be pursued very far, but at least the point is made. (One is reminded of the "think tanks" which helped to prosecute the Vietnam War.) Concerning the nature of information, three quotations should suffice: "What can be doubted is man's understanding of information ... its constitution, generation, use and transfer" (Debons, p. iv); or "The most conspicuous thing is that it is not clear what the information science field is" (J. C. Licklider: "An Overview," p. 453). And finally, Allen Kent: "The title of this paper reveals a frustration on the part of the author who has worked in the field for more than two decades" ("Unsolvable Problems," p. 299).

One is reminded of Miss Twye in Gavin Ewart's little poem:[5]

> Miss Twye was soaping her breasts in her bath
> When she heard behind her a meaning laugh
> And, to her amazement she discovered
> A wicked man in the bathroom cupboard.

Somewhere behind these phenomena and the people who write the books about them, there is always that "meaning laugh."

Naturally the report had to grapple with definitions and it immediately noted the confusion. As one of the Commission members remarked (p. 279), "in a part of the literature the two terms 'information' and 'communication' are often confused or used indiscriminately," and the Soviet representative stated that in Russian the two words usually have the same meaning. In English, at any rate, the word communication usually (but not always) implies a two-way process involving an exchange, while information tends to be one-way; however, even information may elicit a response, usually called "feedback." Here we are not dwelling on this distinction but are more anxious to examine the definition of information only. In the Report, information is regarded as an end product, and this is perfectly sensible. Yet we cannot but be aware that the word is used in other ways, and often it refers to a source of information, or sometimes to a process.

But this is not the end of the matter since the alleged terminological confusion reflects underlying contradictions. A leading Soviet authority[6] does recognize the difficulty, although he dismisses it as unimportant. "What is the reason for evolutions in the meaning of the word 'information'? The reason is its rather strange character, its elasticity that is so loathsome to the scientist." Or again, "No matter what are the variations in the meaning of the word 'information' the important thing remains that it carries intelligence, tells us something, i. e., puts an end to the lack of knowledge, destroys uncertainty" (my emphasis). (Well, yes, perhaps it may do that, but more information data often increase uncertainty.) Elsewhere in the same work he notes that "Scientists are not afraid to concede that they have totally ignored the human value of information." In spite of this admission of doubt, it is clear that this description rests on a materialist concept of Reality and what, I believe, is called the "correspondence" theory of knowledge. From this point

of view information is simply a data system of the world
around us.   These philosophical foundations are beyond our
scope or my abilities, but they have to be mentioned in
passing since everything depends on what we consider Reality to be.   (From evidence supplied by psychologists we know
that more people have been driven mad by epistemological
obsessions than by any other problem in philosophy with the
possible exception of the freedom of the will.)

Returning to our definitions, it remains to record that
Anthony Smith[7] defines information "as a kind of raw material which is contained within the product whose manufacture
depends upon it. "   This analogy is apt and does describe
what happens.   He might also have added that when it is
used, it is not, like other materials, used up.   One is still
left with a certain amount of "loathsome elasticity. "   Why is
this?   The Concise Encyclopedia of Computer Technology[8]
defines information as "the meaning attached to data. "   If
we use this simple definition (as I think we should) the problem is clarified considerably.   There are three elements involved:

1.   The sources (the information data).
2.   Technical and social activity (the information process
     commonly called retrieval).
3.   The finished product (information data organized as
     information for a particular purpose).

I am concerned to emphasize here that the process
(item 2 above) is not only technical but also social.   That is
where the human values are attached and that is the key to
an understanding of the matter.   It is this part of the equation which has been neglected.   It should be clear that data
by themselves are inert and meaningless.   In this sense
there is no information in the world: the data do not become
informative until somebody makes them so.   Who then is the
"somebody" going to be?   Before answering that question we
should note that new terminology has had to be invented to
allow for the wider implications I have described.   The
French refer to the technical components as télématique and
the British use the term Information technology: there is
now a junior Minister of Information who operates within the
government's Department of Industry.   However, these words
refer mainly to the technological aspects.   The totality of information problems can be embraced only by using the word
Informatics, which was coined in the Soviet Union in 1966.
As D. J. Foskett[9] recorded in 1973, the original outline (as

given by Mikhailov and Ciljarevskij) did mention the study of information needs and other disciplines including classification and psychology. It does encompass, therefore, the social content I have stressed. Yet, as Foskett also notes in the same article, there is a tendency to use the term Informatics as if it were limited to information technology only. It is my impression, therefore, that at least in a Western context, these wider social, economic and cultural matters have not been sufficiently explored. This applies not only to Informatics in the widest sense, but also to information itself, which should be regarded as a social process.

Let us now consider who it is that adds meaning to the data. The information scientist does not do this, unless he is exceeding his responsibilities. He does, of course, act as a catalyst since it is he who searches the data file, but he does so only in response to the requirements of his client. This is the traditional limitation inherent in information work and it is a dependence which may give rise to acute ethical dilemmas. One has only to think of the use which, in South Africa, is made of data about race relations to see the point. However, we should qualify this assessment by noting that on a technical level, current trends have increased the status of the searcher since the client is usually unable to use the file and is dependent on the techniques of those who work the system. As an American authority observed, 10 "The researcher meanwhile may sit mutely attempting to conjure up in his mind the magic words to open the electronic cornucopia ... there is the beginning of a technology determining the direction research takes." This raises the possibility, which causes so much current disquiet, that the technicians may take over our lives and that a small group of people will control our destinies. But this has not happened yet and the real issue is more complex, since it involves the relationships among technologists who work the machines, technocrats who run the political and economic system, and the statesmen who are supposed to be in charge. It is the probability of their integration into a new and formidable combination which is disturbing.

Although the importance of information has been constantly stressed, not least by librarians themselves, it is now a commonplace that in most countries (particularly those outside the two communist blocs), a lack of recognition has always been a major obstacle to library development. When the MacBride report appeared, representations were made to the Commission by a committee of the British Library Association that little if any attention had been given to the library's role in communication processes. This has been typical in studies of the kind and it reflects an attitude which is quite general. As one traveler declared:[11] "During 30 years experience as a senior library administrator and a traveller to all but one of the earth's continents, I have not met a human community, however literate and numerate, where there existed a genuine popular understanding of what information services are about."

The usual professional reaction is that librarians have failed in their attempts to demonstrate the key role which libraries and information services should play. And there the matter rests except for occasional speculations. Some more recent contributions, however, have acknowledged that this kind of explanation will not do. For instance, Lamia Salman,[12] in analyzing a report on the information needs of eight developing countries, noted that although in all these countries the essential infrastructure existed, yet there was a "discrepancy between the services and the real needs of users." He then goes on to state (p. 248), "The fact that many potential users are not motivated (or not even interested in) the matter is largely due to social, cultural and educational factors that have yet to be fully classified." This survey is an attempt to provide some pointers towards that classification.

It is clearly ridiculous to stop at a point where we are simply implying that the majority of people everywhere are too stupid or perverse to understand the importance of information services. It seems to me that the real answer is to be found in the nature of information work and our perception of it. For a long time it has been known that information data may not be used even when they are available. The "retrieval" of information is a complex social process where many different factors interact, and if some of these factors are absent and others are hostile to the use of the data, no information will "flow." As I have noted elsewhere,[13] in developing countries the reasons for these blockages are often connected with the nature of political power in society. I have suggested also that they are wholly related to the fact that the information is generated elsewhere in the world. The same or similar obstacles prevent the "flow" proceeding from advanced countries in the "North" to those which are less advanced in the "South." Unless these political and economic factors are understood, our perception about information will continue to be inadequate.

The first requirement is that we should stop making grandiose claims for the role of information. Referring to communication generally, the MacBride report notes (p. 16), "Communication has frequently been invested with absolute and omnipresent powers. Such oversimplification has been made obsolete by modern research. Communication's ability to activate, socialize, homogenize and even adapt people to their own culture has <u>always</u> <u>been</u> <u>overestimated</u>" (my emphasis). Librarians have made <u>similar</u> <u>claims</u>, no less exaggerated, on behalf of library and information services. These statements, when they are not simply professional propaganda, are naive mystifications. It can be shown, for example, that many people need not have died from disease or starvation if certain "information" had been available. But the emphasis has to be on the <u>if</u>. It may not have been available for all kinds of reasons quite independent of the data. Often these reasons are psychological: the obstacles are in the minds of men and women.

Let us take modern Iran as an example. Iran under the Shah was, it appeared, becoming totally "westernized" and the Americans were confident that this process would continue; all the data seemed to confirm this. There was an enormous <u>quantity</u> of "information" to prove it. Yet the predictions all went wrong because the minds of the mass of the people in Iran were influenced by quite other considerations. At the present time (1982), human waves of young boys are being sent by miscellaneous Ayatollahs to certain death in the war against Iraq; they "know" they will enter Paradise. Who is to tell them that they have been misinformed perhaps? (In their world there was no "perhaps.") It is phenomena like these which the new science of Informatics will have to analyze. It will have to take account of the fact that Islam (a closed information network based on revelation) is also international. Similarly, the Roman Catholic church has been transnational for centuries: the internationalizing of information is not a new phenomena.

Because of these non-technical forces, information workers are controlled by other people. So are we all, but there are different kinds and degrees of dependence. All the mass media of communication have these characteristics. For example, a person who reads the news on the radio or television is wholly dependent on those who prepare the bulletin, and they in turn work within guidelines provided by program controllers and so on through many ramifications. Somewhere beyond all these processes are the original data, that peculiar raw material which is itself the result of mental activity. (Charles Dickens' Mr. Gradgrind was mistaken in supposing that facts are things.)

At the present time the library profession's perception of itself has to be modified in response to the rise of the new technological information industry. There was, of course, always a gap between the humanist tradition of general librarianship and the new specialist world of documentation, which, in particular fields carried information processes to a higher level. However, in Britain at least, the organized profession managed to keep some kind of umbrella over the various activities and organizations involved. Moreover, in recent years it has been recognized that a collective approach is necessary in order to negotiate with government agencies which have been set up to promote technical information. These developments, however tentative, are welcome but there are other trends which are more disturbing.

Important new information ventures have been proliferating without reference to libraries at all, and doubtless similar trends are noticeable in other industrial countries. The promoters of these activities are not primarily concerned with social responsibility and their interests are commercial and industrial rather than professional. In Britain they include the Post Office system called PRESTEL, which is a promotive version of high-capacity domestication information which will eventually invade our homes. To illustrate professional reactions, some comments in the official professional journal in Britain are relevant: "Non-librarians and even anti-librarians are now forcing the pace. The information trade is now largely in the hands of systems analysts, educational technologists, marketing executives and post office enquirers. They are doing the research and producing the goods with resources which once might have gone into libraries. "14 This reaction is understandable, but what these developments really signify is still a matter of dispute. We can find evidence for the variety of responses by simply looking at one issue of the Library Association Record (January 1981). There one will find a county librarian saying, "Books are an old-fashioned way of passing information. Libraries should be into electronics. " He proposes therefore to abolish all reference departments in the library system. On another page a prominent member of the Institute of Information Scientists announces the demise of librarianship, while on the contrary a representative from Aslib's research department states that "we are still miles away from designing systems anyone would find easy to use. " Furthermore, "the new information systems are inadequate for the job and they are liable to hide more information than they disclose. " Finally, a director of the Information Industries Association, Washington, USA, says that "he expected studies of how the mind worked to result in equipment that would handle information in a much improved fashion within five or six years. " A spot check of this kind has, of course, a very limited value, but it serves to indicate the contradictions involved.

I am not competent to pursue the technical arguments (and it is on that level which most of the discussions proceed); instead, we are exploring some of the social factors inherent in informatics. In "advanced" countries there is an urgent need to coordinate or rationalize the older library structures and the new information systems. In the USA and Britain, for example, steps have been taken toward that end and new government agencies have been set up. These matters, important as they are, do not concern us here since our theme is international, with particular reference to the relations between North and South. The evolving reality is that the societies of the Third World are dependent, in the field of information as in others, on the metropolitan centers: that was the reason why the MacBride Commission was set up.

It is sufficiently obvious that the Communist blocs do not agree that a free flow of information is either necessary or desirable. It is important to understand why. In a basic reservation to the recommendations of the MacBride report (p. 279), the representative of the Soviet Union remarked, "It is unfortunate that sometimes we are catching up already old-fashioned and used trite formulas such as the notion of a free flow of information. " (The translation is bad but the meaning is clear.) Or again, "The right to communicate is too widely discussed, though the right has not gained any international recognition in any of the countries represented in the Commission. " No sensitive person would endorse the lack of intellectual freedom within the Soviet system and my purpose here is not to defend it. This, however, is not the point at issue, since it is obvious enough. My concern here is to emphasize a different kind of non-freedom in the capitalist part of the world, where the information flow is not "free" because it is determined by economic forces which penetrate dependent countries by means of the new technologies. As Anthony Smith declared:[15] "We are beginning to learn that decolonization and the growth of supranationalism were not the termination of imperial relationships but merely the extension of a geo-political web which has been growing since the Renaissance. The new media have the power to penetrate more deeply into a receiving culture than any previous manifestation of western technology. The results could be immense havoc, an intensification of the social contradictions within developing societies today. "

In this respect the information industry is no different from any other: that is how neo-colonialism works. Instead of quoting further evidence from the literature it is perhaps more useful to mention a concrete example from our own experience in Nigeria, a developing country which is more autonomous than most because of its oil resource. In our town all the modern communication media were available: radio and television are nationally owned: there are indigenous periodicals (printed in Europe mostly), and even some Nigerian publishers. At first sight then, it might appear that communications flow freely, since Nigeria is a relatively open society. Yet the equipment and almost all the messages come from Western sources--when they come at all. Libraries are severely hampered in their book provision because of import controls. National newspapers have to rely on one or two multi-national news agencies. There is the beginning of a film industry but most films--a very popular form of entertainment--come either from USA or most often from Bombay or Hong Kong. Educated people have to get world news either from the BBC or from Time magazine or Newsweek, both of which are notorious for their distortion of African reality. On TV the proportion of good Nigerian programs is increasing but most of the films shown are either British or American. There are also well known American or British series such as Steptoe and Son or At Your Service, most of which would seem to be inappropriate, even incomprehensible. (But one has to remember that they are watched mainly by members of an élite who have often spent years overseas.) This may serve to remind us that in the Third World the mass media are not really "mass, " since only some of the masses are exposed to them. Even radio has a limited impact on illiterate people except for the music. The media are geared towards a minority audience, as is particularly noticeable in TV advertising. In our context the most significant foreign program is Sesame Street, which is discussed below. On the level of personal communication, one feels impelled to add that the internal postal system is spasmodic and telephones rarely work. Power cuts are also frequent so that some communications, especially TV, are intermittent. Not all these limitations can be directly attributed to a dependence on foreign resources, but indirectly most of them can.

Sesame Street, the American children's program which is shown almost daily, merits special attention. Started by the Children's Television Workshop set up in 1968, it was financed from Government and business corporations (the Federal grant was later stopped). It has developed into a major institution with a world-wide impact, since it is now shown in at least 90 countries. It was originally designed to help integrate ethnic (especially Hispanic) minorities and it portrays a world from which all strife has been eliminated, where everyone loves everyone else and where children large or small are assumed to have a mental age of four. Because of this, liberal observers both in the USA and elsewhere have been enthusiastic; it was also warmly welcomed by the Unesco Courier. Linda Blandford ("Amer-Diary," The Guardian, 24 Nov., 1982) considered that it is the only cultural manifestation left from the peace and love movement in the sixties. She reported that "at 123 Sesame Street, the most famous address in America, live the only black, Hispanic and white Americans who exist beyond the stereotypes of colour and race" (class might have been mentioned also). The workshop's successful formula is based on techniques taken from commercial television. It is, of course, highly effective and characters like Big Bird are now universally loved. However, there have been American critics of this dream world, since the USA is not, after all, like that. The possible impact on Third World countries (which are not like that either and usually do not have a color problem) has also been deplored by radical or nationalist critics.

For example, the BBC rejected the program in 1970 and the decision still stands. (It was due, however, to start up on Thames Television at the end of 1982.) The explanation offered by the BBC's Head of Children's Programmes is interesting, even if its superior tone is unfortunate. She stressed that the program (after intensive audience research) is based on the TV experience of American children "who until now have watched endless cartoons, soap operas and crime series.... Do we really have to import commercial hard-selling techniques into our own programmes because Sesame Street researchers tell us that in America, children will not listen to anything quiet or thoughtful? Sesame Street is an outcome of a philosophy of ever-available

'wallpaper' TV programming. American children watch television for hours on end" (The Guardian, 22 December, 1970).
She goes on to claim that BBC programs are designed to dis-
courage passive box-watching. In other European countries
the program has been "adapted, " which is not difficult as it
is designed to be international in the sense that it need not
obviously refer to anywhere.

        Granted that the content is educational and entertain-
ing, why should anyone complain? In the Third World the
main objection is not that children will be positively harmed
by this exposure but that it cannot contribute to the development of themselves or their societies. They usually live in
an environment where class and ethnic strife are endemic.
Our own children, for example, once watched the program
when tear gas smoke from riot police was drifting into the
house. But in the nowhere land on the box there is no tear
gas, only universal love. If it were obviously fairy land, no
one could object, but it is not: somewhere these children do
exist, possibly in America. I have used this industry as an
example of a new culture based on the USA. World-wide
influence is also exerted by Reader's Digest, which bases its
appeal on the use of local languages. It now circulates in
more than 100 countries and is published in 14 languages.
Similarly, Playboy claims 28 million readers in 156 terri-
tories. (In view of its price this is somewhat surprising.)
All these cultural exports are only international in a very
peculiar sense and in this respect they resemble the products
of other American multi-national companions.

        Meanwhile the information industry is making dramatic
advances in space and up there a large quantity of ironmon-
gery is whirling round. (If it were visible we might sit up
and take notice.) After the moon had been visited it became evident that further attempts to colonize the remoter
parts of the universe would be most uneconomic. Bearing
in mind the requirements of the cold war (and the demands
of the armament industry) the super-powers switched their
attention and their resources to the alleged information needs
of this world. Information data could be collected by satellites without let or hindrance, and some of it could be transmitted to people everywhere whether they wanted it or not.
Also in the USA, the multi-national firms produced not only
information but education programs which have been geared
to the special needs of a number of countries, including Can-
ada, Indonesia and several in Latin America. For example,
educational programs have been designed in the USA which

can be transmitted by satellite direct to the TV sets in Latin American homes, and there is no need to go through ground relay stations. Many countries have resisted this kind of penetration, yet they lack the technology to do the job themselves. The companies which install the systems can then open up opportunities for the sale of every kind of telecommunications equipment. (A bizarre footnote to this story was provided by the ill-fated birth-control campaign set up by Mrs. Gandhi in India, when transistor radios supplied by American aid were supplied free to all those who agreed to undergo vasectomy.) Meanwhile, the systems in space have now photographed 90 per cent of the earth's surface. (One wonders about the other 10 per cent: it seems possible that a few penguins or the odd polar bear have escaped observation.)

It will be apparent that in this account I am presenting these developments as somewhat sinister manifestations of cultural imperialism (sinister because they relate to a domination which is disguised). I have taken much of the evidence from the comprehensive survey by Armand Mattelart,[16] who was formerly an advisor to the late President Allende in Chile. Using a Marxist analysis he has assembled a vast mass of data to build up his case against world cultural domination by the USA. "How can the freedom to exchange ideas and information be effectively defined in a situation characterized by such power relations between the metropolis and the rest of the world? The thesis of liberalism in space is framed by the principles of commercial freedom: liberalism equals the liberty to dominate" (p. 94). (The remaining 35 per cent of the world is, of course, dominated by the communist great powers, which make no pretense that they are concerned with freedom of information).

Perhaps it is superfluous to add that the interpretation I have accepted here is not shared by everyone, and that many have welcomed the concept of a free flow with enthusiasm. Such views are naturally shared by the agencies themselves, who tend to claim that the poor countries will stand to benefit because they need not do anything at all apart from accepting the services offered. Yet the countries at the receiving end of these systems are inevitably in a subservient position. As Smith states,[17] "a society with no access to satellite sensoring about itself is unable to control its own economic destiny and can in no real sense any longer be thought to be free." (One might add that it cannot control its own destiny for other reasons as well, and many observers, including some members of Third World governments, adopt a "realistic" line and contend that such lack of freedom is inevitable: that is how the world is and it has to be accepted at least for the time being.) Smith also points out that although information is generated by society as a whole, it has to be allocated to specific interests in order to be exploited. Information, therefore, may "flow" only within special groups or for specified purposes. It may be that the electronic media themselves tend to produce closed circuits. Curiously enough, we are recreating on another level the restrictive systems which are characteristic of "primitive" societies.

Here we are primarily concerned with the use of information by transnational organizations. Russell Doll[18] has claimed that "telecommunication is a revolution in information consolidation and access on a scale unknown in human history." It is a new form of Power which "will be exercised through institutions mainly in business and industry. Those who have access to this form of power will have a greater potential for determining events and these will be the large corporations. The multi-national corporations unlike national governments have no constituency to answer and they have world-wide resource bases and need not support the often wasteful superstructures which comprise national governments." He concludes that the transnational companies will eventually supersede the national states. It seems to me that this analysis is false because it ignores the fact that in the USA especially, the multi-nationals are totally interlinked with government agencies, so that there is a permanent alliance between the state apparatus and the big manufacturers of the new technologies. Universities and other research organizations are also part of the network. Thus, although bodies like Intelsat are presented as international, they are in fact largely controlled by American government agencies. (There is a rival satellite network called Intersputnik linking the Eastern European countries except Yugoslavia, and a West European project called Euronet which was created to offset American domination.)

This electronic industry has potentialities for unlimited expansion. As somebody has said, "There is a gold mine in the sky" and those who participate in the new gold rush are helping to create the new information order in the USA, a country where considerably more than half the active population is engaged in collecting, treating and transmitting information. Yet, as Unesco's Director of General Information has pointed out,[19] "... in the 1980s the developing countries will witness the advent of the information society without being able to participate in it except in a dependent role which is likely to increase their debts. "

We can now return to the possible world order in bibliographical information. For centuries dreams have existed that a system might be constructed which would list all items published anywhere, past or present. Dedicated individuals have been obsessed by this task and have sometimes impaired their health and even their sanity in consequence. Now at last the non-human machines have arrived and the task seems possible. International projects already exist to carry out this purpose: their aims have been defined as UBC (Universal Bibliographical Control) and as a necessary corollary UAP (Universal Availability of Publications). Systems have already been created in particular fields, for example UNISIST and NATIS. At first sight these concepts seem wholly admirable, yet even the terminology is misleading since bibliography is only a process and cannot control anything, while "availability" is almost mystical in its vagueness. On a practical level what the terms refer to is technically possible, but underdeveloped countries cannot be plugged into the world system because their own bibliographic services have not reached the required level. These schemes therefore must remain remote possibilities.

As George Chandler observes, [20] these projects amount to "an attempt to create and disseminate impractical schemes based upon theory, rather than upon the bedrock of reality. " He notes that Unesco "has increasingly followed this road by its advocacy of UNISIST and that of NATIS and now of the General Information Programme and its proposed successor, the New World Information Order. " (I would not myself condemn them because they are theoretical but rather because the theories themselves are inadequate. One would not wish to set up this "pragmatic" distinction between theory and practice.) Whatever the explanation, the needs of poor countries are unlikely to be met. Yet once again twittering voices have been raised as if these schemes were already real. The concept of interdependence must, for the time being at least, remain an irrelevant fantasy and libraries may need to have other priorities. For example, D. E. K. Wijasuriya, [21] referring to Asia, observes: "Viewed from an overall national standpoint we are not as concerned with increasing access to documents from the developed countries of the world--for we already have reasonable access--as we are with providing access to information or published documents for our people,

(a) in a language they can understand, and (b) at a level they can comprehend. "

In any event the listing of items is only the beginning of bibliography: lists of items consist of data which correspond to data in other fields. It is a necessary foundation, but that is all: there is no meaning attached until some kind of selection takes place and this is a social activity moderated by human values. Eventually this will have to be done at local national levels. (It is not always appreciated that bibliographical work is no different in this respect from other information activities. An informative abstract, for example, is a summary slanted towards the requirements of the client.) The consequence is that in developing countries, even when the data are available (which they often are not), they cannot be used because of the low level of indigenous bibliographical activity. It is safe to assume that the promoters of UAP or UBC (or some of them) are aware of these obstacles. The solutions, of course, must eventually come from outside the realms of bibliography.

So far we have ignored the existence of general libraries where the bulk of our intellectual heritage is still stored. They include the sciences, of course, but their unique contribution is to preserve and make available the literature in humanistic fields. Although all the records can be mechanized it would seem that the material in their collections is less amenable to electronic exploitation. For some purposes this will be possible (for example when individuals need to refer to particular known items), but for many other purposes the evidence suggests that these libraries will be used in the traditional manner and that people will read printed material as they do now. However, we should acknowledge that the protagonists of electronic information claim that by the year 2000 we shall not use paper or print any more at all. These assertions rest on faith rather than convincing evidence: in such a case one is permitted to have doubts, and the following are some of them.

Many of the articles (such as that of Lancaster[22] in 1978) which take this line read like an inferior kind of science fiction. Their authors write from within a technical frame of reference only, which the better science fiction writers do not. In science and technology there can be no doubt that it is no longer economic to rely on traditional print methods for the transmission of quantities of information. In these areas the electronic media are taking over and the sooner we are rid of most of this paper, the better. The information "explosion" may be real enough but it is also and perhaps mainly a vast increase in recorded information, much of which is rubbish--or wholly ephemeral. (It is comforting to think that all this will be stored away in electronic form and presumably there need be only one of each item stored anywhere.) In the humanities, on the other hand, the amount of rubbish does not "explode" in the same way: the literature does not "advance" and can therefore be economically contained. One imagines also that even though readers (assuming they have access to a terminal) may read passages which they formerly found in books and periodicals, they will still need paper and print for many purposes: the electronic media will be supplementary. Literature searches in these fields are far from rational. How will the machines help when we do not know what we are looking for? (Formerly we were helped by "browsing" or serendipidity.) There are, no doubt, electronic "insights" but will they correspond with my own?

This last point raises the further possibility that if the data are organized according to principles or a view of the world which I do not share, they may well become inaccessible or unresponsive to my particular needs. Would the information scientist be able to do anything about this?-- presumably not. One can envisage a situation where minority groups would be denied access to a data base either by deliberate exclusion or because their mental patterns did not correspond to that of the base. In such an event they might gain more inspiration from a blank page or a broken terminal.

It must also be said that these visions of a paperless future are ethnocentric and élitist: they are likely to become real only for a privileged minority in metropolitan centers. Theoretically it would be possible to transmit some kind of visual verbal message to someone sitting with a terminal under a Baobab tree outside Ouagadugu, but the image is otherwise absurd. Even in the industrialized countries, at a popular level the common reader of print--meaning Everyman--will survive: recreational and cultural literature will still be required since electronic equivalents will be either inconvenient or too expensive. It has been said that it is science which makes life possible, but only non-scientific perceptions--against all the odds--can make life tolerable.

To return finally to the political implications of the MacBride report, it is indeed true that there are "many voices. " But except in a geographical sense there is not one world, nor any possibility of one information system. The existing "worlds, " whether one holds the view that there are three or two or more, are likely to proliferate. The "free flow" concepts rest on a theory of interdependence which ignores global political and economic realities as they are at the present time. Those who support these ideas often admit that these realities exist but claim that the current relationship between North and South must be changed since the alternative is disaster. This is the message of the Brandt report and represents policies usually adopted by centrist political parties such as the SDP in Britain. (How this change is to be brought about is not at all clear.) A more sophisticated approach, such as that pursued by President Mitterand of France, considers that if the needs of the South continue to be ignored by the North, then the countries in question will turn to some form of communism and/or the Soviet Union.

Both of these policies are sympathetic to the demands of the Third World. Yet such changes could only come about if they were accompanied by radical changes in the social relations within the underdeveloped countries themselves. This is the crux of the matter and it is, in fact, admitted at one point in the MacBride report: "It is becoming increasingly clear that reference to the misdeeds and distortion of communication means in effect reference to the contradictions inherent in contemporary societies. " Yet as far as the Third World is concerned, any radical attempt to remove these "contradictions"--a euphemism for various kinds of gross oppression--are likely to be met, as in Nicaragua and central America, by destabilization strategies from the governments of the USA and some of her allies, including Britain. We are driven back once more to the image of Miss Twye in her bath and the meaning laugh of the wicked man in the cupboard.

I should end by noting what our conclusions have been. I have suggested, first, that it is misleading to use the word information when only data is meant. Information is not "retrieved" but created or manufactured for particular purposes by using the data. Second, the term "information society" refers to the fact that the information industry in the USA (and to a lesser extent in other developed countries) is producing huge quantities of electronic equipment which, for commercial and strategic reasons, is being exported to the rest of the world: the "transnational" companies are the main agents in this process. It is only in this sense that there is a world order. Finally, I have ventured to predict that our print culture will continue to be alive and well. Electronics will complement print and will help us to dispose of a waste-paper mountain.

Meanwhile, librarians and other communication people must continue to act as if a free flow of information were possible. Like all other dedicated workers everywhere, they will do what they can. I have made a plea that they should also know what they are doing.

References

1. Unesco. Many Voices, One World: Report by the International Commission for the Study of Development Problems (The MacBride Report). Unesco, 1980.

2. Independent Commission on International Development Issues. North-South: a Programme for Survival (The Brandt Report). Pan Books, 1980.

3. Schramm, Wilbur. Mass Media and National Developments: the Role of Information in Developing Countries. Stanford University Press, 1964.

4. Debons, Anthony, ed. Information Science: Search for Identity. Marcel Dekker, Inc., 1974.

5. Ewart, Gavin. "Miss Twye," The New Oxford Book of Light Verse, p. 281. Oxford University Press, 1979.

6. Pekelis. Cybernetics A-Z. Moscow: Mir Publishers, p. 152.

7. Smith, Anthony. The Geopolitics of Information: How Western Culture Dominates the World. Faber, 1980, p. 112.

8. Stokes, Adrian. Concise Encyclopedia of Computer Terminology. Gower Publications, Ltd., 1980.

9. Foskett, D. J. "Information Science as an Emergent Discipline: Educational Implications," Journal of Librarianship, Vol. 5, 1973, p. 161.

10. Doll, Russell. "Information Technology and Its Socio-economic and Organic Impact," Online Review, Feb. 1981.

11. Borchardt, D. H. "Aspects of Library and Information Services in the Framework of Social Policy Planning," International Library Review, Vol. 9 (4), Oct. 1977.

12. Salman, Lamia. "The Information Needs of the Developing Countries," Unesco Journal, Oct.-Dec. 1981, p. 241.

13. Benge, R. C. Cultural Crisis and Libraries in the Third World. London: Bingley, 1979.

14. Harris, K. C. E. "Ostrich Librarianship," Library Association Record, December 1980, p. 569.

15. Smith, Anthony, op. cit., p. 114.

16. Mattelart, Armand. Multi-national Corporations and the Control of Culture: the Ideological Apparatuses of Imperialism. (Formerly published in France, 1976). Brighton: Harvester Press, 1979. New Jersey: Humanities Press, 1979.

17. Smith, Anthony, op. cit., p. 176.

18. Doll, Russell, op. cit.

19. Tocatlian, Jacques. "Information for Development: the Role of Unesco's General Information Programme," Unesco Journal, Vol. III, No. 3, Jul.-Sep. 1981.

20. Chandler, George. "The Internationalisation of Library Literature," Focus on International and Comparative Librarianship," Vol. 13, No. 2 (50), 1982.

21. Wijasieriya, D. E. K. "UAP and the Development of National Information Systems," Unesco Journal, Vol. IV, No. I, Jan.-March 1982.

22. Lancaster, F. Wilfrid. "Whether Libraries or Wither Libraries?" College and Research Libraries, Sept. 1978, p. 345-357.

2.   LIBRARY OBJECTIVES IN AFRICA

It has been recognized for a long while that library objectives in Africa need to be more carefully worked out. In this contribution I wish to examine why it is that neither the eastern nor the western models have been suitable, and why it has been so difficult to formulate new goals.   This is, of course, not just a theoretical exercise and we are considering a historical context where Western professional objectives were transferred to Africa as part of the colonial process.   I shall also refer to the role of the library schools and the library profession in that endeavor.

The present library systems in the non-communist world, and especially the public libraries of U. S. A., Scandinavia and the British Commonwealth, were associated with the growth of capitalist democracy in the nineteenth century and librarians naturally reflected that liberal ideology, the main element of which was an emphasis on the reading needs of individuals rather than a consideration of a national system.   The perception is apparent in some of the library slogans once familiar in Britain, for instance, "self-development in an atmosphere of freedom" or "the right book for the right reader at the right time"--very quaint and unsophisticated they seem to us now.   The concept was that people have not only a duty but a right to develop themselves, and this directly reflects the existence of a dominant middle class.   In Britain, for example, the members of this class (mostly in a political, religious or charitable context) carried out multifarious educational and cultural activities outside of the formal education structure.   Such work was also undertaken by the organized working class in Mechanics Institutes and by the Trade Unions, although in their case the social and political objectives were more in evidence.

There was already a tension or conflict between the public and private sectors which has persisted ever since and has been reflected in professional ideology.   This is apparent even in Ranganathan's Laws of Library Science since some of these refer to the individual and others are collective, for example, "Books are for all. "   He was well aware that in his native India books were not for all, if only because the majority of the people could not read yet; the implications were never fully worked out.   Certainly after a struggle it was accepted that local government should provide library service of a very limited kind, but the laissez-faire notion sur-

vived that individuals should be left alone as much as possible.
One trend was exemplified in the liberalism of John Stuart
Mill, which eventually led to the advance of Fabian gradualist
socialism. This movement ultimately brought about the welfare state, where it became generally accepted (in Britain at
least) that there should be an organized national library service as a state responsibility. Meanwhile, in the hundred
and fifty years following the industrial revolution, uncoordi-
nated and separate types of library service had proliferated.
Partly because of this, perhaps, members of the library profession still tended to think mainly in terms of personal service to individuals.

That this tradition is still very much alive was brought
home to me when, in 1981, I was involved in a British Library Association exercise aimed at producing a Code of Ethics. A draft code had been published and members of the
Association were invited to comment. I was asked to sum-
marize their reactions to the proposed code. What impressed
me was that both the code itself and the comments--over one
hundred of them--were largely concerned with individual ethics rather than social responsibilities, presumably on the
grounds that ethical problems are personal.

This is the individualist tradition we have been discussing. Certainly the quintessential professional act is interpersonal, as is evident in the work of lawyers, priests
and doctors. They are crisis professions and their members
are needed when something has gone wrong. (In the same
way the armed forces have a social role until peace breaks
down, and it is only then that they start killing other people--
an interpersonal act.) Philip Larkin--himself a librarian--
expressed this in a striking image in his poem:

Days

What are days for?
Days are when we live
They come, they wake us
Time and time over
They are to be happy in
Where can we live but days?

Ah, solving that question
Brings the priest and the doctor
In their long coats
Running over the fields

In the case of librarians you could say that anyone urgently needing information is in a crisis of sorts, but the urgency is less. Librarians do not run over the fields, either literally or metaphorically, and their consultancy role, however important, is likely to be low key. Their contribution is to be there all the time and to be conspicuous only when they are absent. This is their social role and it can be compared to community medicine, which is very important but not so obtrusive as the individual diagnosis. At the present time, because of recent technological changes involving information, these social responsibilities have become more urgent than in the past. Yet--at least from the evidence of that 1981 Library Association exercise--it would appear that dedicated librarians (both those who drew up the code and those who made comments on it) still tend to think mainly in terms of their relationship with individual users of libraries. It is possible that they are happy to leave the national responsibilities to those of their members who are active in professional organizations. Yet professional leaders and the administrative staff of library associations are supposed to represent the views of their members: this becomes difficult when they have no views. When such a stage is reached professional bodies lose touch with their members. I should add that the code in its draft form was not adopted, an outcome which surprised hardly anyone.

So far I have concentrated on this one aspect because it was a central element in the assumptions which were transferred to Africa as part of the Colonial enterprise. Also, I have emphasized its traditional historical significance because by itself it is no longer a satisfactory objective, even in the advanced countries where it developed. In Third World countries there is, as a general rule, no socially responsible middle class and these societies are not yet pluralistic in the sense that multifarious influences can be brought to bear upon individuals. Certainly there are conflicting voices but the main conflict is between the traditions of the tribe and those of modernization. This is not pluralism in the liberal sense because such influences tend to cancel each other out. Furthermore, you cannot tell an illiterate peasant to go away and develop himself: he has nowhere to go and, except at a material level, he is unaware of his own needs.

The significant exception is and always has been the work done by religious organizations, whether they have been colonial or indigenous. Priests and mullahs have, for their own purposes, brought education and literacy to many people who, again for their own reasons, have been glad to accept these civilizing benefits: this is the credit side. On the debit side is the ironic fact that the great "religions of the Book" have usually been fundamentalist and therefore not interested in multiple influences or other books. In addition, all of them have been exclusive and have fostered the disastrous concept of a Chosen People. (This phenomenon has been noticeable everywhere, not least in the USA and in South Africa.) It is in this respect that they have brought an opiate to the people whose eyes have been directed to a world elsewhere (it has never been suggested that there are libraries in Paradise).

To return to this world and the transfer of library objectives, we must now consider the other library purposes as usually defined. The oldest role for libraries is of course the preservation of materials, and certainly there was no need for this emphasis to be transferred since it was there already. Because of inadequate resources the preservation role receives priority even in libraries where other purposes should be paramount. Such a requirement is often not fully appreciated by impatient visitors from more affluent parts of the world. In my own case I remember recommending that public libraries in small West Indian islands should discard their copies of the memoirs of forgotten generals or the exploits of big-game hunters in a previous century. Such advice could not be acted upon and there were angry complaints in Constituent Assemblies: the alternative might have been half-empty shelves. School libraries also may have to concentrate not on the educational use of their books but on their preservation, since their collections are otherwise likely gradually to dwindle away. The only reason for stressing the role of preservation, therefore, is that it must have greater priority, especially in tropical environments. At one time there was even, for this reason, a demand that there should be a thing called "tropical librarianship." Such a perception at least indicates an embryonic appreciation of the needs of a different world. (The tendency to dwell on climatic factors came naturally to the colonial mind.)

Our next objective to be transferred is the provision of information, and here one runs up against inherent social obstacles, since most of the societies under discussion are still pre-industrial. (Library activity for this purpose has been essentially an urban phenomenon.) I have discussed this problem in the previous chapter of this book and in chapter eleven of <u>Cultural Crisis and Libraries in the Third World</u> The main arguments set out there are: first, that in the modern world most information is generated in the great metropolitan centers of the West; and secondly, that underdeveloped societies are not geared to make use of a "free flow" of information data. I am repeating this analysis here because library activists continue to make the absurd claim that a lack of information data is partly responsible for development failures. Like illiteracy, the absence of information is a symptom, not a cause of underdevelopment. The provision of information is a social process which is generated by other social forces or, alternatively, is repressed by them. The central fallacy is to imagine that if only the data can be made available, then it will be possible to make use of them. What we are faced with are not information societies but what Paulo Friere has called a "culture of silence" which, like a fog, still blankets much of the surface of the globe. Must one then conclude that the information objective should not be transferred? I do not think so. It is simply that traditional methods may not be effective and that new ways need to be developed to meet the information needs of the people, bearing in mind that these are mostly not <u>felt</u> needs and have to be identified.

We come finally to the <u>education</u> role of all types of libraries. Here, at least, it would appear that we are on firmer ground. Every international gathering has agreed that all kinds of libraries in Africa should be linked to formal education and research. This concept required some modification in the goals which public libraries had traditionally maintained in the West, but in schools, colleges, universities and special organizations it seemed to be fairly clear what needed to be done. Furthermore, it could not be said that Governments were not aware of the importance of this role. There is the difficulty, it must be admitted, that in most cases the objectives of Education and Research <u>cannot be fully realized</u> because of economic obstacles such as exchange controls, but at least the objective is valid and that is our main concern here. Yet this, alas, is not the end of the matter, since "Education" is not an end in itself. Education, but for what and for whom? And what kind of education? The official answer to these questions is now usually that the purpose of education is to <u>promote national development</u>. Here at last we arrive at an objective which can be recognized as an indigenous reality. This, then, is also the purpose of the library services.

The next task is to examine how this can be carried out, and at once the practical difficulties emerge. They arise from the fact that in most cases "national development" is a myth and a delusion. Let us take as an example the role of universities and the libraries which serve them. They obviously contribute to the national economy by producing manpower but this, in itself, does not constitute development. Ever since colonial times official reports have urged the need to relate education--at every level--to the lives of the people here and now. In spite of this awareness the practical results were not impressive, and they are not impressive now: the universities, in most cases, have continued to be "ivory towers." (Community units exist, of course, in most African universities and they do have some impact, notably in medicine and health.) In Northern Nigeria our Education Faculty was regularly asked to preside over efforts to translate these aims (which are part of official government policy) into reality. Recommendations were (ritually) made and some staff members and students went into the local township to try to improve social amenities there. But although the expertise was available, these well-meaning efforts were, in most cases, frustrated by the same social factors which had prevented development in the first place. Outside individuals might propose certain much-needed improvements (one group even worked for some long time on building a road) but they cannot provide the political will or remove obstructions which are rooted in vested interests.

The more immediate question here is what can the libraries do towards this end? The most obvious area of concern is that of the selection of materials. Librarians who do not take this task seriously have often concentrated on the acquisition and preservation of expensive historical sources. What is required, on the contrary, is a special effort to obtain material on development studies. Such efforts are necessary because items in this field are inter-disciplinary and cross-cultural. The problem of drought and/or desertification immediately comes to mind. At least a dozen different disciplines are involved and it is not just a matter of providing material for an economics library. The relevant items may be widely scattered among libraries in one country or elsewhere--in which case some kind of bibliographical center should be set up. I understand that there is a United Nations Environment Project (UNEP) located in Nairobi and that one of its divisions is an international information system called INFOTERRA. Even if locations are given for items there is still the problem of obtaining them. One would imagine that national centers are desirable in any event. In Latin America a special organization called CLADES has been set up: this is responsible for coordinating documentation on development in Latin America. In discussing this project Feliu Ximea[1] uses an appropriate term, "Desinformación": she stresses that some of the political obstacles to the flow of information can be overcome by "requiring the commitment of all participants in the development process." Whether participants can be "required" to have such an allegiance is a matter of opinion, but at least the point is made. One cannot, of course, be committed to a "process" and I would claim that a wider political commitment needs to be involved.

The fact that public libraries in Africa should redefine their objectives has also been generally accepted for a long time. The commitment to "education" has been formulated but the main stumbling block has been simply that the majority of the people are illiterate. As Andrew de Heer[2] recently noted, "the Ghana Library Board is working towards a new concept of rural library service." The significant thing about the statement is that it was made at least 30 years after the Ghana Library Board was set up. If the new concept is national development, what can the libraries do? The first requirement was to get rid of the old ideas which, as we have seen, were based on colonial or neo-colonial patterns. Yet that process is still incomplete. For example, it is a familiar fact that African public libraries tend to be filled with what are unfairly called "dropouts" from the formal education process: they use the libraries to study their textbooks. Yet their presence is often deplored and discouraged since it is alleged that they are not really using the library for reference purposes but only as a reading room. Yet if national development is to mean anything, these are the young people who should be catered to. Politicians naturally tend to want a "proper" library which can stand comparison with the best libraries anywhere. The emphasis therefore is likely to be on a prestige building. Such projects can be defended but it is well known that "misdevelopment" has produced such white elephant buildings all over the landscape, and in the process new concepts have been lost.

At first sight it would appear that the only way to build up library services for national development is an integrated plan within which the libraries can "cooperate" with other agencies, notably those for adult education, health and agriculture. The implication is that there should be a national plan; furthermore, that if there is no national integrated plan, then such services should be developed at local level. (This is what the colonialists called Community Development.) The concept is entirely sound but, except in special circumstances and to a limited degree, it cannot be translated into practice. Usually each Ministry has its own plan, but that is all. The following anecdotes may illustrate some of the difficulties involved.

In one small town (an administrative center) in Northern Nigeria there is a school library and, a few yards away, a branch of the state public library. One could be excused for thinking that the two services might somehow be combined since they both serve mostly children. Yet the Minister of Education, who was a Muslim, told me that the school children should not be allowed to use the state branch library because there they would be exposed to social abuses such as drug taking and sexual immorality. This may well have been the case but I should add that the Minister of Information, who was a Christian and responsible for the public library, told me that this was nonsense and declared that I should take no notice of that man. Under such circumstances cooperation is difficult and "integration" out of the question.

The second example concerns integrated community development. I participated in an ambitious project (financed by a Dutch firm) centered on Jos in Northern Nigeria: it was to be based on an Intermediate Technology Unit which already existed. A blueprint worked out by expatriate advisers was admirable--as a blueprint--but it could not be implemented because it took no account of the social realities of that place. There was never even a remote possibility that the various agencies involved would be able to cooperate in the manner proposed. As for the library's role, there was no "information" to coordinate.

Since this kind of integrated planning is so rarely possible librarians often fall back on priority theories, and these, it seems to me, are not helpful. They attempt to show that library provision should be a priority in a list which includes health, education and agricultural development: it is not surprising that ministers remain unconvinced. The infrastructure, meaning railways and roads, must receive priority but after that, all other services depend on each other; hence the need for simultaneous development on several fronts. The Chinese communes are (or were) a response to this need, as are the Ujaama communities in Tan-

zania. It would appear that both have been found wanting in
some respects, but they both arose from a sound analysis of
development requirements. Priority theories, on the other
hand, produce services which cannot operate because they
are disconnected from anything else. Even such a funda-
mental amenity as electric power cannot by itself transform
a community. If other developments are absent, the main
activities will continue to be sleeping and the consumption of
lethal liquor, both of which are possible without electric
light. "I have come," wrote Lenin somewhere, "to abolish
the village idiot." It would seem that we, on the contrary,
have come to put him in charge of the library.

After this brief survey we are obliged to conclude that
although national development is the right objective for libraries, there are inherent limitations which prevent that objective from being realized. I consider, however, that in
particular plans and circumstances some progress will be
made and that libraries are a necessary part of the development process. This view is based on the assumption that
national development as commonly understood is both possible
and desirable. However, it must be noted that there are
those who do not share these assumptions. Most significant
in our context is the book by Adolphe O. Amadi, called
African Libraries: Western Tradition and Colonial Brainwashing. 3 I reviewed this in Focus (1982) and will not repeat that assessment here. The important thing to note is
that this is an African, not an expatriate, contribution and
that it takes the view that Africa is not and never will be
"developed," and that libraries as they have existed elsewhere are wholly irrelevant to African needs. As the title
indicates, Amadi stresses the colonial factor and wants to go
back to the oral tradition and the kind of guru system which
flourished in ancient Timbuktu. He concentrates on the psychological legacy of Colonialism and I am sure that this
emphasis is right.

Much has been written on this need for the "decolonization of the mind" but how this will come about remains
obscure. Although it would be absurd to regard the psychology of individuals as simply a reflection of economic forces,
it is difficult to see how this decolonization can take place
while neo-colonialism remains. (There is every indication
that it will survive for a long while yet.) There will always
be exceptional individuals who may liberate themselves but
most citizens of the ex-colonies are materially still wholly
dependent on the goods and services which are produced in

the industrialized world. These imports include the majority of books, periodicals and television programs where these exist. These are the communication agencies which influence the non-material level of culture and naturally help to inhibit the growth of new modes of perception. Also, within the societies themselves the interests of the dominant groups are tied up with and dependent on external economic factors-- they are usually involved in business, not production. This being so, the "brainwashing" happens as a matter of course, and in this sense the citizens' minds are still colonized. Naturally there are ideological forces which oppose this kind of dependence but they tend to be without a power base and operate therefore in the void.

This radical view by implication rejects any attempt to modify Western library objectives in the light of African experience. The "model" therefore (if we have to use this tiresome concept) is that of traditional Africa which was there before the colonialists came. There is, however, the Eastern or Communist model, which for obvious historical reasons has not been seriously considered in Africa. Communist and democratic socialist ideology has nevertheless made some impact, if only because Unesco library recommendations have become known. These have included the requirement that library planning should be part of the national development plan. They have also made familiar the modern concept of a library service which transcends the various separate types of service which have existed for so long in the west. Finally, they have stressed the library needs of the majority of the people and have rejected élitist concepts, which usually take the form of a preoccupation with university libraries and the reading needs (if any) of the new élites.

It must be said, even so, that the objectives of libraries in Communist countries cannot be transferred at the present time, first, because most African economies are still tied to the Western world, and second, because national planning remains at a rudimentary level, partly because they are not in control of their own destinies. Furthermore, "the masses" remain largely illiterate and live still in a peasant world. The parallel is not so much with Eastern Europe today as with nineteenth-century Russia. From a liberal socialist point of view one must wholly reject the concept that literature should be rigidly controlled, yet one has to admit that communist régimes have been able to abolish illiteracy whereas "Western" policies tend to perpetuate it. (Tanzania is a special case but "socialism" there has not been able to overcome the difficulties inherent in their situation.) One is obliged to conclude, therefore, that the unique circumstances which prevailed in the Soviet Union, and later in China, are not yet to be found in Africa. What the possibilities are in Ethiopia, Angola and Mozambique remains to be seen.

The library schools in Africa naturally have to confront the realities we have noted and they have to prepare their students for the kinds of situations we have described. The ex-student may well discover that the principles of management he has absorbed cannot operate. He will notice that the values of his colleagues, and especially those of his superiors, are incompatible with the professional objectives he has learned. If he is in a senior position he may find that he has little or no control over his own library system. Finally, he may become aware that monies voted for library purposes have mysteriously disappeared. (Some library buildings have been delayed for years, even decades, for this reason.) Such realities are, of course, no more than an extreme variation of a universal human experience, and somehow the library schools must explain why these things are so and not otherwise. It is also the schools' responsibility to work out objectives which are relevant. In so doing they are faced, first, with the way of life of the people; second, with the nature of the library profession; third, with the level of library development in the country, and finally, with the requirements of universities.

Within this context the library schools have to create a new program. Everyone involved is aware that this exercise is required, yet the practical results have not always been impressive or noticeable to outsiders, and we should examine why. One of the first requirements is that the curriculum should be modified, since the new library schools usually used British or American models to start with (they had to start somewhere). My own experience in these matters is discussed in an article (contributed with Tony Olden) to the Journal of Librarianship. [4] Initially, for example in Ghana in 1967, I tended to think mainly in terms of producing an appropriate syllabus, whereas it seems to me now that I failed fully to appreciate social realities there, and it is this which is the most difficult aspect of indigenization. Eight years later, in Nigeria, we modified the syllabus mainly by leaving out traditional subjects which are less relevant or by making the subjects optional. Changes of this kind, incidentally, cannot be implemented in small library schools and this is one reason why they often fail to develop a new orientation. In addition, the structure of the program allowed for individual study of local circumstances both at undergraduate and Master's levels, and there is now available a considerable body of project and thesis material which is entirely devoted to indigenous realities. I would now claim that however important such changes may be, the most decisive changes have to do with the approach used. If a member of staff has really acquired "new modes of perception" (as distinct from lip-service conformity), then any subject can be indigenized: if not, it will not happen. The significant factor is the quality of the staff, and I can recall individuals wholly unable to comprehend what was required.

Beyond all this, the main impact as far as I was concerned personally was on the outlook of individual students-- always an intangible factor to assess. I was confident that many students acquired a wholly new perception of the realities of their own society. Yet at the same time we were aware (and so were they) that they would have to live with those realities, and one could not therefore set forth new objectives without making it apparent that in most cases they could not be realized, for reasons already mentioned. A decisive factor was that I was a European left-wing radical working in an environment which was not radical at all--far from it. (A more dynamic influence in that Northern part of Nigeria, and to some extent in the University, was that of the Ayatollah Khomeini, and who could compete with him?) In any event there are limits beyond which expatriates cannot conscientiously go. Most of our students had come from "the bush" and were determined never to go back there. Who was I to tell them that they should return to their backward villages as "servants of the people"? They had their own lives to live and a future where many of the concepts I had tried to transfer were luxuries they could not afford.

Other library schools in Africa have moved in the same direction, as I know from experience as an external examiner. By various means Dr. Aguolu (Maidugari; Nigeria), Professor Kotei (Botswana), and Professor Aboyade (Ibadan; Nigeria) are committed to the development of an indigenous approach. In some cases it is possible that these moves may constitute little more than the kind of fashionable gimmick which international bodies generate, but at least some kind of commitment is there. My own political approach is not to be expected from African professors who are part of a national establishment (which I was not). But the way is open for further advances.

The important task is to analyze correctly the problems involved. If this is not done, misleading interpretations are made. One such appeared in Libri[5] in 1982. In this article the joint authors point to an alleged failure to develop relevant local programs in African library schools. Their initial analysis is admirable and they note the failures in education and adult education which are now well documented. They also observe, quite rightly, "The problem is that librarians have failed to conceive of themselves or of their institutions within a total social context. The librarian is a member of an educated minority serving an even more élite group." Quite so; the analysis is sound. But then they go on to imply (contrary to what they have already stated) that educationists themselves can somehow change that élitist environment. Accordingly, in addition to a new curriculum (which is difficult to understand), they propose that newly qualified librarians should join a "Library Corps" which would then coordinate the information needs of other agencies. For setting this up, "government commitment is mandatory," they say. Who is going to issue the mandate? Following a thesis produced by Dorothy Obi, their proposals fail to allow for the social realities we have described. The article starts out on the right foot by stressing "the total social context" but loses that context halfway through; but at least the attempt is made. The criticism of library schools is less cogent than it might have been because the findings are based on evidence which cannot be taken seriously (random interviews with African students who happened to be in the USA at the time). Also, the writers appear to believe that one can assess library schools by examining their syllabi.

It remains to note that the working out of library objectives is a task which the profession also might be expected to undertake. Yet one has to remember that individuals are usually not in a position to have much influence. The lack of control over their own affairs, which is probably the greatest limitation librarians have to face everywhere, means that their objectives are officially not their own but those of the parent body, whether this be a university of a government institution or a public authority. In countries where libraries are in their infancy the librarian's position may be very weak indeed. Elsewhere, for example in Latin America and the West Indies, the feminization of the profession does not help its status. In some countries, especially those where middle-class women have not traditionally worked, a post in a library is regarded as a suitable genteel occupation for them. Army officers send their daughters to the library instead of locking them up. Under such circumstances professional ideals may not be paramount.

Finally, we should note that the organized profession is not likely to contribute much to this endeavor. It is often overlooked that the role of the professions is not at all what it used to be in earlier times. In industrial countries the social role of the professions has changed considerably in recent years. For example, their educational role has been taken over by universities, and governments have taken over responsibilities which were formerly theirs. It should not, therefore, be taken for granted that they are "progressive" in the sense that they easily adapt to new national needs. In the new countries of Africa national library associations are still struggling with functions not very different from those of trade unions. It is, in consequence, difficult for librarians to think in terms of national requirements; this is a matter not of priorities but of perception. One is driven to the conclusion that professionalism is not enough.

If that is the case, what then, it may be asked, is enough? The answer, of course, is that nothing is enough, and this comforting thought also applies to the analysis I have made in this chapter. A search for principles or purpose is necessarily an abstract undertaking and all abstractions are dangerous unless one constantly refers back to concrete circumstances. Objectives are often formulated after events and not before them, and nothing is more dead than an idea which no longer relates to material reality. (National development, as distinct from that of individuals, is an abstraction also.) As Adolphe Amadi would point out, these objectives are part of a continuing colonial legacy and circumstances in Africa are such that entirely new objectives may emerge at any time.

We are, in fact, discussing the human spirit and its infinite possibilities. From such an angle the library should be regarded not as an institution, nor as a service, nor as a building, but as a symbol of our aspirations. (Status symbols are another thing.) To illustrate this, let us take note of one reality which has somehow escaped mention throughout this assessment: I refer to the existence of the children who constitute at least two-thirds of the population of Africa. We cannot easily apply some of these concepts to them and their minds are not colonized yet, but they and their unfettered imaginations are the most important element of all. From them will come a demand which the "libraries" of the future, whatever form they take, will have to meet.

References

1. Ximea, Feliu S. "CLADES: a Contribution to Action in Latin America and the Caribbean in the Field of Development," Unesco Journal of Information Science, Librarianship and Archive Administration, Vol. IV, No. 1, Jan-March 1982.

2. De Heer, Andrew. "Ghana and U.A.P. Obstacles and Prospects," Unesco Journal of Information Science, Librarianship and Archive Administration, Vol. IV, No. 1, Jan-March 1982.

3. Amadi, Adolphe O. African Libraries: Western Tradition and Colonial Brainwashing. Scarecrow Press, 1981.

4. Benge, R. C. and Anthony Olden. "Planning Factors in the Development of Library Education in English-speaking Black Africa," Journal of Librarianship, Jan. 1981.

5. Tjoumas, Renee and Robert Hauptmann. "Education for Librarianship in the Developing Countries: a Radical Departure," Libri, Vol. 32, No. 2, 1982, pp. 91-108.

INDEX

Achebe, Chinua 151
Allfrey, Phyllis 97
Amadi, Adolphe O. 214, 219
Amis, Kingsley 148
Auden, W. H. 2, 22, 41, 149, 180

Bibliographical control 200
Bingley, Clive 176+
Boyd, William 154
Brandt Report 203
Brenan, Gerald 183
British Council 93

Carroll, Lewis 159, 176
Caudwell, Christopher 17
Chandler, George 200
Children 219
Civil service 9
Clearwater, Thomas 172
Colleagues
    Dean, John 102
    Dudley, Edward 172
    Evans, Eve 100, 102
    Foskett, Douglas 172
    Hockey, Sidney 94
    Hogg, Frank 105
    Kotei, Sam 101, 104
    Linford, John 99, 100
    Roe, John 101
    Sewell, Philip 173
    Smith, Harold 172
    Villars, Kwesi 101
College of Librarianship, Wales 104+
Communication 186+
    Satellites 19
Connolly, Cyril 178

De Heer, Andrew 212
Debons, Anthony 187
Decolonization 94, 167, 214
Doll, Russell 199
Dominica 96

Eastern Caribbean Regional Library
    School 95
Enaharo, Peter 129
England
    Home Counties 8, 91
    North Western Polytechnic 112+
    Tonbridge 2
    Tunbridge Wells 2+, 74
Ewart, Gavin 188
Exoticism 147

Foskett, Douglas 189

Ghana 100+, 152
    Expatriates 118+, 147
    Police 146
    Sexual relations 120+
    University 102, 105, 118
Ghana Library Board 212
Gibbons, Stella 26

Hardy, Thomas 181
Hauptmann, Robert 218
Havard-Williams, Peter 175
Hazlitt, William 180, 181

Ideologies 150, 152, 177
Informatics 10, 11+, 12, 17, 185, 189
Iran 192
Isherwood, Christopher 149
Islam 192

Kent, Allen 187
Kipling, Rudyard 69
Kundera, Milan 182

Lancaster, E. W. 201
Larkin, Philip 148, 207
Lawrence, T. E. 26
Left Book Club 17, 22

Librarians
  Role 4, 12, 13, 17
Libraries
  Central Office of Information 9+
  Education role 210
  Information role 209
  Latin America 212, 218
  National development 210+
  Objectives 206+
  Preservation role 209
  St. Marylebone 11+
  Tunbridge Wells 3, 74
  West Indies 209
Library Association (British) 2, 7,
    87, 190, 207
Library Education 87+, 172
  Objectives 216
  Part time students 91
  Visiting lecturers 91
  Visits 90
Licklider, J. C. 187

MacBride Report 185+, 203
Machel, Camora (President of
    Mozambique) 166
Marxism 16, 17, 28, 29, 38, 153
Maugham, Somerset viii
Montaigne, Michel de vii

Neogy, Rajat 92
Nigeria 110
  Ahmadu Bello University 113+,
    131+, 156+, 163+
  Communications 195
  Corruption 142, 152
  Decolonization 157+, 167
  Dogs 132
  Education 155, 163+
  Expatriates 113+, 122, 127+,
    155, 157+
  Homosexuality 137
  Interracial marriage 135
  Islam 155, 160, 161, 192
  Magic 143+
  National development 153, 211
  National traits 129+
  Racial relations 127+, 131+
  Religious conflicts 160
  Servants 140
  Sexual relations 125+, 133,
    134+, 136
  Tuaregs 144
  University of Ibadan 158
North Western Polytechnic 112+

Obi, Dorothy 218
O'Brien, Conor Cruse 102
Olden, Anthony 216
Orton, Joe 15
Orwell, George 179
Owen, Wilfred 43, 58

Pacifism 22, 42
Pekelis 188
PRESTEL 193
Priestley, J. B. 21
Public libraries
  Role 16
Publications (personal) 171+
Publications
  Bibliography and the provision of
    books 174
  Communication and identity 176
  Cultural crisis and libraries in the
    Third World 154, 177, 210
  Libraries and cultural change 175

Ranganathan, S. R. 206
Reading
  Function of 15

St. Vincent 96
Salman, Lamia 191
Scannell, Vernon 43
Sesame Street 145, 195+
Smith, Anthony 189, 194, 198
Soviet Union
  Communication 188, 194
  Experience on troopship 74
  Library objectives 215
  Repatriation of "collaborators" 78
  War effort 20, 40, 75
Soyinka, Wole 93
Spain: civil war 7, 22
Spender, Stephen 17

Teaching experience 89+, 106, 111+
Tjoumas, Renee 218
Transition 92
Trinidad 94, 120, 141
Tropical diseases 149

Unamuno, Miguel de 183
Unesco 16, 185, 199
United States of America
  Communication 196+
  Expatriates 118, 129, 162

Wales
    Aberystwyth 106, 151
    Haverfordwest 26
West Indies 94, 175
Wijasuriya, D. E. K. 200
Women
    Expatriate 117
    Exploitation in Africa 120, 133,
       143, 163, 166
    In libraries 218
World War II
    Austria 75+
    British class system 48
    The Buffs 5th Battalion 47+, 81
    Cassino 59
    Codes 33, 68
    Concentration camps 80
    Egypt 72+
    Fear 36, 43+, 67, 71
    Hebrides 27
    Homosexuality 25, 50+
    Hospitals 57, 62
    Italy 58+
    Leadership 36, 65
    Medals (personal) 33, 63
    Montgomery, General 33, 58
    Patrols (personal) 34, 53+
    Promotions (personal) 35, 47,
       81
    Scotland 26+
    Sex 52, 79
    Sicily 44
    Training 8, 23+, 81
    Tunisia 30+
    Vienna 76
    War diaries 38, 70, 71
Writing 178+